OFFICIAL DISCARD
LAGRANGE COUNTY LIBRARY

ON

LAGRANGE COUNTY LIBRARY

THE AIR!

Tom Shales

SUMMIT BOOKS
NEW YORK

Copyright © 1982 by The Washington Post Company
All rights reserved
including the right of reproduction
in whole or in part in any form
Published by SUMMIT BOOKS
A Simon & Schuster Division of Gulf & Western Corporation
Simon & Schuster Building
Rockefeller Center
1230 Avenue of the Americas
New York, New York 10020
SUMMIT BOOKS and colophon are trademarks of Simon & Schuster
Designed by Eve Metz
Manufactured in the United States of America

10   9   8   7   6   5   4   3   2   1

First Edition
Library of Congress Cataloging in Publication Data

Shales, Tom.
   On the air!

   1. Television programs—United States—Reviews.
I. Title.
PN1992.3.U5S48   1982   791.45'75   82-10445
ISBN 0-671-44203-1

This work was originally syndicated by The Washington Post
Writers Group

FOR MY MOTHER AND MY FATHER

ACKNOWLEDGMENTS

The author, such as he is, wishes to thank, for help and encouragement beyond measure, James A. Miller, a former colleague and a friend for life.

He is also exceedingly grateful to Shelby Coffey III, former editor of *The Washington Post*'s Style section, for his stubborn support and good advice; to Leslie Berger for tirelessly researching and typing the manuscript; to Peggy Tsukahira for her dauntless and resourceful editing of this book; to Andrew Bornstein and Ann Beattie for the generosity of their faith and friendship; and to his sister, Mary, who listened with forgiving patience to the first stories he ever wrote.

Contents

FOREWORD, 11
Hapless Days, 13
To Uncle Johnny, Illusion of Light, 15
The Great One, 21
Johnny Carson: A Rolls, Not a Chevy, 24
Saturday Night Lives, 29
Farrah Fawcett-Majors: "I Just Laugh," 37
Today's Dave Garroway: Still at Large, 42
Little Rascals, 49
The First Archie Bunker Award, 56
The Awful Joys of TV in L.A., 59
Hey!!! It's Steve Martin!, 63
Lou Grant: Just What TV Needs, 67
Singing Sausages, 69
Television Kills: The Trial of Ronney Zamora, 72
Edith Bunker's Ordeal, 78
The Fading of the *Hall of Fame*, 81
The Death of Mirrors, 84
Nostalgia for the Future, 88
From L.A., Heeerre's . . . the Newsonality!!, 92
The Initiation of "James," 96
Videoraphobia, 99
Death of a Salescat, 102
Video Noir—TV's Long Shadow, 104
The *60 Minutes* Decade, 110
The Time Was Prime for a Pause for Peace . . . , 114

Forever Howard, 118
Robin Williams Visits Earth, 121
Fast *Feud* with Relish, 127
Oh, to Click Nixon Around Again . . . , 132
The Great Clichés of 1978, 136
The Last of the Media Monarchs, 139
Watching *The Teng Show*, 146
Videoplomacy: Peace According to the Networks, 150
Carol Burnett, 153
The Best Theys of Your Life, 158
The Garner Files: Mashmallow Macho, 162
Moyers' Superb Study of Job Hunting, 167
Everyman Has a Headache, 169
The Glories of Gin: John Cheever's Spirit, 175
Operators Are Standing By, 177
Terrorvision, 180
TV in the '70s, 188
And Now—The End of the World, 193
One Woman's Story, 196
Petty for Teddy, 202
Losing the Picture, 206
Dan Rather's New Reality, 209
Auntie Babsy, 216
Gunga Dan, 218
Live, from Detroit: The Republican Convention, 221
The Man Who, 227
The Light That Failed, 230
January 20, 1981, 232
The Late Bloomer, 239
February Creeps, 244
Trauma and Instant Replay, 246
Going Ape, 252
Jugular Journalism, 254

Rona, 259
Duncan, the Wonder Horse: or, The Commando Strikes at
    Dawn, 264
Wedding, 270
Marty Lives, 274
Sugar Ray and the Media's TKO, 276
The Caution and the Fear, 279
Report from the Betacombs, 285
Gimme an Axe, 288
A Tale of Two Toms, 289
Uncle President, 293
Farewell to Brideshead, 296

Foreword

I love the food at McDonald's, I like the smell of Right Guard deodorant and I'm incurably crazy about television. It was love at first sight, on a summer day in my Midwestern hometown, when a next-door neighbor leaked the secret that while my sister and I were at school, our parents had finally sprung for a set. I raced home and turned it on, and the first face I remember seeing on its screen was the freckled wooden beamer of Howdy Doody. Thus began a life of curtains closed in the daytime and meals served in the living room.

Everyone has been very patient about this. *The Washington Post* even made me its television critic. In effect, this is like being sentenced to solitary confinement; but in my case, it's a self-exile that began a few decades ago and is now irreversible. I used to half-apologize to people for being a television critic and for hanging on to a flicker of faith in the medium, but no more. It's not a matter of learning how to stop worrying and love TV, because the worrying will never stop, ever. Much about TV is worrisome. But now and then I feel grateful not only that I'm alive in the age of television but that, unlike a lot of people I know, I can still find it, on occasion, marvelous. I can be delighted and astonished and exhilarated by it, and appalled.

A terrible interviewer once asked me what I watched on television for fun. I told him *Family Feud*. He reeled, incredulous. Surely, he said, I watched it to laugh at it. No, I told him, I enjoyed playing the game, I found Richard Dawson very funny and I liked to see an American family win $5,000 or $10,000 in a snap. *I enjoyed responding as I was intended to respond.* The program had become for me a dependably satisfying ritual, like Johnny Carson's monologue. Sometimes, days seemed incomplete without it.

The companionship role that television plays is invariably overlooked by pressure groups calling for an end to this or an increase in that and in high lathers about how children's minds and public attitudes are being warped by television in one direction or another. But occasionally a letter from a reader will give me a sudden shock of recognition about what television means to millions of daily lives: something so intimate it can hardly be expressed. Lorne Michaels, the creator and producer of the original *Saturday Night Live,* has called TV "the greatest cure for loneliness ever invented."

I think it has probably dried a lot of tears in its time.

None of this means it isn't proper to panic at regular intervals about the way what's seen on television affects the people who see it, about the distortions it has introduced, about the mass and the individual psychological side effects. If television can cure loneliness, it can also exaggerate emptiness, and encourage dread.

You watch hour upon hour of TV shows in which people discuss the suddenly discussable topic of "relating" to one another and then it may dawn on you that what you relate to best is not the people at the office, or the people on the street, or the people in the same house with you. You find you are relating best to people under glass.

The television environment is changing now. Cable and pay-cable and direct-satellite television, and VideoDiscs and videocassette recorders, are all ostensibly going to free us from the tyranny of television's first 30 years. We are leaving the first age of television and entering the second. But whatever happens to it, or to us, television remains a black silk hat, a kaleidoscope, the car with the thousand clowns inside, Alice's looking glass. The mere fact that hardly anybody works magic with it doesn't mean it isn't a magical instrument.

In an old *New Yorker* cartoon, a bartender and a customer are marveling over the fact that a merrily smiling man at the other end of the bar, whiskey glass in hand, drinks because he actually "likes the taste of the stuff." I like the taste of the stuff. I still watch television because I want to.

Now this:

Hapless Days

DURING THE '50s, television presented us with an amusing counterfeit version of the American family. Tonight's breakthrough in television programming, a new ABC series called *Happy Days*, presents us with an amusing counterfeit version of the previous counterfeit version.

Somehow you get the feeling of a cycle having completed itself.

Happy Days would not be on the air at all but for two strategic facts: *American Graffiti*, that warmhearted picture about lost innocence, has grossed more than $21 million nationally since its release last year; and *Grease*, a rock musical about '50s high school hoods, is the longest-running show on Broadway and a touring hit around the country.

These success stories, along with the continuing rock 'n' roll revival craze, have made '50s nostalgia highly marketable —even to kids born too late to remember this era. The creative forces in television are the last to seize on most trends; now that the movies and records have been selling, TV is ready. At least five new pilots about the '50s are kicking around Hollywood right now, waiting to be sold.

The original pilot for *Happy Days* predates them all, however. Garry Marshall, executive producer and a co-writer of the series, says the first "Happy Days" was broadcast as a segment of *Love American Style* three years ago on ABC. But Marshall could never sell the series until now.

"The '50s theme and nostalgia became more popular during those three years," says Marshall from his office at Paramount Studios in Hollywood, "and the '70s became less popular." The time was right for something new in TV exploitation.

But *Happy Days*, from the looks of tonight's premiere, is not something new. It is TV Traditional—the further adventures of the Cipher Family in Anytown, U.S.A. The kids have problems growing up. The parents have their hands full teaching good old moral lessons (like, tonight, "Truth is the best answer, believe me"). And amiable, bumbling Daddy lounges around the house dressed neatly in a coat and tie.

Ron Howard, once wee Opie on the Andy Griffith Show, later the virginal lad of *Graffiti*, starred in the original *Happy Days* pilot, and his character, virginal Richie Cunningham, will be the pivotal one in the series.

As for the '50s, they are feebly re-created. Token details are trotted in—white socks, penny loafers, baggy pants and high school jackets—without much conviction or effect. Extracts from '50s pop are used haphazardly on the sound track; though "The Song from *Moulin Rouge*" was a '53 hit, Elvis' "Hound Dog" a '56 hit, the Crew Cuts' "Sh-Boom" a '54 hit and Bobby Darin's "Splish-Splash" vintage '58, they all pop up on the opening show. During the '50s, *nobody* listened to last year's songs.

From the looks of the premiere, we can expect Richie to be regularly goaded into embarrassing situations by his brash pal Potsie (Anson Williams). Tonight, Potsie fixes Richie up with Mary Lou Milligan (Kathy O'Dare), a girl with a "reputation" who likes to "French-kiss" and is suspected of having once dated a sailor. Far Out.

It may be futile, though, to complain that *Happy Days* lacks an authentic '50s sensibility, that it eschews honest retrospection for superficial gags. We don't expect from a TV series much in the way of diligent or thorough period portrayals. Nobody can seriously believe that *The Waltons* is an accurate reflection of life in the '30s; if one loves the show, it's not because it tells us all about the way we were. It offers us, obviously, the way we would like to think we were.

Happy Days is engaged in the same sort of subterfuge, but the hoax hasn't been brought off with even artificial sensitivity; there's not even Hollywood warmth. And yet, there are signs that something of consequence or at least interest may

develop as the series continues; the character of Fonzie the tough kid (Henry Winkler) shows promise.
January 15, 1974

To Uncle Johnny, Illusion of Light

UNCLE JOHNNY COONS is just out of reach.

Having eaten lunch with him daily for several years, one can picture the smiling round face, the jaunty derby, the general physical festivity that marked those midday meetings. He was welcome in our home.

And yet you cannot summon him back precisely the way you recall an old friend or those proverbially termed loved ones. Uncle Johnny remained two-dimensional, slightly distant and confined to a gray-and-white universe that measured 14 inches diagonally. This was the mahogany RCA TV set that became the focal point of our living room in the early '50s, and for half an hour each day, starting at noon, it belonged to Uncle Johnny Coons.

We enlarged our family unit by one to accommodate Uncle Johnny, who became almost literally an uncle, and we tuned in faithfully each day to see what funny outfits he would be wearing, what shenanigans he would improvise and what old-time movies he would show. *Noontime Comics* originated from the Merchandise Mart in Chicago and was broadcast over NBC affiliate WNBQ (now WMAQ), but from our living room in a far northwest Chicago suburb, we never thought of Uncle Johnny as "originating" anywhere. He simply materialized, and television was still so new that the best explanation for this appearance was to say it was "as if by magic."

We grew older, left elementary school for junior high and

graduated to the big, fancy, factory-produced network series like *Mickey Mouse Club* and other more elaborate programs. Uncle Johnny remained a Chicago fixture until 1956, when a brief network Saturday-morning spot proved all too temporary.

Years later, *Noontime Comics* with Uncle Johnny Coons far behind, the same smiling round face could occasionally be spotted playing bit parts in TV commercials.

Then, early last month, at the age of 58, John David Coons, Jr., died, in Chicago, of brain cancer. Coons's obituary in *Variety*, the show-business newspaper, was only one inch long. But in Chicago, hundreds who had known him only as an apparition formed by an array of electrons attended a memorial service. Uncle Johnny Coons had been a member of their families, too.

It is difficult to pinpoint precisely which generation the TV generation is. It could be the children of the '50s who have never known life without television. Or, perhaps more justifiably, it could be the crop of late-war and postwar babies—those of us who are the last generation with a conscious memory of television's entrance into our lives and our living rooms, neither of which, as the saying always goes, would ever be the same.

Just how these things will never be the same we still don't entirely know: what we lost and what we gained and which outweighs the other. In the socio-psychological consideration of television's effects on our consciousness, Uncle Johnny Coons may not be among the most significant factors.

Yet he was part of a new reality, and for us, an important part. We "knew" him in a way we hadn't known people before —certainly not in the way we had known disembodied voices on the radio, and certainly not in the way we knew mere entertainers on a stage or movie screen. And certainly not in the way we knew each other. Television by definition gave us insufficient information for a complete, personal relationship; the experience would remain vicarious. Even so, this relationship would affect all those others, and in time theorists would be saying that the television reality did not so much supplement the other reality as replace it.

If we only knew what was happening to us while it was happening! Things would be simpler.

There was an Uncle Johnny, or an Uncle Somebody, or an Aunt Somebody Else, assuming familial status implicitly or explicitly, in virtually every major city where TV took hold in the '50s. Sometimes these kiddie-show hosts were clown-faced rowdies handy with cream pies and well stocked with old cartoons. And sometimes they were like Uncle Johnny—born for television and its capacity for intimate, direct, one-to-one communication, even if they never thought about technique or media theory or wider ramifications.

On a recent episode of *Good Times,* Florida was defending her family's adherence to the largely discarded ritual of spoken prayer before meals. "It's the only time of day the family shares the same thought," she said.

But in the '50s, before television lost its innocence and naiveté, there were other times. When *Noontime Comics* went on the air, our family was together in the living room eating lunch "with" Uncle Johnny, who himself took the meal on-camera, always extolling the virtues of a full glass of milk and, in a way that didn't seem to offend us, the wisdom of shopping at Jewel Tea Company, his sponsor.

My father was home from work. My mother came out of the yellow-walled kitchen where she'd made sandwiches. My sister, Mary, joined me on the floor in front of the set, until, sometime later, collapsible "TV trays" were invented to facilitate the simultaneous watching of television and consuming of food.

Uncle Johnny's technique was simplicity incarnate. To play different characters, never far removed from his own, he just donned different hats. If he was supposed to be driving down the street with his friend George Dummy, a prop windshield was shoved onto the table he sat behind and someone tossed in George, who was literally a dummy and whose spoken voice could be heard only by Uncle Johnny, then interpreted for us.

No committee of educators masterminded this operation. No public funds were invested in the project so that Uncle Johnny could surreptitiously instruct and socialize us while we thought we were being merely entertained. About the only advice Uncle Johnny imparted was undisguised and paternal —drink the milk and, he would tell us, always sit at least six feet away from the television set.

"I always tried to sit too close," my sister recalls now, but Uncle Johnny would insist. And reluctantly, with our live, in-person parents there to enforce it, Uncle Johnny's rule was usually obeyed.

Perhaps we complied because we sensed Uncle Johnny's trust in us—a faith we did not want to betray—and because, through a combination of personal chemistry and the mysterious electronic transmission of it, Uncle Johnny had our trust as well.

For years, Chicago broadcasters clung to the hope that the city would become a center of network production. Instead, probably to the lasting detriment of the entire system, the networks gravitated to the East and West coasts. And yet Chicago television quickly became and largely remained inventive and pioneering, setting trends that later became nationwide (the talk show, for one). The Chicago style of radio announcing is still the industry standard—slick familiarity and a lack of dialect. The Chicago TV market is one of the nation's most economically important and conceptually barometric. Chicago's TV critics have always been known as feisty, avidly read and thorns in the sides of the networks.

In the '50s, some network shows did originate from Chicago. There was the Sunday-afternoon *Super Circus* with the posing "Mary Hartline." For a relatively brief period there was also the trailblazing daily afternoon talk (and music) show *Club 60*, which featured a so-so but personable singer by the name of Mike Douglas.

And the most adult children's television show ever, Burr Tillstrom's ingenious *Kukla, Fran and Ollie,* with its one small set, one live woman, gallery of inspired puppets and off-screen piano soloist, began as a local Chicago show, on WBKB, until the network picked it up as a daily 15-minute feature.

Somewhere between the network's *Howdy Doody Time* and its *Camel News Caravan* with John Cameron Swayze came the locally produced *Elmer the Elephant,* in which announcer John Conrad, dressed as a ringmaster, was regularly reduced to gibberish by the mischievous Elmer, a large rubber elephant's head with a man inside. The man's arm extended through Elmer's trunk, and the ensuing elephant head appeared through the open top half of a Dutch door. Cream pies were always within trunk's reach, and so was a seltzer bottle.

Conrad would endure these assaults and then sputter repeatedly at Elmer, "The Peck's Bad Boy of television! the Peck's Bad Boy of television!" Cut to cartoon.

The show finally died because of a union dispute. It could not be decided whether the man in the elephant's head was a technician or an actor, and this squabble eventually sent Elmer to the elephants' burial ground.

The children's show that demonstrated the greatest longevity, if not the greatest wit, was *Garfield Goose and Friend,* which appeared on several stations and finally settled on WGN—traditionally the most backward in Chicago—owned by the Chicago Tribune (WGN stands for "World's Greatest Newspaper"). Garfield was a puppet goose who thought he was king of the United States, and fat Frazier Thomas, who created the character, played the live "prime minister" who never dared to wise the goose up.

Garfield Goose and Friend is currently celebrating its 23rd year on the air.

There were many other shows local and national, and other cities had their own versions and their own ex officio Uncles. For us, no one ever achieved status in our home, among the kiddie-show hosts, equal to Coons. No one was allowed to get closer to us, no one was embraced so completely and few if any seemed to understand us as well.

When people talk of a golden age of television in the '50s, it is not because they remember programs or specials as having been without variation masterpieces of unfailing technical proficiency. Indeed, the productions were often technically primitive, with corpses known to crawl away on-camera in the middle of plays. It was hardly an era of Shakespeare every night.

But it deserves to be called "golden" because there was about it a tremendous sense of daring and risk. It wasn't just the possibility of peril every time a live camera went on the air. It was the excitement of experimentation as pioneers dabbled and tinkered with a medium that was not yet drowning in its own experience or the sacrosanct theories of salesmen.

Television had yet to develop its own professionals; it could only import them from radio, the theater and movies, and the people thus enlisted were lured partly by the thrill of going on live and unprotected, and partly by the promise of working in a medium not yet suffocating in precedent.

Perhaps it is when a medium develops and educates its own professionals, when it no longer must draw primarily on other media, that it starts to die, or to lose whatever intrinsic excitement it once had. In the early days, people in television didn't have to worry about How It Was Done because it hadn't been done before.

People who succeeded on television were mainly the naturals—those who acted from instinct and not tradition. Coons was able to look into the tiny eye of the enormous camera and figuratively see through it to the people at the other end—to the family sitting around watching him and eating peanut butter and jelly sandwiches. He may get barely a footnote in broadcasting history, but Uncle Johnny Coons, and others like him in other cities, made television work as well, perhaps, as it ever will.

That is why, though I knew him only as an illusion of light, his place in my memory is secure.

August 3, 1975

The Great One

JACKIE GLEASON, in direct defiance of his image, did not blow into town with an entourage. But he will blow out with one. His wife of five months and her son by a former marriage will arrive here soon and accompany Gleason to London Sunday on the new Concorde jet.

The idea of Gleason on an airplane, even the fastest one, sounds slightly incongruous, too. He is reputed to be categorically opposed to flying.

"Well, that's a legend, pal," says Gleason, temporarily enshrined in a Madison Hotel penthouse suite. "And you don't fight the legends. If people want to say I don't fly, that's okay with me."

He is asked if he has ever gone faster than the speed of sound before. "Only a couple times at Toots Shor's," he says.

When Gleason came quietly into town Wednesday night, he turned on the television set and saw himself in 20-year-old reruns of *The Honeymooners*, the hit series he made with Art Carney and Audrey Meadows that is in current revival on local stations throughout the country. He watched and he laughed. "I never laugh at me," says Gleason, "but I *die* at what Carney does. That man is gorgeous." A *Honeymooners* revival special on ABC in February was such a ratings smash that Gleason and company will tape two more for next season.

Gleason is in town because he wasn't having all that big a toot in Columbus, where a golf tournament was interrupted by a piece of meat that got stuck in Bing Crosby's throat (and was successfully removed by a doctor). "I figured, Washington's gotta be better than Columbus, right?"

A waiter enters with a bottle of Beaujolais. He opens it and as he is pouring hears Gleason say, "Go all the way." Gleason would not want us to suggest those four words as his life's credo, but he does say, when asked if there are any things he wants to do, "I've been fortunate. I've done 'em all, and they all turned out pretty good."

Gleason is called The Great One because he is a great one. He is comedian, actor, writer, composer, conductor and championship drinker. To a generation reared on television, and a later one now discovering him in reruns, the man is icon, patriarch and legend. And you don't fight the legends.

Down to 200 pounds from a long-ago top of 280, finally married, after two other tries, to the woman he says he was destined for (Marilyn Taylor Horwich, sister of June Taylor and former June Taylor dancer), nothing less than resplendent in Miami tan, blue blazer, family coat of arms and red carnation, Gleason sits behind a formal desk and is lured into reminiscence.

First, the matter of who actually christened him The Great One. "It was Orson Welles. We used to look a lot alike, and we'd go drinking together at Toots's. We'd get a load on and then we'd talk about things we wanted to do together in the theater—like *Volpone*. So then we'd stumble out and find an empty theater, and con the guy at the door, and then Orson would go onstage and try to impress me with his acting. You know the best line I ever heard about Welles? It was from a cabdriver. He told me, 'Orson Welles hails a cab like God and tips like a Jesuit.'

"So one night, we're in the Stork Club, and Welles is asking me to recite things from Shakespeare. You know, he asks for a speech and I give it to him. But he tried to trip me up. I said, 'Wait a minute, pal, that isn't Shakespeare, that's Aeschylus,' and then I recited the lines. He turns to me and says, 'You're The Great One.'"

Gleason, 61, talks about other comedians. He says he is not that flattered to be called "the Chaplin of television" because "Chaplin, in all of his life, made maybe thirty-six pictures, many of them ten or fifteen minutes long. In my career I've done over four hundred shows. I'd like to see Chaplin have to go on television and be as consistent as I've been."

Bob Hope. "He cannot make me laugh. When I see Hope, I tell him, 'You are the worst comedian I've ever seen in my life.' And he says, 'Whaddayou know?'"

Groucho Marx. "Groucho is unique. He's the only great comedian I know of who never also had the ability to make an audience cry. W. C. (Fields) could do it. Abbott and Costello could even make you cry. But not Groucho." Who besides Carney can make Gleason laugh? "Henny Youngman. He's beautiful. He'll tell thirty jokes and only get laughs with four of them. That kind of heroism is exquisite to me."

In the Great One's greatest days of television, everything was live, and he remembers these with affection, as will anyone who saw him. One night, at the start of his weekly comedy-variety hour, he stood before a curtain that subsequently refused to go up on the show. So he did the whole show by himself in front of the curtain.

During an incomparable *Playhouse 90* production of William Saroyan's *The Time of Your Life*, Gleason, in a straight dramatic role, discovered that the champagne he was swilling on the set was the real stuff. "I was half stiff! We all were. A young kid comes in and sings some Irish song and we're all supposed to cry, and we really did cry. We blubbered like babies." Yet the program went off without a hitch, and Saroyan called afterward to call it the best *Time of Your Life* that had ever been done.

Many of Gleason's jokes over the years—including Reggie Van Gleason's immortal "Mmmm-boy, that's good booze!"— and Gleason's once-conspicuous elbow-bending life-style, have involved drinking as sport and as comedy, but Gleason says drinking has never reached the problem level for him and that he can't tell what it would take to make him actually drunk.

"No one knows when they're drunk," he says jauntily. "That's what's beautiful about it." He takes another sip of the Beaujolais, and his guest takes one too, and his guest at this point is thinking, "Here's to The Great One, pal, and the legends that shouldn't be fought."

May 28, 1976

Johnny Carson: A Rolls, Not a Chevy

JOHNNY CARSON is just thin enough, just funny enough and just vaguely enough defined to have become one of the most enduring and broadly popular figures in the history of television. He is the Walter Cronkite of comedy, a trust symbol for old ladies and young marrieds alike. It is hard to imagine the video city without him.

Yet television has its young Turks and its restless profit-watchers. And the oopsy-daisy innuendo with which Carson has titillated bedtime America for nearly 15 years is starting to look frail next to the nastier satire of *NBC's Saturday Night* or the TV-wise topicality of Norman Lear's *All in the Family* and *Mary Hartman, Mary Hartman.*

This year—for the first time—there's been a hint of a threat to Mister Late Night from another network; ABC has made ratings inroads with an assortment of taped semimysteries and smoldering reruns from bang-bang prime time. Carson himself now can—reluctantly—envision a day when someone else will ascend to his *Tonight Show* throne.

It sounds incredible. But time is ruthless. *How ruthless is it?* "If they had told me when I started that I'd be doing the *Tonight* show for fifteen years, I would have said, 'You are absolutely insane,' " says Carson. "Look at Jack Paar. He did it for five years and then he had to go off to Maine to commune with a moose. People say, 'Jeez, Carson's off the show a lot.' Well, I'd be in a rubber room and fed by paid attendants if I wasn't. I'm fifty now, and I am sure I won't be doing the *Tonight* show in ten years. I doubt if I'll be doing it at fifty-five."

Carson is sitting in his at-home "office," a new building that adjoins his vast house in leafy Bel Air, one step up from Beverly Hills. The room is filled with electronic toys—a Video-Beam TV projector, videotape recording equipment—and wonderfully at-ease California furniture, browns predominating. Carson looks well and well off.

The silently opening electric gate at his front driveway screams success, and Carson clearly has it. Beyond his $3-million-plus annual salary, his profitable men's-clothing franchise, his 15 weeks of vacation and his four-night work week, there remains the fact that after all these years he is still very often very funny, and he is probably called upon to be amusing for more hours a week than anyone else in television. Maybe anyone else anywhere. He has made an art form of survival.

Carson's third wife, Joanna, offers "little cakes" and coffee, then drifts out of the room in her floor-length hostess gown, while out the eastern windows a man can be seen cleaning the tennis courts. Carson, in sloppy-classy slacks and sport shirt, settles into a chair with two packs of Pall Malls.

Has he seen the future and does it hurt? By the future we mean *NBC's Saturday Night,* which has replaced the Carson reruns formerly shown in the weekend time slot.

"Off the record or on the record?" he says. "On, then off," he is told, but he forgets to go off. "I've seen some very clever things on the show, and they have some very bright young people," he says. "But basically they do a lot of drug jokes, a lot of what I would consider sophomoric humor and a lot of stuff I find exceptionally cruel, under the guise of being hip. I mean it is just plain bad taste. That Claudine Longet thing was unforgivable. And during the Patty Hearst business they did some very mean things—after all, that girl was on trial for her life.

"One night the show ended a minute and a half early. There were eight people—*eight people*—standing there onstage and not one of them could think of anything to say."

They can't ad-lib? Carson illustrates his agreement with one of the mildly off-color quips familiar to his nightclub audiences: "They couldn't ad-lib a fart at a bean-eating contest," he says.

And yet one of "them," Chevy Chase, has been mentioned as a possible successor to Carson. "When I go they can get anybody they want. I could not care less," he says, and he lights another cigarette.

Such programs as *Saturday Night* and the Lear shows do seem to have widened TV's available universe of joke topics, however, and Carson himself has definitely been doing more political humor than usual (his writers have even borrowed a joke or two directly from *Saturday Night*—for example, "President Ford bumped into a cow, and Secret Service agents wrestled the cow to the ground").

Carson thinks it's Washington that determines how much political humor is on the air. "Let's face it: Nixon was a humorless man. Then Jerry Ford came along and started bumping into things and opened things up again.

"Now Carter is almost a caricature, but in a way I think he's humorless too, basically. Not that you want the President to be Henny Youngman. But with Carter once you get past the teeth and the smiling and the sixth peanut joke, you're pretty much out of business.

"I think our studio audience is a good barometer of how the country is feeling. Five hundred people can give you a pretty accurate indication; you can see right away what is fair game.

"When Agnew first got started, and nobody had heard of him, he was a great target for jokes. Then when he was in trouble, you could sense that a lot of people were pretty hard hit by that in Middle America. Wilbur Mills was funny for a while; then you find out the poor guy's an alcoholic. We try not to be cruel or take cheap shots, and I try to stay completely apolitical, not to get involved. I'm too visible night after night to start taking one side or the other; people wouldn't want it. I'm an entertainer, and I go right down the middle."

The jokes that go over best these days are those directed at Ronald Reagan, whom Carson described in one monologue as being "slightly to the right of the Sheriff of Nottingham."

"Well, maybe so," says Carson. "You say, 'Ronald Reagan couldn't be here tonight; he's posing for the cover of *Guns and Ammo*,' and that hits a chord. But I know Ron well; he has a sense of humor."

There have always been those who said the Carson show was lightweight, that the book guests are always last and least, that 90 minutes a night is given over to trifles when serious topics could be discussed. Recently, though, Carson spent a full half-hour of his show talking Mars with astronomer Carl Sagan. On the other hand, two nights later Carson dropped his pants on the air to get a laugh.

"I'm a comedian," Carson says defensively. "I'm not out there to lead everybody out of Armageddon. All the guys who have tried it—from Les Crane to David Frost—have gone off.

"Sure, I'll have Paul Ehrlich on from time to time. But basically, it's an entertainment show. If you start taking yourself too seriously and try to make great social change, you might as well hang it up. The ratings will go right down the toilet. It's different with an actor like Paul Newman. He can go on screen and be somebody else. But I'm out there every night. I'm 'Johnny Carson.'"

He smiles and blinks. "You know, Jack Benny used to tell me people don't like to feel a comedian is terribly much brighter than they are. I don't mean that in a patronizing way, either, but it's true."

Some of Carson's material has been controversial in nonpolitical ways. He has been criticized for making too many jokes at the expense of old people, women and homosexuals. "You can't do a joke without offending somebody," he says. "We're not unkind to old people. My Aunt Blabby character is lively and feisty, and dressing up like an old lady is a staple of comedy."

(Ed McMahon to Aunt Blabby: "Is the situation grave?" Aunt Blabby: "Never say 'grave' to an old person.")

One actress, Carson is told, has complained that he makes too many jokes at the expense of her breasts. "Who said that?" he asks. Valerie Perrine. "I have never made any jokes about her breasts," he says.

"She says you look down her neckline and roll your eyes," Carson is told.

"Well, then, she shouldn't wear those necklines. These actresses come on hanging out of their dresses and then act offended at jokes about breasts. Now, come on. Who's kidding whom! If you ever look at the women's magazines, all you see is ads for breast development—'Develop Your Breasts.' So there you are."

And homosexuals? "We don't take cheap shots. The other night we said the sky on Mars was orange and yellow and that maybe we'd discovered the first gay planet. So I suppose now we'll hear from the gay Martians."

Carson sounds exasperated about the need to please everybody, but that's his business. Like the door-to-door salesman whose smile must be infinitely adaptable, Carson's kind of entertainer might be an endangered species. One hates to risk overdramatizing him into a dying breed, but maybe the Mr. Nice Guy, Something-for-Everyone, Middle American mischief-maker is doomed. Maybe it's the niceness that's the most endangered part—a kind of good manners of comedy that won't hold up in the cynical '70s. Maybe people want more blood in their humor.

"Professionally, I feel very secure," says Carson. "People basically like me. They have to feel some kind of rapport with me or I wouldn't have been around for so long. Show biz isn't everything to me, but I need that acceptance from an audience. My wife says to me, 'You're only happy when you're performing.' I don't think that's completely true. But it is a great high. If I quit tomorrow, I don't know what the hell I would do.

"I feel better physically now than I did when I was twenty-five. I'm more active physically now. I have a gym in the basement and I work out. When I was twenty-five, I didn't have time; I was too busy trying to make a living."

He is asked how he keeps in touch with the real world from behind electric gates in upholstered Bel Air. "I can get it in perspective," he says. "I just have to remember driving through this very place with my folks in 1937 when I was twelve. It's all relative. It doesn't become that difficult to live with."

And what will he do when time catches up and he leaves the *Tonight Show*? "I'll be perfectly willing to say, 'Hey, warm up somebody else.' I could do six or seven specials a year. Or write a book, although I don't want to write a book just to write one. When you get something to say, then you should write a book. I don't have lots to say that's new. It's not playing Harry Humble. It's just that I don't have that much interesting to say."

What seems outrageous today will probably look tame tomorrow. In five years, we may be well beyond *NBC's Saturday Night*. Carson is certainly a man who has changed with the times. His style is a compendium of comedy history—right down the middle. But no one is infinitely adaptable. The new offensiveness may bury the old innocuousness.

Carson recalls a *Saturday Night* joke about a comic named Professor Backwards, whose cries for help as he was being bludgeoned to death were ignored because he said, "pleh, pleh."

Carson thinks that kind of joke is "incredibly vicious," but then says, "that kind of joke you tell at a private party. You don't tell it on television." Carson's humor may seem cruel to some people too—all comedy has its cruel side—but he thinks there are boundaries that should be observed.

This charming idea may someday earn him his last laugh.
August 8, 1976

Saturday Night Lives

LARAINE NEWMAN is sitting on the floor of the greenroom above NBC's Studio 8-H. She brushes her hair, sips some Chablis, sticks out her lower lip like a mopey Shirley Temple and moans, "I miss Chevy. I really do."

They all miss Chevy at NBC's *Saturday Night Live*. And as Newman speaks, it is in fact Saturday night, and the cast is recovering from one of the gloomiest dress rehearsals in the show's one-year history. Jokes and sketches are being cut, the producer is arguing with the censor, painters are still working on the sets and in less than one hour all these people are going to be right out there on television.

So it's like New Year's Eve on the S.S. *Poseidon*, with the tidal wave scheduled for 11:30. Coincidentally or not, this is to be the first program since the official departure a week earlier of Chevy Chase, whom the fickle eye of TV singled out from among the talented company and turned into a star. But the show is a star too; its bright, hip satire has made it an oasis of television hope for a generation raised on television.

Saturday Night has been called the best TV comedy since the reign of Caesar, and like Sid's show, it is done nakedly, brazenly and perilously live.

Moreover, thirty-five additional NBC stations are carrying the program this season after its smash splash last year. Ratings are up and ads are sold to the hilt.

Still, things are grim in the green room as 11:30 approaches. "Chevy's dead," says staff member Neil Levy, who plays a bee on the show. Newman picks up the refrain and makes it a blues ballad: "Chevy's dead . . . That's what I said."

CHEVY IN LOVE

Chase is not dead. He is 33 years old, living in Los Angeles, and he left the show not just for better offers but, says Lorne Michaels, to get married, on December 4, to longtime love Jacqueline Carlin, an actress. Now he's gone. Gone, gone, gone.

Except that he'll be back on this week's show. Briefly Michaels wants him to appear during the opening as a bum on the street outside the NBC studios. They've joked about his departure on previous shows. During a game-show sketch called "Jeopardy 1999," one question was to name the "famous comedian whose career fizzled after leaving *Saturday Night*."

"The show isn't hurt," says John Belushi. "All of us get restless and think about leaving. I get restless every week.

The show is hard, it's tough, but you have to remember it's the best thing on television, so how bad can that be?"

Dan Aykroyd, at 24 the youngest of the show's players, says he'll miss Chase too, but that now the group identity will come through more strongly on the air. Chase once said of Aykroyd, "Danny has more talent in his right hand than I have in my whole body." Chase resented as well as loved the fact that the media and public leaped on him with attention.

Chase hit the road about the same time Gerald Ford is taking a walk; Chase's fumble-bumble Ford routine became a *Saturday Night* ritual. Jimmy Carter arrives, meanwhile, to the tune of Aykroyd's achingly accurate impression of him.

"I'm afraid of that Carter thing a lot," says Aykroyd. "I don't want to be just 'the guy who did Carter' when I go looking for another job. I remember what happened to Vaughn Meader when Kennedy died. Besides, I was in Atlanta on election day and that town is filled with people who can do Carter." Aykroyd met Jack, Jeff and Chip Carter; they didn't comment on his impression. "They just sort of acknowledged that I did it."

Like Belushi, Aykroyd has his restless moments, even though the show has had a rousing public response. "I give myself one more year starting now. By next winter, I'll be gone."

LAST YEAR'S SENSATION

Such talk adds to the expanding cosmic headache of Michaels, television's hottest young producer—he turns 32 today—whose dark hair is being noticeably invaded by little gray troops. Chase had been threatening to leave since last spring, partly because Michaels wouldn't move the show to Los Angeles, where Chase's ladylove lives.

"Chevy was a member of the family, and he is one of my best friends," Michaels says. "But I think he should have stayed the rest of the year and then moved on. It takes two or three years to make a real impression in television." The Chase bolt does help with one of Michaels' other woes, however: finding reasons to change a show when viewers seem to like it the way it is.

Michaels isn't worried about being Last Year's Sensation. "The media will continue to pay attention because we can be a new sensation each week. There are certain kinds of controversy we create by being unlike anything else on the air. *Playboy* is here right now; they're doing the first group interview since the Beatles on us. *Cosmo* is here too. What we have to worry about is being too much too fast. The danger is, you start to think you're everything the reviews say you are. You begin to believe your own hype."

For this Saturday's show Michaels has scored a coup. A gag offer of $3,200 for a reunion of the Beatles on *Saturday Night* has inspired George Harrison to make a rare TV appearance on the show—for the standard minimum fee of about $320. The segment had to be taped in advance because Harrison wanted to be in India for a religious holiday. Paul Simon will be the guest host.

FRIDAY AFTERNOON

But now, as Michaels talks, it is Friday afternoon and much remains to be done. He is interrupted every two minutes by people who rush into his small office above the studio, all of them with urgent problems, some with screaming crises.

Music director Howard Shore is virtually hysterical; the risers for the band are still in Brooklyn, where *Saturday Night* originated in October when its space was taken over by NBC News for election coverage. A woman enters: guest-host Dick Cavett wants to wear a wig for the "Blonde Ambition" sketch. Another woman enters: Al Pacino wants two tickets to tomorrow night's show for relatives. Another woman enters: Ralph Nader is coming in at 6:30 to discuss being a future guest host.

"The pressure would kill a lesser man!" says Michaels.

A telephone man enters. He wants to know if there are any telephones missing. There are.

"If I don't get them, I'm quitting," says Michaels.
"Is that a promise?" asks the telephone man.

Alan Zweibel, who writes most of the weekly "Update" news satire, says he has a great idea for Cavett's monologue. They'll run a "crawl" of printing on the screen over Cavett's face, and it will contradict everything Cavett says.

It's not precisely the style of the staff to laugh while they work, but as he and Michaels discuss the bit, throwing ideas at each other, Zweibel occasionally breaks up, shyly covering his eyes with one hand when he laughs.

Later, after Zweibel has written it, Cavett will nix the whole routine and it will be thrown out.

LATER THAT DAY

In the studio below, the level of pandemonium dwarfs the opening-night opera bedlam of *Citizen Kane*. Cameras on cranes, dollies and tripods are being whirled around the room; painters are painting sets in all four corners: the musicians rehearse the *Saturday Night* theme; Cavett is tap-dancing by himself; regulars Gilda Radner, Jane Curtin and Newman, waiting for technical adjustments, pass the time by singing the Ladies Garment Workers' song; and behind the false walls of an alleged luxury hotel, two men are doing feverish printing with grease pencils on big white cue cards.

Cavett and the others begin rehearsing a "Crossroads" sketch that spoofs TV religious dramas. He reads a line. "We cut that!" interrupts script coordinator Ann Beatts, who looks like Woody Allen and dresses like a 1914 newspaper reporter. "Lorne cut that. I think it should go back, personally." It's cut. A man emerges to change the cue card.

Rehearsal continues. Aykroyd pretends to whack Belushi in the mouth. Belushi tumbles to the floor, yelping and whooping in make-believe pain. The normally somber cameramen start to laugh. Then a kitchen cabinet falls off the wall and hits Belushi on the shoulder, and he is in real pain. Someone asks, "Is Buck Henry behind that flat?" because on last week's show he was struck by a sword being swung by Belushi and was cut enough to bleed profusely from the forehead. A bandage was applied, the show went on, and the regulars donned bandages of their own in an expression of solidarity.

Two more sketches are rehearsed—one with Aykroyd in a billowy antebellum red dress, playing Jimmy Carter as Scarlett O'Hara, the other "Foxhaven," a spoof of good-life wine commercials. Both sketches will be cut from the final show just before dress rehearsal, which begins at 7:30 Saturday night. "Foxhaven," by staff writer Michael O'Donoghue, has now been cut 10 times from the show.

"It's a weekly ritual murder!" O'Donoghue scowls from behind dark glasses. But cutting is religion around here. Nothing makes it from conception to birth on-the-air without changes. Changes continue until air time, and in fact, during the show two writers still argue about which prop will be used in a sketch that will go on the air in minutes.

THE CENSOR

And then there's the censor. The former censor on the show was a man named Jay Otley, whom most of the staff on *Saturday Night* considered a reasonable man. He was so reasonable, according to writer Tom Schiller, that he didn't like working on Saturday nights. So now the censor is Jane Crawley, a buxom middle-aged woman who walks around with three handbags and a ready blue pencil.

Crawley spots Michaels in the hall and asks him to cut a joking reference to Serbo-Croatians from a sketch about pressure groups. She tells Michaels, "I'm no writer. I'm not a creative person. But couldn't you just make it ridiculous—you know, some group that isn't even a minority?" She is afraid that Serbo-Croatians might be offended.

The line stays in the show. Others do not. After the dress rehearsal on Saturday night—the first time the "Update" script is rehearsed—Crawley goes at it with a pickax. Two of the jokes O'Donoghue contributed are censored. One is about a reformed segment of the Catholic Church introducing a ceremony in which the "host" is augmented by the "cohost," which represents "the body of Mike Douglas." The other joke is about a "new strain of gonorrhea" showing up in all the states where Ronald Reagan campaigned. "Reagan said he was only spreading conservatism," went the joke. And the joke went. Out the window.

O'Donoghue is furious. "Crawley is ruining this show!" He vows to sell all cut jokes to *Hustler* magazine to embarrass NBC.

SATURDAY NIGHT

At 6 P.M. Saturday, the cast gathers for a photo to promote their new Arista album due out in two weeks. They are joined by rock-music mogul Clive Davis, who produced the record. They sit on the steps and take turns making devil's horns behind one another's heads. Garrett Morris is wearing a black tie and an undershirt. "This has got to look sophomoric and juvenile—the stuff we're famous for," says Belushi.

"Hey-hey, we're the Monkees," sings Aykroyd.

Tension is building. The painters are still painting. Director Dave Wilson is yelling over the studio intercom. In the greenroom, Newman is still practicing "Frankly, Dick, I don't give a damn" for the Carter-O'Hara sketch because she doesn't yet know the whole thing will be cut. Dress rehearsal, in front of a studio audience, will run 18 minutes long. The previous week's dress rehearsal ran 25 minutes long.

The dress-rehearsal audience proves viciously comatose. "The King Kong Dirge" leaves them numb. It will be cut. Curtin has taken over the "Update" from Chase, and it flounders too. "I'm not confident with it, yet. It isn't mine," she says later in the greenroom, having changed into a "CHEVY's GIRLS" sweatshirt left over from another era.

At 10:15, the full staff "cut" meeting begins. Michaels announces the cuts and makes changes. He ends the meeting on a note of soft sarcasm: "It's the best show we've ever done." Everybody knows it isn't. But the gloom gives way to a frightening kind of energy. This is an energy sometimes known as fear. It can be tremendously rejuvenating. It is hard to be among this ensemble at this particular time and not feel your heart doing somersaults and your arms quiver. The meeting ends at 11:10. In 20 minutes THEY WILL ALL BE ON TELEVISION.

THREE-MINUTE WARNING

With three minutes to air time, rushing, dodging and painting still continue on the studio floor. Through a slip-up, NBC pages have neglected to admit more than half of the studio audience. Michaels refuses to panic and begins to drink white wine from a glass near his command center against one wall. Announcer Don Pardo, a broadcast veteran who associates more with the old-timers in the crew than with the kids in the cast, jumps up and down in his persimmon sport coat and exclaims, "Ready or not, we go at eleven-thirty!"

With one minute to air time, the audience is still being seated; many have to stand behind the bleachers that look down on the studio. Morris, in position for the opening joke, begins babbling in frenzied Spanish to a cameraman, and Radner, standing center stage, hops up and down and squeals.

Exhilarating terror is sweeping through the room.

"Twenty seconds" is called out. Michaels lets out a loud, pep-talking war whoop.

"Ten seconds" is called out. There are wild shrieks from the boys in the band.

On the Air. And the passive disdain of dress rehearsal has been exorcised. The audience is up, the cast is up, the giant camera cranes roar through the room like bulldozers. The show goes on—not the best, not the worst. Whatever it is, it is live, riddled with ideas and in wildly different order from the program that Michaels had mapped out with index cards on a bulletin board in his 17th-floor office less than 24 hours earlier.

Guest artist Ry Cooder's song is one of the few things that

have remained the same: "True love can be such a sweet harmony, if you do the best that you can..."

The cast heads downtown for a ritual after-show party that is surprisingly sedate. That may be because they are in shock. They have just put themselves through the kind of ordeal usually reserved for spies, traitors and people caught buying dope in Turkey.

"The show gets to be repetitious; I get tired of doing it," Aykroyd had said earlier. "But then, it's also like an institution now. It's like a magazine. And, you know, it's great, you write something down on a piece of yellow legal stationery, and three days later it becomes—reality."

November 17, 1976

Farrah Fawcett-Majors: "I Just Laugh"

MAYBE IT'S THE HAIR. Maybe it's the eyes. Maybe it's the teeth. Maybe it's the intellect.

No. It's the hair.

The sign on the door of the trailer says, "FARRAH F. MAJORS. RESTING. UNDER NO CONDITION DISTURB ME." But the magic kiss of a publicist's telephone call wakes her, and America's newly anointed reigning princess opens the trailer door. And there it is, the hair. The hair! So fluffy, so billowy, so ultra-tawny. It cascades and tumbles to her shoulders like a waterfall straight out of *Bambi*.

Farrah Fawcett-Majors, 29, is told her hair looks great.

"Oh, it's awful!" she says, running a hand through it but failing to dishevel it. "Do you know I have never in my entire life come to work without washing my hair until today? I like clean hair, and my hair looks terrific when it's shiny, but do you know what time I had to get up today? Four A.M.! So I thought to myself, I'm not gonna do it. I'm not gonna get up half an hour early just to wash my hair. And now it looks awful." There is the suggestion of a pout.

Of course, the hair actually looks wonderful. Farrah Fawcett-Majors looks wonderful, in a loose-fitting sweat suit and little fuzzy-bunny slippers, sitting cross-legged in her trailer with two tennis racquets and a collapsible bicycle nearby. Sun is pouring through the windows; we are in Westlake, a squeaky-clean L.A. suburb where the cast of *Charlie's Angels*, the biggest new hit of the TV season, is doing location filming.

A few days earlier Farrah's press agent had told her that someday she will be "bigger than Monroe," and she just laughed. She shouldn't have. Lithe and bubbly and noncommittal and innocuous, she absolutely epitomizes the outdoorsy '70s California ideal, at least as supplied by Los Angeles.

You can't walk down a street of New York City without seeing a Farrah Fawcett-Majors poster beaming at you from the window of a store. She is dressed in a wet red swimsuit and she is smiling like 36 Rockettes. "FARRAH" is the fastest-selling poster in the country; Pro-Arts, Inc., of Medina, Ohio, says it is now "bigger than THE FONZ" and selling "several hundred thousand" copies a month. One million have been printed, and more are on the way.

"They wanted me in a bikini," Farrah says. "I said no. Then they wanted me looking out from behind a tree—you know, acting seductive. I said, 'No, that's not me.' I wanted to be smiling. Happy. The reason I decided to do a poster was, well, if you don't sign a deal to do one, somebody does one anyway, and then you get nothing. Now they're calling me about putting my picture on bed sheets and pillowcases!" The thought of that makes her giggle.

She is asked if she knows she is a sex symbol. "If I am I don't feel it. I don't know what it would feel like. I haven't done anything really sexy, you know. Sure, on the show, maybe I don't wear a bra, but neither do the other girls. Neither do ninety percent of the girls you see on the street. I go to Beverly Hills and look around and I say, 'Wow!' Now my agent says my poster will be bigger than Raquel's. I just laugh."

And what does she think of the thousands of people buying and, for all we know, worshiping those posters? "I think, Oh, ho, ho—silly people."

Certainly it is the illuminated evanescence of Farrah Fawcett-Majors that is largely responsible for the success of *Charlie's Angels*, the farfetched adventures of three women detectives and one of the most vacuous and insipid hits in TV history. People must be tuning in just to watch Farrah bounce around; on a recent show, one character likened her appearance to that of "pudding on springs." In recent ratings, *Angels* has consistently been among the top five programs, which puts it high above *The $6 Million Man*, which is also on ABC and happens to star Farrah's husband, Lee Majors.

"I can't really put my finger on why the show is such a big hit," she says innocently. "People in the business tell me, 'That script was so bad, you couldn't follow it,' but there must be a lot of people out there who watch it and say, 'Gee, that was interesting.' I think people want to see some glamour, some clothes, some hairstyles; you know—they want to see girls."

Coproducer Leonard Goldberg has said of the show's three female stars, "We love to get them wet, because they look so good in clinging clothes," but Farrah says he was only kidding and that *Charlie's Angels* is not the cool porno for middle-aged males some have said it is. She doesn't even think the show is sexy.

"That's a little shocking. Is there that much, kind of, uh, sex on the show? I don't think so. Aren't there more sexy shows on, or is ours the sexiest? We really don't have sexy things happening, do we?" This is ingenuous enough to break your heart, and she seems to mean every word of it. "I don't know, maybe people watch the show because they think it's good.

"Of course, everybody appreciates watching women. I know I have a big following among young little boys. Now, that can't be all sexual, can it? We just changed our phone number, but before we did, these little guys would call up and put on a deep voice and say, 'This is, er, James with the William Morris Agency'—they're smart, these little kids. Then I'd get on the phone and the voice would become this little adorable squeak.

"And I'd say to them, 'This is very wrong, to say you're somebody else,' and they'd say, 'I love you. You're the most beautiful person in the world!' Now, how can you be mad?"

Farrah can no longer rush home at 7 P.M. each day to fix dinner for husband Majors, the way she likes. She's hired a housekeeper to do it instead, "although I still sort of supervise things." Nor can she stroll as frequently or as freely in public. People want to touch the wiry tube goddess for themselves.

"I guess I have a memorable face," she says with brazen understatement. People recognized her on the street previously from her 100-or-so TV commercials. But they didn't always know her name, so they'd call out "Hey, Ultra-Bright!" or "Hey, creamy!" (Noxzema skin cream.)

Now they know her name; but not all women are thrilled with the characterizations on *Charlie's Angels*. The three heroines take orders from the voice of John Forsythe, who as Charlie is perpetually attended by cuties and honeybunches. Farrah does not find that discomforting.

"I know I am still limited as an actress and there are things I cannot do, and one of them is play Christie Love with guns blazing. God made men stronger, I think, though not necessarily more intelligent. He gave women femininity and intuition. If there's something I want and I can draw somebody in with my femininity and catch them off guard and get it, well, what's wrong with that?

"I don't think all the flak this show gets from women libbers is justified. I don't think it would be a better show if we went around karate-chopping everybody. We're females, not males."

Farrah offers a tangerine from a basket. The trailer is filled with flowers and fruit and sunlight.

"After all, we do have a show with three female stars, and that's a step forward for me and a lot of girls who happen to be pretty. Thank goodness we're not just decorating the background. I got so tired of people saying I was 'too pretty' to play a waitress, or telling me, 'No one will believe your husband left you.' "

The only changes she wants made in *Charlie's Angels* are expansions of the character she plays, so she'll be more than pudding on springs. "I want them to start showing she's had some hard knocks, too, and cries, and is sad. Who's gonna care about her if all she does is say, 'Ooo! This week I get to play the hooker'?"

Being a bigger hit on TV than her husband, Majors, has not been a problem, Farrah says. "Imagine the pressure it would have put on him if I'd had a bomb!" Do they watch each other's shows? "Well, we watch his more. He kind of falls asleep in mine. But I love his show. I never really think he's bad. I'm still a lot of notches behind him as an actress."

If Majors loses at ratings, he still wins at tennis—when he plays against his wife. "Let me tell you, I have much better strokes. But he is a man. I can't beat him. When he socks the ball real hard, I just cannot keep up. How these women think they are equal to men I do not know."

Once bored with her husband's tales of high ratings, Farrah now finds herself fascinated with her own. Once addicted to eating chocolate-chip cookies and Cheetos ("the hard kind," not the puffy kind) in bed, she now finds herself craving high-protein foods like tuna and pot roast. "Something very physical is happening to my body," she says. She is getting less sleep, and she has less time for domestic rituals like making big deals out of Majors' morning departures. "He'll say, 'Darling, honey, I want to kiss you goodbye,' and I'll say, 'Oh, goodbye already!' " Things like this happen when you become a star, a symbol and the nucleus of an industry all your own.

We'll still see Farrah in an occasional commercial. "I have one more Wella to do. I like doing commercials because they spend all day lighting you and making you look terrific." The California sun is lighting her as she talks—and fiddles with the toes inside her fuzzy-bunny slippers—and she does look terrific.

Movie scripts are coming her way, and she likes the new

luxury of picking and choosing. She was in *Logan's Run* ("Oh, but that was so awful") and wants to do a "picture with real woman's emotions" about an "emotional woman" who has "woman's emotions." No, it won't be Lady Macbeth. Told that only the sky is the limit for her, she just rolls her crystal gray eyes and laughs. ABC executives naturally don't like her to be told such things. They want her to stay at the same job. At the same price. They want her to be satisfied with *Charlie's Angels*.

Oh, ho, ho—silly people.
January 5, 1977

Today's Dave Garroway: Still at Large

A FEW MELLOW BARS of "Sentimental Journey" are hanging in the air. "When did that first become your theme song?" Dave Garroway is asked.

"About 1949," he says, "when we went on television. You know about television? That's when the pictures are here and what's going on is someplace else."

"It'll never catch on," he is told.

"I didn't think it would. And it hasn't, really. There are almost no live shows any more. There's no television."

Garroway, now 62, was present at the creation of this brave new medium—the one that was going to show us the world in our homes; the one that was going to bring people together.

"It brought people together," says Garroway. "It brought them together in little rooms to gather around a tube and not say anything to each other, just look. That's the saddest part."

Garroway, however, remembers his own years in live television with pleasure, and so, probably, do those who remember watching him. From *Garroway at Large* in 1949 through nearly a decade as host of the *Today* show and three years of *Wide Wide World* as well, Garroway was the coolest, the least grating, the most seemingly trustworthy and one of the most assuring intruders ever to enter millions of American homes. He was tutor, guide, inquisitor, philosopher, maestro and companion. He was born to television.

Now he can't even get a job in it. "There haven't been any offers," he says.

Garroway doesn't have to be coerced into reminiscence about the early days of television. He complies half-willingly. He recalls how *Garroway at Large* got started, and why. The manager of the Chicago station where he worked in 1949 got a wire from New York asking if the station could "fill" the 9-to-9:30 network time slot on Sunday evenings. Starting the next Sunday evening Garroway and friend Charlie Andrews threw a show together with a $5,000-a-week budget for an NBC network of 23 stations.

"And," says Garroway, "there were no sets." Meaning TV sets. So the audience was somewhat limited, though the show couldn't help breaking new ground. "We did some things first because, like Columbus, we got there first. We were pioneers —how could you lose?"

Garroway thought it would be funny to close the first *At Large* by chopping the coaxial cable attached to the camera in half with an ax. "We proposed this to the engineers, who gave kind of an engineering laugh, and I said, 'I'm not really gonna do it' and I sure did. I still have a piece of that cable at home. And it did end the show."

Chicago broadcasting was going "phffft," says Garroway, because the networks were basing operations on the East and West coasts, "where show business was." So after two years of *At Large* he was out of a job. Then he read about the new *Today* show proposed by NBC programming whiz Sylvester "Pat" Weaver. "They were considering big names for it, like Fred Allen and Bob Hope. My agent said, 'I'll see what I can do,' and then I talked to an NBC executive named Mort Werner for half an hour, and the next day my agent called and said, 'You're in.' It was that easy.

"Things haven't been so easy lately."

Today said its first "Good morning" on January 14, 1952. "I remember it as though it were now. I mean, I don't remember exactly what and who were on the show, but I remember the great feel of it. I was delighted with it. I felt pleased with myself as I perhaps never have before or since. And when it was all over, the whole crew applauded. It was the best sound I ever heard."

The *Today* gang—including Frank Blair, Jack Lescoulie and Betsy Palmer—got along well because they remained strangers off the air, Garroway says. "Jack Lescoulie was a very private person. In all those years on the air, he never gave anybody his address or phone number."

One cast member, however, was a shameless prima donna, a temperamental ham and a blatant egomaniac. He also bit people. He was J. Fred Muggs, the chimpanzee hired by Werner not long after Werner hired Garroway. The man and the monkey never got along.

"That monkey sued me finally for a half a million dollars. His owners sued me. They said I had insulted his character by saying that he bit me. I never said that on the air, but in fact NBC has a record of twenty inoculations for chimpanzee bites, for tetanus. He bit me and he bit everybody else. As he grew older, and meaner, we were trying to phase him off the show. Now, this is how much loyalty I had to the image: one morning he got his teeth right through my cheek, and blood was coming out. I was actually shielding him so the blood wouldn't be seen, because if the picture on the screen had shown him with a grip on me like that, and I was bleeding, his value to the program would have been destroyed. 'Look,' they'd say, 'the chimp is biting Garroway.'

"I got him out of camera range and disentangled the dear little fella. I sacrificed all that, and still they sued. The funny thing is, NBC defended it but after five or six years of litigation I'll be doggoned if the network didn't pay them off five or six thousand dollars."

Guests could be difficult as well—though Garroway was never bitten by one.

"Once a guy who didn't know we were on live—he thought we were rehearsing—told a perfectly innocent story and all of a sudden interlarded it with six or seven four-letter words. What do you do? We were sitting on a couch, and I simply got up and slowly walked away, picked up a piece of paper and started reading it into the camera. And you know, hardly anyone noticed those words. I guess I have said every bad word you can think of at least once on the air, but if you don't pause or change the continuity of your speech, and just keep on going, almost nobody will be sure that what they heard is what went on."

The *Today* show was far more leisurely and nonabrasive on those less madly competitive days, but it did kill off seven shows—including vehicles for Jack Paar and Walter Cronkite—that CBS sent into combat against Garroway and company. One of the more charming and seemingly daring *Today* features was to aim a live camera out the window of its ground-floor 49th Street studio in New York and let passersby look through a window and into the eyes of the nation. NBC vice presidents did "all sorts of agitation" against that idea because they thought people would hold up "indecent" signs, Garroway says. Instead, they held up signs with such messages as "Look, honey, I'm sober."

Wide Wide World on Sunday afternoons was 90 largely live minutes that toured the country by television. A single show would use as many as 127 cameras at various locations, with Garroway perched on a stool in a Manhattan studio twenty-five feet away from the nearest person and narrating the hour. Some of the remotes were amazing. And some were fantastic flops.

"On one *Wide World* a man jumped out of a plane, at twenty thousand feet, with a live television camera. We set it up for weeks in advance. Well, he jumped, and we cut to it. *Black.* The only thing he failed to do was turn the camera on."

Garroway's wife Pamela died suddenly in 1961, and that was among the reasons he left the *Today* show, Garroway says. By then this once-shaky experiment was earning the network $8 million a year, and Garroway had been dubbed "The Indestructible" by a TV critic. In the following years, however, the niches he found tended to drop out from under him. A brave attempt to revive live—not taped and edited—TV with a syndicated show out of Boston was "just getting off the ground," Garroway says, when the station decided to go to filmed shows instead. Film is cheaper and safer and "you can put it on a shelf" and it doesn't give you the problems live human beings can give you. Television may have deteriorated in many ways over the years, but it has triumphed in eliminating the unexpected.

The mystery about Garroway is why he was able to succeed so quickly and naturally where hundreds would later fail, at the elusive art of relating directly to the inhuman specter of the television camera.

"It's the funniest thing about looking into that camera," he says. "I didn't have any idea what it would be like that first time. But when we got on the air, I felt very warm and comfortable—strangely so—instead of being frightened. The lens seemed to be so direct and friendly, really, almost as if I could see somebody there. It was a black channel to the people, a neutron star. I still think that way. It stuck with me all my life. I am much more comfortable and more in communication with whoever is at the end of that black hole than I am with someone in person."

He learned how to look into a television camera from a woman he knew while stationed with the Army in Honolulu. "She never looked away while she was talking to you. The power she had was remarkable. It was unique. So I tried it on television. You do not look away, except during what I call periods of politeness. You see, we are animals with a kind of shell around us. If I get six inches from you suddenly, you'll back away. If I move eight feet away, you'll come closer to hear me. It's the same with this eye phenomenon. So on television, you drop your eyes every so often so you aren't staring. You have to kind of feel when to do it—maybe every four seconds, or whatever."

Garroway looks older now, of course, but not 62. He still wears glasses, but they are modder than before, and he tapes them onto his head with "wig tape" ("it won't melt from the heat of the body") so that journalists will no longer insist on calling him "owlish."

He keeps busy, but he wants a job. He wants to be back on the air. He doesn't watch TV much himself because he doesn't consider today's version to be *television*. It's not live; it's not real; it leaves your mind limp. "I know a girl who is a booker for a big network and she's almost going out of her head because they don't want *any* content in the guests—no writers, no thinkers, not a poet—no, only movie stars, rock stars, people like that."
August 28, 1975

Two years pass, and on a cold day in January of 1977, Garroway shows up for the 25th-anniversary broadcast of the Today *show. It's almost as if D. W. Griffith were attending the dedication of an automated movie theater in a suburban shopping center. Garroway and other past cast members have walked through a time warp to sit in the same studio with their squeaky-clean, hair-sprayed, 1977 counterparts.*

It was a face-off, with a battery of fat color cameras forming a line between them.

"Good morning," said Jack Lescoulie to about 6 million TV viewers. "This is *Today*, January 14, 1952." It wasn't, of course. It was *Today* celebrating its 25th anniversary on the air by inviting its founding fathers to participate in the show and in a party thrown right there in Studio 3-K when the show was over.

Only in television would they serve champagne and Bloody Marys at 9 A.M.

Garroway looked portly, benign, baronial. Lescoulie seemed puffy but spirited. Newsman Frank Blair, who didn't leave the show until 1975, was the live wire in the room throughout and after the show. During a commercial, Blair, who has previously expressed his dislike for former *Today* host Barbara Walters, put his arm around current cohost Jane

Pauley, 26, and laughed, "Eat your heart out, Barbara! Look what I've got!"

But conspicuous by absence was J. Fred Muggs. "His handlers called us from Florida and wanted to know why we hadn't invited him back," said producer Paul Friedman. "He's down there doing an act that ends with him playing 'The Bells of St. Mary's.'"

Then he paused. "You want me to say it? Okay, I'll say it: I didn't want that damn monkey on the program."

Friedman said at the party after the show that he thought certain things about the original *Today* show were "embarrassing" and he wouldn't do them today. But then during the program, an old clip of Garroway prankishly observing "National Donut Week" was shown, and this broke up everybody in the place. Television may have been silly or crude or makeshift in the '50s, but there was something civilized and humane about it too, at least on shows like Garroway's.

The man credited with the invention of the *Today* show—and with the *Tonight* show, *Wide Wide World*, and other innovative concepts—was at yesterday's silver anniversary: Sylvester "Pat" Weaver, a former NBC president who looks as tall and dapper as William Powell in a *Thin Man* movie and now lives in Santa Barbara, California.

"What's lacking in television today, mainly, is that network managements have no real design, no real plan," said Weaver at the party. "I had a grand design—a system of programs to reach and influence and enlighten and entertain the people at home. You've got to care. The great communications entities of the world were always made by people who cared. If they cared, they made them great, and when you ran a great anything, you made money."

A veteran cameraman spotted Weaver talking and muttered to a colleague, "We had our highest ratings under him. This company was number one. We need him back again."

Naturally, reminiscences shot through the early-morning air. Former news and features editor Lee Lawrence, now with the White House Conference on Handicapped Individuals, recalled the time she installed four Cessnas on the Rockefeller Center ice rink to illustrate a piece on aeronautics, and the time a space capsule was sawed in half to get it into the studio. "And remember when the TelePrompTer boys threw me into that fountain in Rome?" she asked another *Today* alumnus.

Garroway said he still watches the *Today* show. Sometimes. But he also watches the ABC competition that gave the program its first serious challenge. "Oh, yes, I watch *Good Morning America*, too. In fact, I like it better. It's looser."

By and large, the two *Today* show casts, past and present, kept their distance on and off camera. Friedman seemed amazed that the show hadn't exploded right in his face. Maybe he thought the old-timers would fall apart, but they're the ones who showed the most life. During a discussion of social change in the past 25 years, Pauley, off-camera, gave a long and uninterested yawn, but Garroway, over on his side of the room, stood up from his desk and listened intently.

"I think," historian Daniel Boorstin was saying, "the fact that mankind has survived television is an encouraging sign." Not too much later, Garroway raised his right hand to the TV camera and said, "Peace"; and that, years ago, was the way *Today* ended and the day began.

January 15, 1977

Little Rascals

TELEVISION LAND is Kiddie Land.

Ad agencies drag kids in to sell everything from tires to Ravioli-Os. Kids are added like chemicals to formulas for situation comedies and other shows, to raise the cuteness quotient and snare more viewers.

These kids are the victims of television even more than the most addicted of TV-watching children are. And we are victims of them.

And yet, among the hundreds of children's faces plastered across television screens every week, some belong to kids who have managed, even while being manipulated, to retain their dignity as children.

By luck, through perseverance or just because they are superior to the others, these children can still convey the integrity of innocence. Even if their incomes are approaching six figures a year and they are thinking of getting a better agent. And they have a pilot in the can. And they read the trades by the swimming pool.

These are the great kids of television.

It's worth enduring all the others to come across the likes of them.

MASON REESE

"Kids need TV," says TV star Mason Reese. "They really do. They need something to watch besides their parents."

Mason, now 11, is the dean of American children, the grand old man of tots. He is just under 50 inches tall, but has the enlightened countenance of a philosopher, and seems also to possess an incredibly incisive perspective on what it means to be a kid. Especially a superkid.

First skyrocketed to pudgy fame with an award-winning Underwood meat-spread commercial in 1973, Mason went on to be a frequent cohost on *The Mike Douglas Show*, the youngest reporter in the history of WNBC-TV in New York and the star of an unsold comedy pilot, *Mason*, shown earlier this week on ABC. Currently he is the national spokesman for Dunkin' Donuts and the living motif for a new Birds Eye campaign that has begun in print and hits TV in the fall.

Of course, like all of us, he would like to be on TV regularly —"if I had my own series." He prefers to play himself. "I don't think I could do a *Police Story*. I couldn't play cops very well. I play myself very well," he says. Could anyone play him better—say, Robert Redford? "Maybe. If he cut his legs off."

Mason is just as unquestionably a pro as he is questionably a kid. Boston ad man Bob Schmalenberger, who put Mason in the Underwood spots and handles the Dunkin' Donuts campaign, marvels at Mason's ability to read lines perfectly the first time and advise different on-camera techniques and light placement. "He says, 'That light is a little too high,' and he'll be right," says Schmalenberger. "He doesn't mean any harm. He's just bright."

Yet for all the sophistication, Mason remains approachable. He didn't like it when *People* magazine recently called him a "media brat." And though he pitches doughnuts called "Munchkins," he isn't too thrilled about being referred to as a Munchkin himself.

"At first I thought it was kind of cute," he says. "Everybody was callin' me 'Munchkin.' Now, since I realized I am small and I am kind of weird-looking, it now seems to bother me, the word 'Munchkin.' It's not something that people say meanly, though. It's kind of a compliment, I suppose."

Schmalenberger says the fact that Mason doesn't look his age is an asset to his career—he can still pass for 7 or 8. But Mason complains that he is 4 inches shorter than he should be.

"The doctor I'm going to is very concerned with my growth, and for some reason or other the allergy shots he's been giving me are making me grow. I'm allergic to almost everything. But the shots, I think, are just for pain. To give me a little pain. I told the doctor he'd better get off his butt and start making me grow a little more."

As for *People* magazine and its cracks, he says, "They have the right to do it, but really, the right should be taken away from them. No, I'm just kidding."

Acting is only a temporary gig. "What I'd like to do when I grow up is I think be a writer for comedy. I've had a bit of experience writing comedy because I've written some stories for my class. Mostly satires. Let's see, I wrote one—'Airport '87'; no, it was '86—and I did one called 'Superjew.' It was about a guy who goes into a delicatessen, eats two kosher pickles, goes into the bathroom and turns into Superjew.

Superjew can leap tall kreplachs at a single bound. He can dive into matzoh-ball soup. He can hold up Hebrew books. Not that many kids in my class are Jewish, but there are a few Jews, and they all understood my jokes."

Mason lives in Manhattan with his parents. Of them he says, "I like my mommy. Except when she says 'no.' Then she's just a problem. That's when I lock myself in the bathroom."

MIKEY

Advertising history was made in 1971 when two little boys, confronted with an untasted cereal called Life, used their brother "Mikey" as a guinea pig. "He likes it!" one exclaimed as the silent Mikey munched the oats. The commercial was a sensation, resulted in a sequel referring to "the cereal Mikey likes," still plays on network and local television six years later and got Mikey's picture placed prominently on every box of Life.

Where is Mikey today?

In the first place, the kid's name is not Mikey. He is John Gilchrist, of Yonkers, New York. He was 3 when the commercial was made, and he doesn't even remember making it. When he sees it on TV now, he says, "I laugh."

His two brothers, Tommy, now 14, and Michael, now 12, are the other two boys in the commercial. But John is the one most often recognized as the immortal Mikey.

"When we went to Disney World," his mother says, "people got more excited at seeing 'Mikey' than they did about Disney World. It happens so often."

John still "works" a little, his mother says, doing commercials, but one knowledgeable Madison Avenuer says the kid has already made at least enough money to put himself through college. At the very minimum, the Life spot brings the Gilchrists $12,000 every year it's on.

Mrs. Gilchrist is shy about "publicity" and says she usually turns down interviews for John. But, coaxed, she calls him to the phone. He was in the backyard. Playing baseball. Just like a real kid.

Asked if he would like to stay in acting, John says, "Yeah. I like the business." He would like to be a singer, too. When he is asked for an autograph, he says, "I sign it *'John Gilchrist'* and then in parentheses I put *'Mikey.'*"

Fame does not seem to have been a burden for him.

Mrs. Gilchrist and her husband, Tom, have six kids. "We're trying to keep them very normal," she says. "We try not to make too big a thing out of any one of them. John's just a regular kid, and we want to keep him that way."

BUDDY

Kristy McNichol got her start in an Opel commercial. "I was seven. I thought it was great." Now 14, she plays the continuing role of Buddy in the popular ABC prime-time drama series *Family*.

"Burt Reynolds called me and he wants me to do a movie with him," she casually mentions when reached at her Sherman Oaks, California, home. Her mother had been cautious when answering, because Kristy has been getting crank calls from overzealous fans.

Still, Kristy has no doubts about the show-biz life and doesn't think she's missed much by not having a normal childhood.

"I think that I've gained, not lost. In all ways," she says. "I love acting. Everything about it. It doesn't get boring. I've done billions of commercials. At least fifty. I've done Hostess Twinkies and McDonald's, and Kraft Cheese. A lot of them. When I have free time, which is hardly ever, I go off and do a commercial.

"But now I'm too busy to work on anything but *Family*. I'd like to do more *Afterschool Specials*, but it's just a rat race. I don't think I can."

Kristy is asked if acting is good for her ego.

She says, "What's ego? It doesn't make me feel better,

seeing myself on TV, if that's what you mean. I usually just crack up. I sit on the floor and watch myself and I just crack up laughing."

Kristy McNichol is blasé.

REV. JIMMY

"I've never taken advantage of being a star," says 9-year-old Marcus Gordon Issoglio, whose professional name is Sparky Marcus. "I'm not really a star yet. I'm just an actor now. I don't really see how acting could go to my head. It's just a job. If you have it, you gotta do it. It's like owning a house. If you have it, you gotta pay the taxes on it."

Sparky has appeared in *Afterschool Specials*, movies like *Freaky Friday*, and TV specials like *The Night That Panicked America*. But the role that brought the young lad with the overintelligent face to prominence was Rev. Jimmy Joe Jeeter, the pint-sized evangelist, on Norman Lear's *Mary Hartman, Mary Hartman*.

He stayed up late to watch Rev. Jimmy expire on the show —electrocuted, as the script went, when a TV set fell into his bathtub.

"Instead of dropping a TV, they threw water balloons into the bathtub," he explains from his home in suburban Los Angeles. "The first time I got in the tub they had pure hot water in it—well, not that hot, but after about five minutes my head was getting wet, my shoulders were sweating, my knuckles were sweating—ugh!"

Sparky's mother, Lylene, put him in show business when a friend insisted, "Sparky should work, Sparky should work." Sparky went to work.

"I can remember as far back as, I think, five," he says. "I did a McDonald's commercial and then some other commercials until I was around seven, and then I really hit it *hot*."

Sparky, 48 inches tall and irked when "people call me 'small,'" says he watches television every day, but not the violent shows. "It's very disgusting, the violence. All the bloodshedding is for nothing. What does fighting solve? Nothing! You know what I mean?"

He watches the Saturday-morning kiddie shows and gueststarred in one of them. "I did six weeks of *Sigmund and the Sea Monsters*. My parents woke me up at seven-thirty in the morning to watch it. I was supposed to be a sea genie. See, Sigmund used to have a genie and then the genie went away and then he was walking down the beach—I think his sister was at a fat farm losing weight—and, anyway, I played a little brat. I whacked my uncle's whammy, and I turned Sigmund into a chicken. And Fran Ryan into a pig."

"And millions of other crazy things."

Sparky is asked if he is enjoying life. "Yes," he says convincingly, "I certainly am. Without life I wouldn't even be talking to you."

MELISSA GILBERT

She is lying on the floor of her Los Angeles home in her ballet clothes, having just returned from class.

"Oh, I just dropped a shoe on my face," says Melissa Gilbert, 13, into the telephone. "It's a plastic shoe. It's a new kind of shoe. And—oh, there's a hole in my stocking. No, two holes. My God, the whole thing is coming apart! Now there's a third and a fourth hole. This is a play-by-play description. . . ."

For three years, Melissa has been stealing scene after scene as Laura Ingalls on the low-key NBC pioneer saga *Little House on the Prairie*. Melissa plays Laura not just as a cute little girl, but as a cute little girl with intelligence and brass. It is one of the best continuing jobs of acting on series television.

But Melissa sounds quite unfazed by her celebrity, even by the mysterious fan who sends her crystal champagne glasses in the mail (she calls him a "nutto"), and, indeed, she is a veteran, having first acted in a diaper commercial at the age of 2. "Then I retired."

56 / ON THE AIR!

Now, a hit series part of her everyday life, she also manages to do things other girls do—falls out of trees and collects wooden dollhouse furniture. And watches television.

"I'm a TV weirdo. I'm a TV freak," she says. "I *love* television. My mother is constantly yelling at me not to watch it. I say, 'It's educational, Mom.' She says, 'Is *I Love Lucy* educational? Is *Gilligan's Island* educational? Is *Charlie's Angels* educational?' I say, that all depends on how you look at it. I love television. It doesn't take too much energy to watch it. And, um, you can plug one in anywhere if you can find a socket."

She watches *Little House* every week, she says. Her favorite episodes: "The one where the baby died and I climbed a mountain and found Ernest Borgnine at the top" and "The one where the raccoon bit us and we thought we had rabies."

Utterly unimpressed by success, casual even about the fact that she regularly eats lunch with Fonzie (Henry Winkler) because "we both shoot at Paramount," Melissa isn't worried about her future or that of her series.

"Oh, it'll vanish eventually, and I'll go on to bigger and better," she chirps. "I like everything. I'll be on anything. What do I want to be when I grow up? Oh, a nurse, a doctor. I'd like to perform open-heart surgery. That is, of course, if I can't make it as an actress."

July 8, 1977

The First Archie Bunker Award

AMERICANS THINK THE Alaskan pipeline is a klutzy farce, the neutron bomb a cruel joke and Anita Bryant a big pain in the neck.

These findings are the result of scientific study: a content analysis of the ongoing monologues of Johnny Carson, star of

The Tonight Show Starring Johnny Carson. When you follow Carson's nightly topical musings religiously—or, let's say, loyally—you get a provocative picture of what a popular entertainer thinks it is safe to say about current events. Carson is not on the cutting edge of social change or public attitudes, but what he says is acutely barometric because he's so brilliantly expert at gauging and exploiting what the traffic will allow. In recent months his monologues have grown increasingly audacious and topical, and it's his handling of the Anita Bryant business that has proved most interesting to observe.

Gay-rights activists said they feared a new era of "McCarthyism" when Bryant began her crusade against homosexual visibility. On the contrary, she may have unwittingly done them a favor, because Carson and other comedians have turned her into a new symbolic stock comic figure; Anita Bryant has become the female Archie Bunker, a living caricature of abrasive bigotry.

The image of Bryant that emerges from the Carson monologues—repeatedly to the cheers and laughter of, one presumes, a largely heterosexual studio audience—is that of a prudish, self-righteous fanatic. Was the New York blackout an "act of God"? No, said Carson, because "Anita Bryant would never have given Him time off."

In a routine about mock predictions for the future, Carson prophesied that this year, "at the insistence of Anita Bryant, the Muppets will undergo a sex test."

He also promised his audience, "A little later on, Anita Bryant will be out here and try to knock off Truman Capote's hat with a Florida orange."

The tone is not hostile, but clearly derisive. Other talk-show guests have spoken against Bryant but not quite so effectively, because they all lack Carson's inimitable and incomparable guileless credibility. Guest host Rob Reiner sounded nearly as self-righteous as Bryant when he implored into the camera, "Why doesn't that woman stop? Stop, Anita." This did get a big hand, however.

It's very likely that Bryant jokes will be particularly plentiful on the new fall comedy shows coming up. They all did *Gong Show* jokes last year; they'll all do Bryant jokes this year. *Laugh-In* producer George Schlatter, contemplating topics for the new version of the show to be seen on NBC, was quoted recently as noting, "You don't have the war anymore —but you do have Anita Bryant."

Pollsters could be more conclusive about this, but it does begin to look as though Bryant has solidified public opinion against what gay activists call "homophobia" more effectively and—thanks to the speed with which television affects social attitudes—more quickly than any amount of homosexually generated propaganda could have done.

The image of homosexuals projected by television, meanwhile, has become as squeaky-clean and wholesome as was the image of blacks during the most sensitive years of the civil rights struggle. In those days, stereotypes were avoided so scrupulously that from TV you got the impression blacks were just like whites, except they didn't have any flaws.

From TV today, the impression given of homosexuals is that they're just like heterosexuals except they have no hang-ups.

Many series had stories with prominent homosexual characters last season, and, because the networks are touchy about the demands of activist groups, these characters were so removed from the old fey stereotype as to seem utter supermen. When "Alice" fell in love with a homosexual man on that series, the guy was brawny enough for a Brut commercial.

ABC has already capitulated to premature homosexual protests and refined the gay character on the upcoming comedy *Soap*. He will no longer be referred to by a sarcastic brother as a "Froot Loop."

When CBS recently aired the movie *Made for Each Other*, star Joseph Bologna was not allowed to say, when he stumbled into an encounter-group session, "I don't know why I'm here; I'm not a fag or anything." That kind of censorship may seem like a victory to homosexual activists, but in fact "fag" was just the word that a character like Bologna's in the film would have used. Obviously accuracy in dramatization is being sacrificed in the name of tact.

What Bryant and Carson may have done is help speed up the process that will allow television to treat homosexuals with the same disrespect with which it treats everyone else—which is in its way a kind of 20th-century media realism, and perhaps even fair. At the moment, homosexuals are a privileged class in television, and Anita Bryant, at least in the telltale monologues of Johnny Carson, has assumed the Earl Butz role of national village idiot.
July 31, 1977

The Awful Joys of TV in L.A.

WELL, LET'S TAKE a little trip, out old L.A. way. Let's sit indoors and watch tee-vee on the sunniest day.

It's something to do whenever you find yourself getting too optimistic about the human race, the state of the nation or the next 25 years. Watch a little local television in Los Angeles. That'll cure you.

L.A. TV is so terrible, it's wonderful.

Los Angeles is the second largest TV market in the country. TV here is what much TV secretly or overtly wants to be—junky, slick, relentless, mindless. It's 24-hours-a-day on several stations, so you can get a fix anytime. L.A. and TV were made for each other; television in other cities looks quaint by comparison. Yet what happens in television in L.A. is likely to happen to television elsewhere sooner or later. It's a trend-setting town.

The commercials are just great. They reflect the Southern California fetishes of personal appearance and self-gratification at any cost, and they constantly congratulate their audience for having moved to Southern California and thus become the envy of everyone else in the universe. In a Western cult sci-fi book called *Ecotopia*, soon to be a mass-market paperback, California and some other Western states simply secede from the Union because they don't want to go down in a cloud of pollution and blubber with the rest of us.

It would be naive to pretend there's nothing infectious about this spirit of El-Ay Lucky Us–ism. It bespeaks faith in one's environment and one's future. You won't find much of that in New York.

Dodge Cars and Trucks have a special line of "Adult Toys" that were "created especially for Southern California," gabs a lean male skin-diver type surrounded by bikini-clad cuties. "Start your own collection of Adult Toys," he says, winking—the idea being that people in Southern California don't just have fun; they have funnnnnn. And this sun-saturated playground in which they play with their adult toys must be preserved in all its pretty perfectness. Hence a toilet-paper commercial for ecology-minded "Aurora—the paper products that care about The West."

Perhaps only in L.A. would you see commercials for a "School for Bartenders," for "Home of Mobile World" and dozens of other "RV" (recreational vehicle) dealers, for "Spa-Arama," who'll help turn your house into a playpen, and for all manner of self-improvement emporiums. They'll make you stop smoking, stop drinking, stop eating and, of course, build a beautiful You that everyone will want to play with. "Feel better about yourself," says an ad for an alcoholics' hospital.

"Ever since I started at Jack LaLanne, I get great compliments on my body," boasts a buxom blonde. "People really tell me I look good." And that's what counts, right?

The morning exercise show on one station is called "Body Buddies." It's presided over by a husband-and-wife fitness team so screamingly healthy and robust as to shame Adonis. "Dr. Bernie Ernst," identified as a "chiropractor-nutritionist," and his wife, identified as his wife, do the exercises and do commercials for such body-boosting products as raw certified milk and an exerciser called the "Trim with Win Trim-Ex." During that spot, he kneels in all his sun-tanned blond healthiness while she lies on the floor in a fetching leotard, trimming like mad with this big slingshot and bubbling, "Turn yourself on to a trimmer, firmer, shapelier you!"

A regular feature of the show is "Gyrate and Lose Weight." Mrs. Ernst jiggles and wiggles rhythmically to rock records. Dr. Bernie says, "Now let's disco-dance with my wife, Jeannie!" It's a real waker-upper.

The news here is a circus, sometimes of horrors. One of the most popular personalities in town is KNBC's Kelly Lange, who'll be graduating to network soon enough. Lange once ended a series of interviews at the homes of stars with a "mystery guest." Guess who. Kelly Lange, the news star! She interviewed herself in her own home.

Much more recently, she returned from vacation after the helicopter crash that killed traffic reporter and former U-2 pilot Francis Gary Powers. Lange paused for a moment and made a Very Serious Expression. "While in New York, I joined your great sorrow over our Telecopter tragedy," she told her news buddies, without mentioning the pilot's name.

For the sleazy side of the news you turn to Metromedia's KTLA, which has a comedy news show called *MetroNews, MetroNews* but whose actual newscasts tend more to the ghoulish than the amusing. "We'll Show You the Violence that broke out when Queen Elizabeth visited Ireland," promised a station "newsman" a few minutes before a nightly newscast. This was accompanied with newsreel footage of a soldier being kicked in the head. What more would they show at news time?

At the top of the newscast itself, the head-kicking footage was repeated as another lure to viewers. "By satellite we'll Show You the Violent Demonstration..." began another newscaster. Finally the time came for the news itself. The head-kicking footage was repeated yet again, the third time it had been aired within less than 20 minutes. You can imagine the jolly time they had with the Son of Sam story.

But if you want uplift, you can get uplift; KLXA in nearby Orange County broadcasts 24 hours a day of gospel music, religious talk shows and pop religion. The message is unceasingly jubilant. "It's just so beautiful being a part of the family of God!" says a suntanned woman with glistening lips. "My goodness!"

A program originally called *Let's Just Praise the Lord*, later retitled *Praise the Lord* and referred to on the air as *PTL*, is seen several times daily. A husband-and-wife fun religion team—Faith Buddies—read letters from viewers, describe the growth of their industry and request donations.

On another recent show, another couple were making their daily "Prayer Reports."

"Little Evie's here with me, my lovely wife," said a burly man. "We're going to be going to the Lord with our prayer requests in a moment, but right now, honey, what have you got for us?"

Little Evie, wearing a big yellow flower on her dress, had several reports of answered prayers. One was from a woman who was sure she would not have survived "sixteen hours of surgery" without prayer. Another was from a couple, Evie said, "who sold their home" after praying they would. "They not only sold it, but they sold it to some Christians! And they're just so grateful for the way the Lord handled it."

There are also reports from people who were "financially healed" after praying for fiscal repairs.

For me, though, the perfect crystal moment of L.A. TV occurred one evening in April 1975 on the ABC affiliate's tons-of-fun *Eyewitness News* show. A woman reporter was interviewing a stewardess who had just returned from a three-month trip to war-wracked Laos. "We have a real nice California person tonight," the reporter promised.

Her big question to the stewardess was phrased like this: "What did you learn about the Laotian people; or—more important, I suppose—what did you learn about yourself?"

The woman said she had learned about herself that she can get along without "hamburgers and ice cream," at least for three months.

"Thank you," said the reporter. "I guess we can see that idealism is alive and flourishing among young California people."

Let's go back to L.A. soon.

August 28, 1977

Hey!!! It's Steve Martin!

HEY—WE'LL GET TO those Revealing Interview Quotes in just a minute. But first—how about some Witty Media Journalism? Steve Martin bounds onto a stage. "Hi, I'm Steve Martin," he says. "I'll be out in just a minute!" A little later: "Okay—let's go with the Professional Show Business!" And still later:

"I just remembered—I am *so mad* at my *mother!* She's a hundred and two years old, and she called me the other day, and she wanted to borrow *ten dollars* for some *foooood!* I said, 'Hey! I *work* for a living!' "

At this a normal audience roars, only to be reassured, "Hey, we're having some fun, though, aren't we, kids?" A secret of Steve Martin's success is making a huge point out of never leaving well enough alone.

Steve Martin: Boon or Boor? Steve Martin: Gross-out Champ or World's Greatest Comedian? Steve Martin, by his own admission, "a ramblin' kind of a guy . . . a cuh-ray-zee kind of a guy . . . a yew-neeek kind of a guy" who once began a guest-host gig on the *Tonight* show with "I know what you're saying—What's this guy doing hosting the *Tonight* show? Well—I have hostages!"

Martin, whose fluffy gray hair doesn't belong on a 32-year-old head (first gray hair: at 15), was not having some fun himself when he came into Washington yesterday for tonight's two sold-out concerts at the Kennedy Center. His cab had a flat tire on the way from the airport; the Sheraton-Carlton lost his reservation and sent him to the Sheraton-Park. He sat there in his room glum and tired late yesterday, but tonight he'll be just entertaining people to pieces—until they can't *stand* it anymore.

Martin may seem like just another of those 15-years-of-hard-work overnight sensations, but he's bigger than a stand-up comic's been in maybe a decade. He is beginning a 50-city,

60-day concert tour selling out right and left, and his new album, *Let's Get Small,* has been out only half a week but will appear on *Billboard*'s what's-hot chart next week.

"There's no age group he doesn't appeal to," marvels a flack at Warner Brothers Records.

What does he appeal with? With everything. He throws the book at his audience—a history of American shtick that includes the old arrow-through-the-head gag, the funny nose, the balloons twisted into animal shapes ("This one's a venereal disease"), the joke for joke's sake. He plays the total ego, the clod, the self-assured master of virtuoso ineptitude and the fool who takes the audience riding for a fall with him.

And he's not very political and he's not even very dirty. Does he think he is a sign of the times?

"Yes," he says, "Apathy."

He does not feel a part of any generation. "But I feel like we're part of a new society, a changing society. We're kicking the '60s goodbye, and I'm enjoying that extremely. There's a new formalism now, I think. In the late '60s, it was a very informal period. You could say dirty words and insult people and it was okay to get up and dance at a movie. All that's just fashion—not good or bad or anything: just the way things were for a while. Right now things are going back to formalism. I like the change."

It's Martin's yew-neeek kind of style to constantly call attention to form when on stage. He'll say, "We're having *some fun,* though, aren't we, kids?" or, "Okay—that's enough Funny Comedy Gags!"

Once, when guest-hosting the *Tonight* show and being faced with grumbled reaction to a joke, he shot back, "Hey, folks—*comedy is not pretty.*" In fact, he gets a louder welcoming ovation from the Carson audience than any other guest host.

And he'll open the season for the youth-seducing *NBC's Saturday Night,* where his guest-host appearances helped put him over the top into the total consciousness of all humanity. He's made it by defying the current; he doesn't rip any jokes out of the headlines.

"I'm just tired of topical humor," he says. "I am consciously atopical. Number one, topical is old hat, and number two, my act's different. It's personal. It's about what happens in the moments you wake up, or the moments before you go to sleep —little personal, private observations of the world in general. That person I play on stage is oblivious to newspapers. He's full of opinions about nothing.

"I think people are distrustful of government, distrustful of organizations, distrustful of everything. They just want to get back to their personal lives, and let those other guys do what they want."

Steve Martin is a cranked-down prophet for a new age of Self.

But our story doesn't start here—*obviously*. It starts in the shadow of Disneyland, where Steve grew up, eventually going to work at the Magic Kingdom and once or twice even meeting Unca Walt, though he was too paralyzed with awe to say anything to him. "The balloons? They came later, but the seed was planted there, at the joke shop where I worked. We sold arrows-through-the-head, funny noses—all those things that at first were funny, and then when you were in college they were metaphysically funny, and then they got just funny again.

"But I don't use them much anymore."

He was a philosophy major in college, later got a job working for the *Smothers Brothers Comedy Hour* on CBS, where he found the censors to be "just idiots, just people off the street that they turned into censors." Years of performing in small clubs, then as the booed-upon opening act for rowdy rock groups, prepared him for the giant step he took in the past year.

He elbowed his way into our hearts with a loud "Well Excuuuuuuse Me!" that has, like some of his other trademarks, waddled its way into the language of the times.

At his solar-powered home in chic Aspen, he lives a vegetarian life without drugs or booze, he says, which completes his refreshingly reactionary image.

"I quit drinking two years ago and I quit smoking dope ten

years ago and my life changed a hundred percent. I don't mind drugs, but I do mind blithering idiots. When some guy at a concert walks down to the front and stands there just swaying, I can tell he's stoned out of his mind. I don't mind drugs, really; I'd like to get drunk every night. But I just don't want to pay the price."

John Denver comes over to his house now and then and he goes over to John Denver's house now and then. Sometimes they play horseshoes. Such a healthy life for a comedian. Comedians are supposed to be neurotic wrecks born on the lower East Side of New York.

But Martin is part of a—I hate to say it, but it's true—New Breed of comedian that includes people like Lily Tomlin, Richard Pryor, Chevy Chase. And he's also a living parody of comedians when he's up on stage. Martin doesn't exactly tell jokes; he does comedy about joke telling.

"I don't like to offend people," he says on the album, recorded at a San Francisco club. "I don't do any fag jokes or anything like that." Pause. "How many fags do we have here tonight, by the way?"

He picks up and plunks at a banjo and dares the crowd to sing along: "Now, I ask you very confidentially way down upon the Swan . . ."

He tells the crowd he had to break up with his best girl. "One night she said, 'Please drive me home.' I didn't want to, so I shot her."

He admits, "I love bread. I'm into money. I love everything about money," and lists some of the luxuries he's bought himself—"a three-hundred-dollar pair of socks. A fur sink. An electric dog polisher.

"Of course," he says, "I bought some dumb stuff too, you know."

Finally, he gives the crowd his benediction: "Laugh once a day—because a day without sunshine is like . . . night."

The world's greatest comedian's hotel room is invaded by his manager. They're playing cuts from Martin's comedy joke album on WFIL radio in Philadelphia, he tells Martin—and they *never* do that! It's unheard of. This Steve Martin is some phenomenon. Martin does not look impressed.

"I hope it's not a flash-in-the-pan career," Martin says later. "You know, one year and it's all over. Right now we're having a nice rush of concerts and this record thing, but you know, it all comes to an end, no matter who you are."
September 15, 1977

Lou Grant: Just What TV Needs

LOU GRANT is the best new show of the season. Like the man in the title, it is a bracing, reassuring combination of an essentially gentle spirit and good, old-fashioned guts. This may be not only what television needs, but what America needs.

Certainly there's not a prime-time network entertainment series more intelligently crafted or more demonstrably concerned with human nature. Grant, as played with bluster and sensitivity by Edward Asner, could be the first major character in TV history to walk out of a comedy series *(The Mary Tyler Moore Show)* and into a dramatic one. The transition is smooth.

There are laughs (though no laugh track) on the premiere tonight on CBS, and pretty rich ones at that. But it's a serious, thoughtful show, and as we remeet Grant, we find him going through one of the loneliest and most unnerving of passages —out of work and dropped into a town, Los Angeles, that he once knew but that no longer knows him.

"I'm fifty years old and I have two hundred and eighty dollars in the bank," he mopes. He's also lost 40 pounds—as has Asner—but people keep telling him, "I liked you better fat."

The creators of this MTM production—writer Leon Tokatyan, director Gene Reynolds, producers James L. Brooks and Allan Burns—hit the right tone right off, and early shots of Grant arriving at L.A. Airport, his rumpled countenance silhouetted against glass doors leading to the glare outside, set us up for a moving, engrossing hour.

Grant goes to see an old pal at the *Los Angeles Tribune* (the *Los Angeles Times* was the principal model for this fictitious daily) and is offered the job of city editor, as long as he can win the approval of the wealthy, feisty woman publisher, played by Nancy Marchand. Their first meeting suggests that a rewarding relationship will develop.

The last scene in the premiere, in which she offers Lou a ride in her black Cadillac and then reconsiders, is a hoot. Throughout the program, writer Tokatyan leads characters to the brinks of clichés and then turns them away at the last minute to something inventive and credible.

A few lapses don't hurt the overall good impression. The creators of the show obviously didn't want to spend a lot of time on exposition about Grant breaking into his new job; they wanted to tell a free-standing story, so once Grant is hired, he jumps right into the job with no ado. It's abrupt, but probably a wise course.

Great care has been taken to portray newspaper life realistically—certainly more so than in such unlamented howlers as last year's *Andros Targets* on the same network. It isn't documentary-dull, but *Grant* does give reporters a break, which is not to say an unqualified kiss on the face.

Lou Grant is not so much upbeat or downbeat as sensationally sane. Unlike most of the new shows, it doesn't see the viewer as someone to be coddled, bamboozled or coyly titillated. There's a small scene near the middle that epitomizes the style; Grant is faced with a tough decision, so he sits down on a park bench and silently thinks it over while midday church bells chime. It's not a flashy or witty moment; it just strikes you as wonderfully, quietly plausible.

For Asner, *Grant* represents an especially trenchant triumph. Grant isn't just the kind of editor a writer would like to have; he's the hard-knock old pro anyone who relishes people would like to know.

Chewing his pencil at a news conference, regarding a prematurely adult 16-year-old with a melting double take, testing out approaches to impress the lofty publisher, Asner proves Grant completely worthy of center stage.

"You're not afraid of me, are you?" he growls at a young reporter.

"No."

"Awwwww," Grant says. "That's too bad."

The supporting cast includes Mason Adams as managing editor Charlie Hume. Adams is recognizable if you close your eyes and listen to him talk; his has been the unseen voice in dozens of TV commercials. He'll be proud he showed his face on *Lou Grant,* though. It is a gruff and lovely credit to all involved. And to television.

September 20, 1977

Singing Sausages

WHAT WOULD WE DO without the National Association of Broadcasters? Just when it looked as if our geese were cooked, the NAB has stepped forward with revised "personal products guidelines" for TV commercials. Whew!

The new regulations specify the hours in which feminine-hygiene products can be advertised on the air, prescribe a "restrained and inoffensive" approach for selling underpants and get very specific on the matter of how laxatives may be hawked.

"Graphic representations of symptoms," the laxative guidelines say, "and/or product mechanics shall not be permitted (e.g., rain, rivers, gelatin, concrete blocks, etc.)."

Concrete blocks? If we can take *The San Pedro Beach Bums,* we can take concrete blocks. This NAB code really isn't very good. It doesn't speak to viewer needs. I have a better code of my own to cover all TV commercials, and I hereby submit it for NAB approval, knowing full well that anything this sensible doesn't stand a prayer:

- Pork sausages shall not be allowed to sing and dance, live bulls shall not be permitted to enter bars where liquor is sold and cats may no longer do the cha-cha-cha unless accompanied by an adult.
- The following phrases are not permitted in commercials: "Me and my," "Now, there's," "A whole new way to," "Nothing artificial," and "natural."
- Unnecessary violence must be avoided. Ferocious snow tires, marauding odor eaters and aggressive scrub bubbles are forbidden.
- Close-ups of dirty shirts will not be permitted, and the phrase "ring around the" as applied to collars is out.
- Viewers shall not be given the impression that packages of gum grow on trees, that new cars come equipped with beautiful girls or that insurance companies send out handsome middle-aged announcers to pay off claims.
- Karl Malden's nose shall not appear on the screen for more than five seconds at a time.
- Innuendos about deodorants that tickle, Bics that flick and "getting stroked in the morning" shall be eliminated.
- No male athlete may do automobile commercials unless it has been proved he can read and write and get dressed by himself. No female athlete may be propositioned by any product on a golf course or anywhere else.
- The institution of marriage shall not be undermined by scenes in which husbands or wives attempt to pass off a dandruff shampoo to each other as a baby shampoo.
- No one, especially Bess Myerson, who has ever served in an official capacity as a consumer adviser shall be allowed to appear in any television commercial. Further, all commercials for pain relievers must be accompanied by the spoken phrase "This product may not do you any good at all."
- Toilet paper shall not be squeezed, petted, played with, bandied about or otherwise flaunted in public. Models shall not fondle automobiles.
- Commercials for wine and beer that show happy people enjoying the product must also include scenes of fat old men dead drunk and lying in the gutter.

- Showers and baths shall not be portrayed as wild, sensual fiestas.
- The following personalities are not permitted to appear in television commercials: Joe Namath, the mother of Dr. Joyce Brothers, Dr. Joyce Brothers and Aunt Blue Bell. In fact, Aunt Blue Bell is not to be permitted to appear anywhere.
- Oil companies and other huge corporations are not allowed to spend more than $250 million on messages about how they are working to save money and energy and how they do not make excess profits.
- Little girls shall not be shown receiving praise from their mommies and daddies for having baked something that came out of a can or a box.
- Employees of airline companies, such as pilots and mechanics, shall not be permitted to sing and dance in television commercials unless they also perform these functions in the course of their work.
- So-called "real people," such as those photographed by so-called "hidden cameras" in supermarkets, shall not be permitted in television commercials. Only attractive models and actors who are obviously not real people are allowed.
- There are special regulations governing the advertising of fast-food establishments. Viewers shall not be led to believe that they will actually encounter such celebrities as Roy Rogers or Ronald McDonald, the well-known clown, when they visit these establishments. Nor shall they be led to expect a Philadelphia Mummers parade, an army of Donny and Marie clones or a sudden appearance by the Mormon Tabernacle Choir and marching band.
- If a station or a network receives more than 25 letters of complaint about any commercial, it must be taken off the air and thrown away. Should this regulation result in more than 90 percent of all television commercials' vanishing by tomorrow morning, then my code will have precisely served its purpose.

October 5, 1977

Television Kills: The Trial of Ronney Zamora

AT 9 O'CLOCK LAST NIGHT the TV viewers of this city could have watched *Charlie's Angels, Learn to Paint,* a CBS movie about child abuse, the National League playoffs—or *Florida v. Zamora,* the first trial in state history to be televised.

A few hours earlier in the day, the trial could be watched live and in person as it happened in the Dade County courthouse, where 15-year-old Ronney Zamora stands accused of first-degree murder in the fatal shooting of an elderly neighbor, Elinor Haggart.

If Zamora's lawyer gets his way, Zamora will be the first person in history to be found not guilty by reason of television. Attorney Ellis Rubin's defense is based on the idea that excessive viewing of TV violence led to Zamora's temporary insanity at the time of the shooting.

Psychiatrist Michael Gilbert, a key defense witness, told the jury yesterday that for Zamora, "the pulling of the trigger was in effect a conditioned response," brought on by his 'habituation' to television and his fondness for viewing violent crime shows like *Kojak.*

Zamora's addiction to television started early in life, Gilbert said—long before he was indicted, along with another youth, in the fatal shooting. "It almost became a way of life for him. It replaced the spoon-feeding and the pacifier, as it were, of a child. In his later life, the choice of programming centered on violent horror stories and things like that."

Even as Gilbert spoke of TV and TV violence, a TV camera in Dade County Circuit Court was watching him. The first trial of television has also become the first trial *on* television, at least in Florida. A State Supreme Court ruling has opened the courtrooms to TV cameras for an experimental one-year period.

The single, stationary camera was placed in the courtroom—three seats in the press gallery were labeled "RESERVED, TV CAMERA"—by public TV station WPBT, which airs about three hours of taped trial highlights each night.

Station program director John Felton says the coverage is costing the station about $3,000 a day, but that so far about 800 phone calls have been received at the station and 97 percent of them are favorable to the coverage. Felton estimates that more than 80,000 Miami households see part of the trial each night.

Late Tuesday, ironically or not, one hour of WPBT's Zamora trial was in direct competition with a CBS network rerun of *Kojak*, the very program specifically cited in court as one of Zamora's favorites.

Actor Telly Savalas, who plays the tough, bald cop on the show, had even been served with a subpoena by defense attorney Rubin and was about to leave Hollywood for Miami yesterday when Rubin released him as a witness. Judge Paul Baker had reportedly rejected Rubin's attempts to make TV violence an issue in the trial, and it was unlikely that Savalas would be allowed to testify anyway.

And yet *Kojak* did come up in testimony. Psychiatrist Gilbert said that an episode of *Kojak* flashed through Zamora's mind after the gun went off and Haggart fell to the floor.

"Kojak was his hero," Gilbert said. "His mother told us that he even wanted his stepfather to shave his head like Kojak's."

During all of the psychiatric testimony, Zamora was absent from the courtroom at Rubin's request. He was present only at the start of yesterday's long session, his dark eyebrows usually in a position that suggested fear or puzzlement, although the expression on his face remained one of indifference.

He probably does not realize that he represents the fulfillment of dire predictions by sociologists, psychiatrists and the massed foes of TV violence. The defense has depicted him as a socially deprived, love-starved child who escaped from depressing reality into the fantasy world of television and became himself the victim of its excessive violence and emphasis on stories of crime and criminals.

According to the picture painted by his lawyer, the young man is the first martyr to television.

From trial testimony by numerous psychiatrists and psychologists and the boy's mother, a portrait of Zamora emerged that seemed somehow a sign of its time. "Sociopathic," or antisocial; alienated from his environment; severely beaten by his stepfather; a scholastic underachiever though he has an average IQ of 101, Zamora used television as a barrier against reality and, according to Rubin, got a warped view of life as a result.

"He interprets the world in a hostile manner" and "lacks emotional closeness with others," said one psychiatrist. "He does not know how to express aggression in a socially accepted way," and he "explains his reactions based on things he saw on TV," said another. Dr. Helen Ackerman called Zamora suicidal and said he had once thrown several knives up in the air and then waited for them to hit him.

And still another psychiatrist said that after the shooting, Zamora felt "as if he could wake up and find it was a TV program or a dream."

Zamora is also a hypothesis come true: according to testimony, he epitomizes the very kind of unfeeling, uncomprehending, television-dominated child described in abstract terms in such books as *The Plug-in Drug*, by Marie Winn, and in such research into effects of TV violence as that done by Dr. George Gerbner at the University of Pennsylvania.

In other words, if Ronney Zamora is found innocent, television will have been found guilty.

Because it is rife with all these ramifications, the trial is getting heavy media coverage, not only in Miami but nationally. Tuesday night's *CBS Evening News with Walter Cronkite* devoted about five minutes to the trial, using taped excerpts of Zamora's mother, Yolanda, on the stand, as provided by WPBT. Mrs. Zamora wept as she described her son as a hopeless lad who "felt that there was nothing else to do but kill himself" and spent long hours in front of the television set without talking.

And yet television, whatever its guilt in this case, also has the role of bringing the trial itself into thousands of Miami homes. Local newspaper coverage has been distinctly nonsensationalistic; this may be because, for the first time, Miamians are able to see what a trial is like for themselves in their own living rooms.

The only still photographer allowed in the courtroom is from *The Miami News*. *The Miami News* is advertised around town on vending machines as *"the newspaper for people who watch television."*

A carnival atmosphere predicted by some does not exist in the courtroom, but there are more spectators on hand than the court can hold (they wait in the hall behind a rope for empty seats), and at least one young spectator said to a friend upon leaving the courtroom yesterday, "Hey—I was on television!"

On Tuesday, the last piece of business conducted from the bench by Judge Baker—who has a wry, rumpled style that suggests a chubby David Brinkley—was to deny the jury's plea that they be allowed to watch the trial on TV as well.

"I have received the request of the jury to watch themselves on television with the sound turned off," said Baker. "They said they just want to see what they look like on TV. But I cannot grant that request during the trial." Some of the jurors moped in disappointment.

Although witnesses are not allowed in court while other witnesses are testifying, the judge has not forbidden—only discouraged—them from watching the trial on TV when they get home at night. Some witnesses yesterday made veiled references to previous testimony they could only have seen on TV.

The TV camera sits in the front of the press box, with one man operating it and another standing by. The camera is rarely referred to during the proceeding, and then only indirectly. When Rubin and Assistant State's Attorney Thomas Headley seemed to be ignoring a ruling he'd made on an objection, Judge Baker grumped, "I only have a small role in this production."

On television, the trial looks orderly and organized, its participants inhabiting neat little rectangles. In person, one has to sit through the frequent breaks or recesses that are edited out of the TV tape, and one gets to see the courtroom in all of its not-so-neat municipal-modern garishness. Because the TV camera never pans up or down, viewers never see the six hanging lamps over the judge's podium that look as if they came straight from a motel coffee shop in nearby Miami Beach.

After seeing the principals on TV, one feels a certain sensory jolt at confronting them in three-dimensional person. Their faces are suddenly completed, with the once-missing details supplied; their clothes appear less tidy, and they look thinner, though the courtroom seems suddenly huge and has two more corners than on TV. Lawyer Rubin, though, still comes across as a nervous combination of Ralph Nader and Bruce Dern.

Whether attorneys and witnesses are performing for the camera no one can say for sure, but it doesn't look that way. Known for his courtroom flamboyance, Rubin pounded his fist dramatically on a table to drive home a point Tuesday, but this seemed to be for the jury's sake and not for the entertainment of viewers whose previous exposure to courtroom activity on TV has been limited largely to reruns of *Perry Mason*.

Richard Carpenter, director of the telecast for WPBT, says, "We try to be as objective as possible" in choosing what and whom to shoot during the trial. When Zamora's mother began to weep during her testimony and turned to one side with her hand covering her face, was she avoiding the spectators or the TV camera? "Probably both," said the cameraman.

In pretrial conferences, Rubin was forbidden to make TV violence the issue of the trial. But it has remained central to his defense of Zamora. After repeated attempts to introduce testimony about the effects of TV violence on children—and having the prosecution object, and the judge sustain the objection—Rubin exclaimed, "Your Honor, involuntary television intoxication is a new defense, but so was insanity at one time a new defense."

Zamora's plea is not guilty by reason of insanity. Rubin has to prove him insane at the time of the crime according to the accepted Florida definition—that the youth did not know right from wrong when the shooting occurred and that he was not aware of the nature and consequences of the act. Through Gilbert's testimony, Rubin tried to show that Zamora's concepts of right and wrong were distorted by excessive lifelong exposure to television and that he was unaware of the consequences of his act because for him pulling the trigger was a Pavlovian response conditioned by watching violence on TV.

"This boy had been exposed to thousands and thousands of situations where he has seen 'When you're threatened—bang, shoot,'" Gilbert said. "This is an emotionally disturbed child who never held a gun in his hand before but who was conditioned that the proper thing to do is shoot it."

Others have testified that Zamora and the other youth were not armed when they entered the home of Elinor Haggart but that a loaded gun was discovered on the premises. When Haggart surprised the boys in the act of robbing her home, the shooting occurred, according to testimony.

The television industry already has been shaken by antiviolence crusaders, congressional investigation and public-opinion polls about violence on the air. Some measure of reform is apparent in new programs on prime time this season, but old programs with old violence standards continue to air late at night. Some local stations may be showing violent programs from years past at virtually any hour of the day. Television is still not and perhaps never will be free of violence. This is the first time that TV violence has specifically been held responsible in a court of law for an act of violence in real life. It may be impossible to overestimate the effects on television that this case could have.

October 6, 1977

On October 7, 1977, Ronney Zamora was found guilty of first-degree murder and, one month later, was sentenced to life imprisonment.

Edith Bunker's Ordeal

EDITH BUNKER IS A national treasure. She is the crowning achievement of a 30-year evolution—the lineal descendant of all the sit-com housewives who have gone before her, yet more real and more universally cherished than any of them. Edith Bunker is the TV mother of us all. How heartbreaking to watch as a man tries to rape her on television tonight.

The Bunkers have gone through many true-to-life traumas in their seven years on CBS, but tonight's special one hour episode is the most nerve-shattering and one of the most brilliant of all. To some, subjecting an icon as beloved as Edith to this sort of indignity may seem too cruel, but that is the point of the program—that rape is not only a crime, but a desecration, and that its victims may remain victims long after the crime itself has been committed.

How many times Edith has lumbered cheerfully across that living-room floor to answer the Bunker doorbell. This time, her friend Sybil Gooley is waiting, angered that she wasn't invited to Edith's surprise 50th-birthday party. Sybil leaves and a handsome stranger approaches. Edith closes the door and fastens the chain bolt before she'll talk to him; "You can't be too cautious," she says.

The ordeal that follows may be all the more shocking not only because it is happening to Edith, whom we revere outlandishly as a symbol and a person, but because the sorrow and the terror of the situation are punctuated with comedy. The rapist has removed his shirt and forced Edith onto the couch when he tells her, "You know, you smell wonderful."

"That's Lemon Pledge," says Edith, and the studio audience roars nervously.

Certainly producer Norman Lear and the writers of this episode, Bob Weiskopf and Bob Schiller, will be criticized for sweetening the subject with laugh lines. But without the laughs, the program might in fact seem too polemical—just another of TV's social-problem shows—and have less impact. Edith's indefatigable daffiness validates her, in a way, as a believable character; like Archie, that magnificent, pathetic specimen to whom she is married and devoted, she reminds almost all of us of someone we know. Most TV-series characters remind you only of other TV-series characters.

And to keep an audience simultaneously on the brinks of laughter and tears is one of the most difficult feats a writer can accomplish. Schiller and Weiskopf, along with director Paul Bogart, bring this off beautifully. Ironically or not, both writers worked previously together on another television milestone, *I Love Lucy*. It is true Lucy was never in straits to equal Edith's plight tonight, and yet the kinship between the two is undoubtedly there. The attempted rape of Edith Bunker is in effect the attempted rape of Lucy Ricardo, and of all the TV surrogate mothers created in their images.

When Archie and son-in-law Mike learn of the attack on Edith, they return to the Bunker house to search for the rapist. Suddenly they are bopping into each other in a slapstick panic that recalls such moments of *Lucy* lunacy as when Ricky, Fred and Ethel tumbled around hysterically when Lucy announced it was time to go to the hospital and give birth (to "Little Ricky").

Television has given us new ways to measure the passage of moments, years and our lives.

You could watch a hundred poshly produced Shakespearean plays on public TV and never feel as devastated as you do watching the assault on Edith Bunker. Television is at its best when it sidesteps aesthetic considerations and connects on an intimate, personal, emotional level no other medium can duplicate.

There are flaws in the show. When Archie first learns of the incident from a distraught Edith, everything we know about him tells us he would be enraged and ready to wreak vengeance. Instead, the writers make him appear something of a coward, and this weakens the program considerably. They also underestimate our concern over Edith and the other characters by going too far with the comic relief, especially at crucial junctures of peril.

Lear will probably get some flak for treating rape at all in a comedy show (though, as mentioned on tonight's program, daughter Gloria suffered a similar ordeal in a previous season). From Hollywood, Lear is naturally indignant at the thought of such criticism, and at the notion that he is topic-dropping again by doing a rape show now that the subject is so popular.

"How could we be reaching for sensationalism when we're taking something right out of our national life and dealing with it?" he says. "Rape is the fastest-growing crime in America. We worked on this script for over a year to get it right."

The program was being taken seriously by some viewers days before its scheduled telecast. On Wednesday, Representatives Herbert Harris (D-Va.) and Peter Rodino (D-N.J.), cosponsors of legislation to protect the privacy of rape victims, held an advance screening of the program for 175 people on Capitol Hill. Among the guests were women who work as volunteers at rape crisis centers in the Washington area. Some of them have been through experiences similar to Edith Bunker's. And some of them wept as they watched her struggling to escape and, later, reacting with horror to the sound of the doorbell ringing again.

The weekly performances of Carroll O'Connor and Jean Stapleton as Archie and Edith Bunker are the best acting regularly on television. They continue to expand on characters who might have become caricatures in other hands. But tonight's program, as one might expect, is Stapleton's particular triumph, an eloquent portrayal of fear, vulnerability, dignity and, finally, victorious resolve.

October 16, 1977

The Fading of the *Hall of Fame*

WHAT HAPPENED to the *Hallmark Hall of Fame* is that the program became just another of the company's greeting cards. Indeed, in newspaper ads heralding the 27th season of this once-prestigious series, the company declares that the real purpose of its televised dramas is "to touch your life, fill you with joy and warm your heart."

What was once a showcase for illustrious playwrights and the noblest actors has become just another instrument of advertising. In fact, the program has become the province of the NBC Television Network and the Hallmark ad agency, Foote, Cone and Belding, in Chicago.

Tonight's season opener for the Hallmark series, a new television adaption of Edwin O'Connor's *The Last Hurrah*, was produced by actor Carroll O'Connor's production company and Columbia Pictures Television, a TV-series factory. O'Connor, who stars in and wrote the static, amateurish script, tried to sell the program to CBS, which turned it down, and then got NBC and Hallmark to pick it up.

In the old days, the *Hall of Fame* acquired some shows from outside sources too, but somehow, these were on a slightly higher plane—films like Laurence Olivier's *Richard III*, which had its American premiere on the *Hall of Fame*, and a splendid color film of *Macbeth* starring Maurice Evans and Judith Anderson.

Did *Richard III* touch our lives, fill us with joy and warm our hearts? In the way that great plays and great players can, yes—in a way to which O'Connor's *Last Hurrah* couldn't hold the tiniest candle.

Most of the memorable *Hall of Fame* shows were aired during its first 10 years (it premiered on Christmas Eve, 1951), when producer-director George Schaefer had artistic control. Schaefer returned to network TV last year with a magnificently revived *Our Town*, but it was sponsored by The Bell System, not Hallmark. He had tried to sell Hallmark on the project several times in recent years, Schaefer said yesterday from Hollywood, but he kept getting turned down.

"I think they had the funny feeling that it wasn't uplifting enough—that it was somehow downlifting," Schaefer says.

Just a list of old *Hallmark* productions is enough to generate goosebumps: Julie Harris in *The Lark* and *Little Moon of Alban;* Helen Hayes and Mary Martin in *The Skin of Our Teeth;* Alfred Drake re-creating his Broadway role in Cole Porter's *Kiss Me, Kate;* and Maurice Evans' modern-dress version of *Hamlet,* among dozens. Schaefer staged *Winterset, A Doll's House, Pygmalion, Cyrano de Bergerac, Alice in Wonderland, The Green Pastures, Saint Joan* and Noël Coward's *Blithe Spirit.*

Just about anybody who saw it would probably rank *Hallmark*'s production of *The Magnificent Yankee,* with Alfred Lunt and Lynn Fontanne, as one of the indelible viewing experiences of one's television lifetime.

The memory of *Hurrah* will be lucky to linger for 15 minutes.

O'Connor's attempt to remake and update the O'Connor (no relation) novel is especially presumptuous since director John Ford did the book nearly every possible justice in a swooningly sentimental 1958 movie that starred Spencer Tracy as old-time Boston mayor Frank Skeffington. Tracy's scenes with character actor Edward Brophy, as his infallibly loyal and unquestioning right-hand man Ditto Boland, were beauties.

By updating the time of the story to the present, O'Connor robs the character of its poignance, and since he plays the role himself with barely the movement of a single muscle, Skeffington lacks human definition as well as symbolic resonance. When he finally crawls off to Irish heaven at the fade-out, we haven't the slightest idea why we should care.

It's not the passing of the Frank Skeffingtons so much as the passing of the *Hall of Fame* that *Hurrah* really commemorates. Schaefer thinks its decline began with the retirement of company founder Joyce C. Hall as president in 1956 (he remains honorary chairman of the board). Hall had taken an active interest in the program and saw it as a goodwill gesture, not just a greeting-card hawker.

"One day a week, I used to meet with Mr. Hall," Schaefer recalls. "We'd discuss the plays that were coming up, and sometimes he had his own ideas. He's the one who suggested we do *The Lark*, for instance. I remember how skeptical he was when I told him I wanted to do Gilbert and Sullivan's *Yeomen of the Guard* but the night it went on, he called me up to tell me how much he loved it.

"He never really cared that much about numbers of viewers. We had five million or ten million who were really devoted, who always watched, and that seemed fine with him. When he retired, I think they decided to reach out with more generally popular stuff. They got out of the classics completely, to my sorrow, and then the network, which had left us alone, became more active in it. That, frankly, is the reason I left; I missed the wonderful independence of being able to do exactly what we wanted to do."

In those days, once the program graduated from half-hour to 90-minute or two-hour specials, commercials were adjusted to fit the program. "If a play broke up into two long acts, then they'd only have three commercials," says Schaefer. He doesn't seem anxious to bad-mouth the *Hallmark* shows that followed his tenure, but concedes that in recent seasons they've done some "really, just awful things."

ABC's Fred Silverman, suffering a chronic case of logorrhea in recent weeks, has been making speeches defending television programming as it is, claiming that TV has to be good or else millions of people wouldn't watch it. It could be that millions of people have nothing else to do.

One begins to wonder if the Last Hurrah for network television, as well as the *Hallmark Hall of Fame*, wasn't sounded some time ago.

November 16, 1977

The Death of Mirrors

BY 1995, THE MIRROR will be dead. You can kiss it goodbye. In the 21st century children will say, "Tell us about the mirrors, Mommy," and ask, "Daddy, Daddy, what's a mir-ror?" The mirror image will have been replaced by a new image; the iconography of the self will have been electronically restructured and a software explosion will have ushered in a golden-glitter age of pampered human vanity.

In other words, You're going to be on television, dummy.

We are all going to be on television. We're all going to get to see *what* we look like on television—and what we look like on television will be the new standard for what we look like, period. Andy Warhol said everybody would be a star for 15 minutes, but oh, Andy, you stopped short! Everybody is going to be a star, and everybody is also going to be a guest host, and everybody is also going to be an auteur.

Audience shall become show, show shall become audience; viewer will be viewee; performer and observer shall be each like unto the other. And, oh yeah, the world will never be the same. Actually, it will be exactly the same, except that instead of staying home and looking at Fonzie's kisser sprayed across a phosphor screen by an electron gun, we will all be able to stay home and look at our own.

This Christmas, a few thousand families will form the vanguard of an invading army in the next great media war. For the first time, home video recorder systems are being aggressively hawked through mass advertising by several different manufacturers, and RCA, which in August introduced its SelectaVision outfit, predicts home video recorders will be a "billion-dollar industry" within three years.

Of course, the home video recorders now being sold by RCA, Sony, Zenith and many others are being pitched as luxury conveniences, components that permit a limited alternative to regular TV viewing. There's been little mention yet of photographing and watching yourself, partly because the costs of a video camera remain prohibitively high (the recorder cost itself hovers around the $1,000 mark). Instead, the viewer-consumer nation is being instructed on the benefits of recording TV programs to play them back later.

"Now you can make the TV schedule fit your schedule," says an ad for the Zenith Video Cassette Recorder.

And Sony's Betamax "lets you program your own television, so you can call your television your own."

All very nice, but that's not what we're waiting for. We don't just want to call our television our own. We want to call our television ourSELF. Can't you just see it now—The I-Me-Mine Network... Channelo Uno... Station WIII...

"Ladies and gentlemen... I present... MYSELF... starring... ME... produced and directed by... YOURS TRULY... with special guest stars... MY wife and MY kiddies and MY aspidistra, who appear with the gracious permission of... *moi!*... Filling in for ME tonight will be none other than... MYSELF... And now, heeeeeere's *I!*"

Yes, a new horizon is in view. We are about to cross another great threshold and fall flat on our faces.

There are some obstacles in the way of this revolution. Don't go-to-the-mirror-boy yet. First, the industry has to iron out some problems. One is that, as with quadraphonic sound, that other great nirvana machine that was going to alter the course of the universe but didn't, different companies have different home video systems, so that the cassette you can play on your RCA SelectaVision will not play on somebody else's Sony, Zenith, Sanyo, Toshiba or Pioneer machine, and no one else's cassette will play on Quasar's "Great American Time Machine" recorder. The manufacturer of each system claims its to be the best—no surprise, that. A standard will have to wait while they slug it out in the marketplace.

There is another little problem—a teeny-tiny lawsuit pending in a Los Angeles federal court that could make it legal for people to own recorders but illegal to record on them, or at least record anything off the TV set, like, say, the 444th rerun of *Destination Tokyo* complete with 16 commercials for a sponge on a stick that enables you to paint a ceiling in your tuxedo. (What a ceiling is doing in your tuxedo...) Obviously, this is the most preposterous lawsuit since Jack the Ripper tried to get *The Times* of London on defamation of character (this didn't really happen—but *who* knows?). But if history has taught us anything, it is that what Lewis Carroll was really writing was investigative journalism.

Nothing is too ridiculous to happen.

MCA and Disney, who brought the suit, fear we'll all be busy recording shows off the air and then—*Hey, wait a minute! Just whom do these guys think they're kidding??* Do they really think we want to tape that crap? Here we are, poor little viewers, who have been suffering through TV shows night after night after night since Harry Truman was still in the kitchen—so now we're going to want to record all that drek? Whoa, boy; pardon us while we split a side. We don't want to *save* that junk; we want to avoid it.

Ah, but the recorder companies themselves tell us that the new wonder-toy will enrich our lives by enabling us to record one program while we watch another. That way, we won't have to miss our "favorite" shows.

What favorite shows? What do you mean, *what* favorite shows? You know—your fayyyyyyyyvorite shows. Like—uh, well, like—uh, well, like—oh, you know. Like on a Monday night, when you can't decide whether you want to tackle the subtle cerebral nuances of *Little House on the Prairie* or savor the witty pas de cinqs of *The San Pedro Beach Bums*. Or when you can't choose which you'd rather avoid: a smarmy piece of slop about rich people having intercourse, or another protracted eruption by that legendary national geyser commonly known as Howard Cosell's big fat yap.

Oh, how have we ever made such choices? Won't we wonder how we ever got along without a BetaVision or a SelectaMax?

No, we won't. Not at first. But obviously, this is a transitional phase—just the first dainty step toward total video armament in every middlesex, village and farm. A nice beginning, but the camera's what we're waiting for. It's not access to *Harry and Walter Go to New York* that we want. It's access to us. Obviously, too, this is a transitional paragraph; because we are going now from the pleasant, amusing, wispy-thin but tasty-yummy area of light entertainment on a Sunday morning and into the heavily holistic, helical-conical, horizontal linearity of far-out Media Theory.

You can go-to-the-mirror now, boy.

When the video image replaces the mirror image, it will allow all of us to see ourselves not as others see us, which hardly matters to a narcissistic species with a long history of onanistic excess anyway, but rather to see ourselves as the camera sees us. In the early days of TV, performers looked into cameras and tried to imagine people inside them, to give them someone to relate to. Now, in the Video Era, people look at other people and try to imagine a camera there. "Remember," says a Maryland video group, "sooner or later, everyone will be on television." When WE are on television —on camera, as it's called—we will at last be the equals of Grizzly Adams, Johnny Carson, Madge the Manicurist and all our other culture heroes and role models and identity figures.

WE will be our own culture heroes. WE will be our own role models. WE will be our own identity figures.

The Camera will validate us.

The Camera will certify us.

The Camera will tell us we exist and pull us outside our own bodies to look at ourselves. And find ourselves rather delightful, if we do say so ourselves.

The Camera will help replace the mirror, yes, but it will also take the observer roles now filled by our peers, our psychoanalysts, our wives, our husbands, our lovers, our children, our Peeping Toms, our Polaroids that are out of focus anyway and our watchful aspidistras.

And, oh yes, God, too. The camera will have a God's-eye view of us. And when we see the tape played back, we will have a God's-eye view of ourselves.

Recorded history has taught us one thing: the only purpose for history is to be recorded. The TV camera will become our guarantor of posterity. Nothing that happens will really happen until the camera sees it, the machine records it and we play it back. Therefore we will move into an exalted state of higher consciousness never known to the human race; we will come to realize that the RECORD button is less important than the PLAYBACK button and that the replica is more important than the original.

The replica will become the original.

Reality will take on a new meaning: no meaning whatsoever.

We are about to take a trip into ourselves that'll make Keir Dullea's journey to Jupiter and The Beyond look like a visit to the 7-11 store to pick up a box of Hostess chocolate-covered doughnuts.

A new day of Self through Video awaits. Every I shall be dotted. Thou shalt know loneliness no more. Neither shalt thou care whom Mike Wallace is beating up this week.

Technology is about to put the ME back in MEDIA. Comes the revolution, we will all be all.

And to all, a good night.

December 4, 1977

Nostalgia for the Future

TECHNOLOGY WILL BE THE RELIGION of the '80s. The media are paving the way now. Enormously popular movies like *Star Wars* and *Close Encounters of the Third Kind* signal a sweeping reconciliation between human beings and science. If *Dr. Strangelove* taught us "how to stop worrying and love the bomb," the new science-fiction fantasy tells us to stop worrying and love the computer.

In television, this new embrace of the technocratic millennium is less evident in programming than it is in commercials. TV commercials have long been more responsive to the immediate preoccupations of our culture anyway; they can be initiated more quickly, and they are by nature and design incomparably more succinct.

The commercials of '77 say, among other things, that a giddy matrix of benign technologies—space exploration, cybernetics, electronic communication—is ushering in a cool nirvana, a new age of media euphoria and light shows in the living room. What we may see in 1978 is the greatest wave in history of nostalgia for the future.

Except perhaps for those viciously distressing smoke-alarm ads—replete with body counts of barbecued families—all television commercials are messages positive in intent (Do this, Do that) and carriers of real or imagined Good News—of gums that go squirt or furniture polishes that cure "the blurs."

More and more of these optimistic extravaganzas are set in outer space or among futuristic trappings, and more and more large corporations are investing in image-boosting ads that herald marvels at hand and marvels yet to come. "ALCOA can't wait for tomorrow," says the announcer, and a viewer's response to all this insistently rosy romanticism may very well be "Neither can I."

TV commercials have always been oases of spectacle in an arid medium; if not for them, there would be almost no special effects on TV, since most regularly scheduled programs have mundane themes and prosaic settings. The small budget for a series requiring special effects, like the short-lived *Logan's Run* on CBS, prohibits anything even remotely eye-boggling, but the budget for a single one-minute commercial can run as high as $250,000 and allows for all kinds of visual wonders.

Many of the commercials of '77 were embodiments of technological surge as well as endorsements of it. Several advertisers followed the lead of Levi's and 7-Up in using dazzling luminescent animation to impart commercial messages in phantasmagorical and nonlinear ways. Youth-appealing record-company commercials, like a current spot for MCA artists

Elton John, Olivia Newton-John and Neil Sedaka, make the most elaborate use of these new techniques.

But there's lots of other stuff incongruously, though significantly, floating through space in TV commercials—Orbit Gum "for a taste that's out of this world"; the Toyota Celica Liftback, "car of the '80s"; and, of course, Ford's Futura, "a dramatic combination of styling and technology for 1978 . . . and beyond."

Revlon's Moisture Release takes us through a neon infinity tunnel ("as you move through time") decorated with *Star Wars*-like explosions. Glass Plus is demonstrated by a friendly robot à la R2-D2. Essence Rare by Houbigant sits smoldering in an eerie and unearthly landscape. Pioneer and Marantz stereo components pointedly and graphically promise trips to the moon on gossamer wings.

But the watershed commercial campaign, the one that verifies the trend, was actually introduced late in 1976 and will continue through 1978. In fact, it's an example of another major theme in TV commercials today: nostalgia for the past. But this one is implicitly wistful about things to come as well.

The spots were produced for General Electric through the BBDO ad agency and star actor Pat Hingle as Thomas Alva Edison, who founded the company that became GE. Hingle's Edison appears in soliloquy, in these two-minute and one-minute spots, to extol the virtues of experimentation, electricity, capitalism and competition with biblical reverence and incredibly convincing low-key, semisubliminal salesmanship.

They're so beautifully produced, so movingly acted by Hingle (almost unrecognizable under heavy makeup) and so suffused with love of technique that coming upon one on TV is a little like finding the Hope Diamond in a pawnshop. The Edison series is the *Roots* of commercials; as a body of work, it's among the very, very few productions ever on television that you might reasonably call a masterpiece.

Indeed, Karl L. Koss, manager of corporate advertising for GE, says the viewer mail response has been "unprecedented" for the Edison series. "Usually when we sponsor a show, eighty percent of the mail praises the program and twenty percent says, 'The commercials were good, too.' But since we started with Hingle, it's been eighty percent saying 'I like the commercials' and twenty percent saying, 'Oh, by the way, I like the show, too.'"

The ads, which will next be shown during a February 1 *GE Theater* special on CBS—and which won Hingle a best-actor "Clio" award, the Madison Avenue Oscar—have been so effective that GE is producing a 30-minute live version which Hingle will perform for trade groups in 22 cities during 1978, the year of the company's centennial.

Among the other amazing things about the ads is that they were filmed with no cuts, no internal editing, so that Hingle had to deliver the Edisonian spiels in single continuous takes. Certainly this series of commercials has given him his most challenging TV role in years; one need only compare it with the cipher he was required to impersonate in the recent and idiotic CBS movie *Tarantulas—the Deadly Cargo* to see the point.

In an October interview for *Videography* magazine, media philosopher Marshall McLuhan declared, "The advertisement, because of its concern for effect and its understanding of the media for getting that effect, is the greatest art form there is. Years from now, the advertising of our century will be studied by all the great art experts. They will all be saying, 'Oh, boy, that artist was totally unknown, anonymous and ignored all his life. He was one of the greatest guys who ever lived.'"

Most television programs are produced to fill time. Production may be sloppy and loose because there is so much time to fill. Commercial production is just the opposite: a lot of production time to fill a small dot of temporal space on the air. "Advertising men know the effect they want before they start —they want sales," McLuhan says. "That's why the art of advertising is the greatest art form in the world."

This hardly means that all TV commercials are works of art. Most continue to be terrible, some are intentionally grating. Tucker Inn, alas, has yet to be torched by vigilantes; rings are still found around collars; Parkay margarine still thinks it's butter; and men dismounting horses continue to make their first remark to companions "Do you think I need a shower?"

And yet at many levels, commercials in 1977 proved balm and salvation when considered in relation to the programs they interrupt. Even the smut was of a more rarefied tone, as TV commercials exposed a bit more skin and dropped a few more innuendos. Generally, however, this was on a far more cheerful, less furtive, less guilt-ridden plane than the smut in shows like *Soap*, where an actress recently got a big howl by describing another woman as being "in heat" after an apparent tryst in an airplane lavatory.

By contrast, who could repress a guileless, wily smile when confronted with the interlocking "Man" and "Woman" perfume bottles by Jovan? The flicking Bics have ceased to be amusing, if indeed they ever were, but there's a wholesome sort of squeaky-clean sexuality to the assorted American types who sashay out from behind blue barrels to dance about in bath towels as they sing "Take care of your birthday suit" for Nivea Skin Cream.

As frequently noted in recent weeks, Nielsen ratings show a distinct decline in viewing levels as the television year ends, but it just can't be the commercials that are driving people away. Viewers may even have already learned how to stop worrying and love The Sponsor.

December 31, 1977

From L.A., Heeerre's . . . the Newsonality!!

"Look, you've got your boredom," says Kelly Lange. "You've got your misery. You've got your tragedy. You've got to have your laughs, too. You've got to have your chuckles.

Otherwise you're just asking too much of viewers who've been hassled all day long."

Lange is defending the fact that local TV newscasts tend to be salted with levity. Sometimes they are, in fact, levitycasts salted with news. In a way, she is also defending her own status as an up-and-coming news personality. Now a busy anchorwoman, interviewer and talk-show host for the NBC-owned station in Los Angeles, Lange also pops up on the network from time to time. Expect more such popping; among the dominant industry rumors is that Lange will soon move into a *Today* show berth, though she says she doesn't really want to.

Her current duties include cohosting, with Michael Landon, the Tournament of Roses Parade. This year the parade will be preceded by a 90-minute program generously and lavishly promoting the network's ailing prime-time and daytime programs, with Lange interviewing their various stars.

This doesn't sound like a hard-news assignment. But we have to remember what Kelly Lange represents. She is not a reporter.

Kelly Lange belongs to the new breed of pop TV journalist. She's a newsonality.

"We do one hell of a good newscast," she says of KNBC's early-evening two-hour all-star news revue. "We have the highest-rated news in Los Angeles, which is a big market. When the last sweeps came out, we had a twelve, ABC had a nine and CBS had a five." Lange says she and her colleagues do not do the bouncing "happy talk" trivializing kind of news show. That's on the ABC station. In fact, she thinks KNBC keeps frivolity to a minimum. "We are less guilty, let us say, than are most other local news operations.

"We don't even look at the ratings. We see them when the sweeps come out, and if we won, they put them on the bulletin board, which is how I saw them."

Still, not everything on the news is the news. Lange does occasional special features in which she visits movie stars' homes. Hmmm. "Well, look, here in Washington you've got all the politicians and there we've got all the celebrities.

They're all there because that's where we do all the product, so we have them on all the time. They're our hometown people."

Is Lange in show biz or news biz? It seems obvious. "When you put the news on TV, it's a show," she says. She's even at work on a screenplay, like everybody else in Hollywood (who can so much as blink). "I love it out there," she says of Tinselania. "The weather! The ambiance! That's why I don't want to move to New York. The NBC building in New York is rigid, right? A different atmosphere. But Los Angeles is where all the production is: there's very little left in New York; Jackie Gleason is in Miami and . . . what else? But this is where all the stuff is. So you walk down the hall with your news script and you say 'Hi' to Johnny Carson walking by. And an elephant walks by. It's fun, you know—people in their cut-off jeans or whatever—a much more relaxed atmosphere.

"Also, there's a caring as far as production is concerned. The people out there really care. It's a known fact that the guys and gals out there seem to be more together as far as putting things together.

"It's not an easy business. It's structured so the weak of heart don't make it. A lot of people get hardened and let it roll off their backs. I've never been able to be that way. *I care.* I care, you know? Maybe that's silly, but that's the way I am."

The way Lange is happens to be the way more and more imparters of the news on television are; Kelly Lange is hanging 10 on the wave of the future. Sure, there are good, solid reporters in TV news, but the TV news directors no longer insist that their reporters have a background in the grittier and perhaps less ego-boosting world of print. In college, Lange thought she was going to be a teacher; she broke into TV news spotting traffic jams from a helicopter.

Newsonalities tend to look good and sound good—they come across on the air—and their function is often that of picker-upper. They sometimes deliver non-news about fellow celebrities—soft-core gossip, idle chatter and pleasing tales of retrieved orphans and redeemed bums. With sunny smiles and shiny teeth, they spread the gospel of everything's-going-to-be-all-right. After all, we've got to have our chuckles.

And we know they care because they say they care.

Then, too, there is the discomforting fact that the big TV news stars all have agents who sweat and strain to get them zillion-dollar deals. Lange is hardly alone in this. Her agent is Norman Brokaw. He's also Menachem Begin's.

"I don't see anything disreputable about having an agent. *Do you?*" Well, do you? "It does seem a little glitzy for the news biz. Tom Brokaw was always that way about it—conservative, you know. Aw, the jugglers and the clowns, whatever. And then he turned around when the big money was coming down the pike, and he signed up with one of the most showbizzy agents there are, a guy they call The Hook [Ed Hookstratten]." Right. "Well, I would not sign with The Hook. Hook asked me to sign with him. I would not go that far, because he has certain tactics that do not agree with my way of doing things."

Brokaw—Tom, that is, who is not related to agent Norman—started at KNBC like Lange (who entered the TV-news biz under the name Dawn O'Day). And so did the man with the million-dollar eyebrows. Tom Snyder, another big news star at NBC. "Snyder and Brokaw—they're the two heavyweights that I learned so much from," Lange says.

She credits Snyder with introducing what she calls "interplay"—chitchat between news persons—on the KNBC news. Here's how he did it: one night 15 seconds before air time, he grabbed Kelly's script out of her hand and threw it in the wastebasket.

So came the revolution in broadcasting.

"I've never had it so good," Lange says of her NBC position; but late last year when her contract came up for renewal and ABC made her an attractive offer, she couldn't refuse and decided to leave. Under the terms of the old contract, though, NBC could keep her if they matched the new offer. They did. Lange stayed on. "I remember crying. Not that I didn't love NBC. They're very good to me. I do my work. I do my thing. And consequently, there's a lot of respect on both sides."

96 / ON THE AIR!

But enough talk of journalism, for now Lange has to leave Washington to continue a multicity tour promoting the Rose Parade coverage. Before going, she extends an invitation to visit the city of Los Angeles and offers to help get tickets for the Johnny Carson show.

Tickets for the Johnny Carson show? Thanks just the same. But hey—next time you see him in the hall at NBC, do say hello.

Say hello to the elephant, too.
December 28, 1977

The Initiation of "James"

JAMES IS NOT GOING to lose his virginity without a fight.

But the fight is between Dan Wakefield, creator and story consultant for NBC's critically acclaimed *James at 15* series, and the network's department of broadcast standards, also known as the censor.

The master plan for James was drawn up weeks ago. The young hero of the weekly series would become 16 in early February and undergo his sexual initiation in an episode titled "The Gift."

Now Wakefield says he will quit the show and already has had his name removed from the "Gift" script because of changes called for by the NBC censor.

More is at stake than a teen-ager's virtue. Wakefield's credentials are considerably loftier than the usual TV writer's. He is a Columbia graduate, a former Neiman fellow, has been a contributing editor at *Atlantic Monthly* since 1969 and has won considerable praise for such journalism as "Supernation at Peace and War," which took up an entire *Atlantic* issue, and such novels as *Home Free, Starting Over* and *Going All the Way.*

He is therefore just the kind of writer who usually wouldn't touch television with a 10-foot pole; the kind of writer downfall and heartbreak are predicted for the moment he gets his own office at a studio. But Wakefield says, "I am not another sensitive novelist, all upset by Hollywood. I'd love to work in television again. I think some of the best stuff being done is on television.

"I said I would write a script about James having sex and losing his virginity only if we could at least refer in some way to birth control in the show," Wakefield says. The censors ruled out any direct reference to birth-control devices, so Wakefield devised this exchange between James and the 16-year-old girl he falls in love with:

JAMES: I love you and I want to protect you. I've heard about teen-age pregnancies and all that and I think people ought to be responsible.

GIRL: I am responsible, James.

JAMES: You are? That's great!

Wakefield says the censor would not allow the word "responsible" as a reference to birth control. "The censor told me, 'the American people will not stand for any mention of birth control on television,'" Wakefield says. "It just boggles the mind. How can they ban the word 'responsible'?"

But Ralph Daniels, the chief NBC censor, said from New York he didn't think birth control was the crucial problem with Wakefield's script. He said there was not enough "remorse and concern" on James's part after the great moment has passed (none of the actual lovemaking was ever in the script).

"We thought if James lost his virginity in a marvelous love affair and that was treated as a mature relationship, that would not be realistic," said Daniels. "It had to be in a moment of passion. Then later he thinks about the consequences."

"Oh, yeah—guilt," says Wakefield. "The network said James couldn't have sex unless he was punished. I'd already disowned the script, by that point, over the birth-control issue. In the new version, which they're shooting right now, the girl thinks she's pregnant afterwards and both kids do some suffering. I'm not sure how many pages of suffering are in there. But it turns out she's not pregnant, anyway."

Censors also cut a reference by the girl to a past affair of hers. Previously, censors had cut a reference to a birth-control device from the two-hour movie pilot for *James at 15*, which scored high ratings when shown last summer. James had asked a friend to lend him "that thing you carry around in your wallet" because he thought his magic moment was imminent.

But it wasn't.

And the censor said nix anyway.

"The censor told me that I lived in L.A. and didn't know what things are really like in the rest of the country," says Wakefield. "Well, I grew up in Indiana and I taught in the Midwest and I have some notion of what people's values are. Out front I'd said I'd only write the script if there was a reference to birth control. There's something like seven hundred thousand unmarried teen-age pregnancies in this country every year, and a big venereal-disease problem. I thought it would be irresponsible not to deal with that.

"It gets to be a little like Vietnam—you say, 'Well, we'll just give in on one more little thing,' and pretty soon there's nothing left."

Daniels was asked if it wasn't inconsistent for the network that aired *79 Park Avenue*, a bio of a high-class hooker, and *Aspen*, a jet-set sex saga, to become upset over Wakefield's *James at 15* script. Daniels said there was a difference between what characters in a "one-time-only" show can do and what characters in a continuing series can do.

He also said the censoring of the script was "a complex issue."

At any rate, even if Wakefield makes good on his vow to leave, the altered "Gift" will air February 9. Presumably, Richard Baskin's lyrics to the title tune will remain intact, if perhaps more pertinent than usual:

"Is it a feeling in the heart, or is it somethin' you can't name? Oh, oh, oh, oh, oh, oh, James . . ."

January 10, 1978

Videoraphobia

AGORAPHOBIA, OF COURSE, is a fear of leaving the house. Now there's videoraphobia, a disease so new even Phil Donahue doesn't know about it. It is the fear of leaving one's television set—a crippling killer first identified by Rand Vander Kand, doctor of public relations at the Institute of Chic Ailments in Chevy Chase, Maryland.

We happen to have Dr. Vander Kand right here to talk about videoraphobia. Tell us, Doctor, what are the first symptoms?

"Well, young man, the first symptoms of videoraphobia—before dilation of the pupils sets in, that is—are that the victims begin to talk in gibberish. To the simple question, 'Hi, Mom, what's for dinner?' videoraphobes are likely to answer, 'A sandwich is only a sandwich, but a manwich is a meal.' The next thing you know, they will insist on calling their grandpas Walter Cronkite."

How horrible.

"There is worse, my boy. Videoraphobes develop strange illusions and tolerances. They actually get wrapped up in the plots of *Charlie's Angels*. They began to imagine that insurance agents are their best friends on this earth, and they will swear on a stack of hot cakes that 'Moon River' is really supposed to go, 'Lip Quencher, wider than a mile, I'm cross-ing you in style, someday' . . ."

Yes, but Doctor—

"Old dream maker, you, heartbreaker, wherever you're going'—"

Doctor, please, is there anything else to watch for?

"Ah, yes. Members of the family should look for telltale signs that the victims are clinging to their TV sets. For instance, at 3 A.M. you may find them sitting in the living room watching the 384th rerun of *Andy Hardy Meets a Debutante*. From there it's just one tiny step to *Sermonette* and the test pattern and then that fuzzy white stuff they put on at five-thirty in the morning . . ."

But don't these people have to eat, and sleep, and so on?

"Sure. Sure. Especially and-so-on. But they do it all in front of the set. The only times they will get up and leave, we have found in our studies, is occasionally to spray their underarms with deodorant and to gargle with a mouthwash that tastes like a candy cane. Otherwise, television becomes for them the be-all and end-all, how shall we say—well, in doctor talk, we call it the Booby Tuby."

Now, what happens if the disease is not treated?

"In doctor talk or people talk?"

In doctor talk.

"In doctor talk, if the disease is not treated, their brains turn to mush, and they become walking stewed prunes, except that they never walk anywhere."

How many known cases do you think there are in this country?

"Oh, I'd say—somewhere in the neighborhood of one hundred million."

One hundred million? But that's about the number of people who watch TV every week.

"Harsh questions call for harsh answers, my boy. I never promised you a brighter day. If you want to search for tomorrow, you can go all the way to the edge of night. We have only one life to live, you know."

Yes, yes, doctor, but tell me—can these people be saved?

"If we catch the disease at an early stage, it is fairly simple. We have what is called the hot-turkey treatment. We hook up the poor shmo to a special television set and bombard him with a succession of unbearable images to drive him away."

What sort of images?

"Oh, you know—Karl Malden's nose, Tommy Snyder's eyebrows, Howard Cosell's hairpiece and Helen Reddy's shoulders. If that doesn't work, we have Bob Hope walk on without his girdle. Or we show them a tape of Robert Conrad coming on the screen over and over and over and daring them to knock a little battery off his biceps."

Isn't there a less cruel way to cure videoraphobia?

"No. Sometimes it takes as many as sixty-seven episodes of *The Brady Bunch*. We have to induce vomiting somehow."

And if none of this works?

"Well, the networks were kind enough to give me advance copies of their new fall program schedules. One peep at these and the videoraphobes realize life is hopeless and they give up television. Sometimes they go to monasteries or nunneries, and other times they just dash straight for a copy of *The House at Pooh Corner* and read it with all their might."

Can you give us tips on how to avoid videoraphobia?

"Well, of course you can't avoid watching television—I mean, what would life be but an endless series of real experiences? No, no. But we have found certain products that contribute to the spread of videoraphobia—Spray 'n Wash, Sweet 'n Low, Shake 'n Bake, and Wipe 'n Dipe. Anything with an 'n in it.

"Then, too, it's a good idea to develop some other diseases so you have something to worry about, because otherwise, TV eats up that portion of the mind which should be used for worrying. Also, you'll get a pain and ruin your tum-tum."

Can videoraphobia be fatal?

"Ah, yes. Sad to say. Only last week a family in Truth or Consequences, New Mexico, went to court to get permission to pull the plug on their daughter's television set."

And?

"And the poor dear shrank down to the size of a little white dot."

Anyway, Doctor, what are you doing to fight the disease?

"For one thing, we are trying to get the networks to put some of their shows on public TV so that nobody will be tempted to watch them. So far, they have only volunteered to give us old shows. ABC would let us have *Mr. T and Tina* and *The San Pedro Beach Bums* and CBS gave us *Me and the Chimp* and *Planet of the Apes*. But both networks insisted we retitle the programs *The Freddie Silverman Show*."

Is there anything else that can be done?

"Money, money—we need lots of money for research.

We've got to get millions of dollars so we can stamp out this scourge of all mankind."

But how?

"Well, we thought a telethon would be nice...."

February 15, 1978

Death of a Salescat

HE WAS BIGGER than Krazy. He was bigger than Felix. He was bigger than Puss 'n Boots.

But he has stuck his little kitty-cat nose up for the last time. The longest-running finicky act in television history is over.

Morris mortuus est; Morris is dead.

The nationally famous cat, who starred in 40 commercials for 9-Lives Cat Food over the past 10 years, keeled over at his veterinarian's office in Chicago Friday and died, a spokesman said yesterday, of "cardiac complications related to old age."

Morris was believed to be 17, but his exact age was never known, because he was plucked from the shadow of the gas chamber at a Chicago animal shelter in 1966 and turned into a star.

Bob Martwick, who discovered Morris and remained his trainer after selling him to 9-Lives as the company's official spokescat, could not be reached for comment yesterday. But Pam Talbot, to whom all inquiries regarding Morris were referred by the Star-Kist company and its ad agency, Leo Burnett, said of Martwick, "He's probably taking it personally."

They were very close.

Talbot, who works for a public relations firm retained to handle Morris' affairs, expressed amazement yesterday at the extent of interest in the fallen star. She had heard from every major news organization, including all three TV networks and all the wire services, and found the response "truly incredible."

"The oddest thing," Talbot says, "is that people have been calling and asking where to send flowers. We just tell them to make a contribution to the American Humane Society."

Morris would have liked that.

At the Stuart Kennels in suburban Lombard, where Morris resided throughout his show-business career, a casket manufacturer telephoned offering to donate a tiny coffin for the tabby. But Morris had already been buried over the weekend near his trainer's home. There was no ceremony. Morris would have liked that, too.

However, it was by appearing not to like anything—except 9-Lives Cat Food—that Morris became a household pet in millions of American homes.

Aloof, urbane, acerbic and wry in his screen appearances, Morris was, behind the scenes, a quiet, shy and private sort of cat, survivors say. "He was a personal friend of mine," Talbot recalled, "and I would have to say he was definitely a special cat. He was finicky just as portrayed, but he was also very friendly. He was a cat with charisma, there's no doubt about it."

Temperamental? Not Morris. "He was independent, though," Talbot said. "When he felt like taking a rest, he took a rest." That, of course, meant that the director, the sound man, the cameraman, the lighting man and all the other members of the production crew took rests too. When Morris was through taking a rest, filming would resume.

Morris traveled in limousines, stayed in luxury hotels and flew in an unmarked cage—lest he be mobbed, his trainer used to point out, by adoring fans. Yet he retained the common touch he may have learned in the alleys of his youth and never appeared spoiled by stardom.

When he visited the offices of *The Washington Post* in 1973, he sat patiently on a desk while staff members stood in line for the opportunity to pet him. And these were hardened journalists who'd managed to keep their cool even when Robert Redford was on the premises making a movie. Actually, Morris and Redford had almost the same hair color—a kind of goldish orange.

Morris completed filming a few more commercials before

his death, but Talbot said all Morris commercials will be pulled off the air "briefly" in memoriam. The memoriam won't last forever, because *big* advertising dollars are involved.

Thus it is that a replacement for Morris has already been found and is waiting to face the cameras. "I haven't met him," Talbot said. "In fact, I don't even know where he is at the moment; but we do have a successor, and he was found in the same way Morris was. He will be called 'Morris.' We don't think viewers will notice the difference."

Morris might not have liked that.

The same actor who did Morris' voice and said all those finicky things will do the voice for the new Morris, but Talbot would not reveal his name. "It's a secret," she said. "Like Santa Claus."

In addition to his commercial work, Morris costarred with Burt Reynolds in the 1973 movie *Shamus*. He played the part of a cat.

Throughout the country yesterday, fans of Morris reacted to the news of his passing each in his own way. In Long Beach, California, a little girl may have spoken for them all when she shouted "Oh, no!" and then, scooping up her own fat orange cat in her arms, cried out, "I don't want to lose my kitty."

July 13, 1978

Video Noir—
TV's Long Shadow

THEY PROBABLY do not realize it, nor do they likely give a hoot, but a number of local TV stations in this country are running perpetual *video noir* festivals. Most people do not even know what *video noir* is—but then, the term has just this minute been invented. Yet the genre goes back to the earliest days of television, and reruns of shows like *Perry Mason, The Untouchables* and *The Twilight Zone* help keep it alive.

Video noir programs have certain things in common. First, they are all in black-and-white. Second, they may defy the traditional theology of the television series that says everything will be all right after the last commercial (Perry Mason always found the real killer, but often the murder victim was someone so despicable that he clearly deserved to die, and the killer thus implicitly deserved to get away).

A *video noir* episode might have a downbeat or even slightly hopeless ending; it might deal with death as a subject and not just scatter miscellaneous deaths about as easy scenic decoration and it frequently would wander midst the realms of the supernatural, the faintly perverse or the existential.

Just as there are *film-noir* classics like *The Big Sleep, Murder, My Sweet, Blue Dahlia* and *Laura,* there are *video-noir* classics and sometimes these are cop or detective stories, as many *films noirs* were: *Naked City, Peter Gunn, Mike Hammer, Richard Diamond, M Squad, The Untouchables.* Often these programs even have an authentic *film-noir* physiognomy, with low light levels (something color television virtually obliterated), heavy shadows and sound-stage city settings under artificial suns and neon moons.

The fact is, a good print of an old *Perry Mason* can be visually beautiful—actually *beautiful,* in a stark, high-contrast, heavy-'50s way unattainable now that all filmed shows have the same muted bluish factory tint. *Perry Mason* is a landmark in *video noir* from its urban-primal musical theme (by the gifted and underrated Fred Steiner)—which sets the ritualistic tone for the minimally mysterious mystery plots—to its unusually handsome monochromatic cinematography. *Perry Mason* looks like the best of the '40s B movies, and it upholds the idea of Los Angeles as the dark dream city of freezing heat that Nathanael West and F. Scott Fitzgerald immortalized.

This vision of L.A. was shattered by color TV, its accompanying inescapable use of actual exteriors (as opposed to back-lot streets and studio sets) and the arrival of boyish and outdoorsy cops like the insufferable and uncharismatic Starsky and Hutch or the insipid vanilla teammates on *Adam 12*.

Such dudes can hardly compare with the imposing sight of those two incredible hulks, Raymond Burr as Mason and the late William Hopper as detective Paul Drake, when they went out together in their padded-shoulder suits to haunt a suspect or intimidate Lieutenant Tragg or the District Attorney, both of whom, with an infallibility peculiar to true-blue bureaucrats, were always wrong. *Perry Mason* said the system works, but generally by accident and always through the intervention of civilians and of fate.

Perry Mason has hardly been absent from television for an instant since the program premiered on the CBS television network in 1957. An attempt to update it, in color, with a lithe and youngish hero, was a ridiculous and doomed failure in the '70s. People watch episodes of *Perry Mason* over and over and over—reruns have been a fixture in Washington for more than a decade—not because they are hooked by the sometimes ludicrously rudimentary plots but, partly, because they get from Perry Mason a pervasive, transporting and consistent sense of comparatively exotic video atmosphere. There is little sense of atmosphere in any current filmed TV series because now they almost all look exactly alike.

Threats of violence were a more elemental aspect of *video noir* than actual violence was, but explicit violence certainly existed. Perhaps no TV shows in history have matched *Naked City* and *The Untouchables* at making violence awesome and intimidating week after week. At ABC's 25th Anniversary Party in Los Angeles, before he'd left for NBC, Fred Silverman watched a frantic old *Untouchables* clip in open-mouthed admiration. "That was a great series," he said. "I wish we could do it today—but they'd kill us."

"They" are, of course, the antiviolence groups who have helped clean up television and, while undoubtedly improving its moral tone, have also helped prevent it from re-creating the furtive, perilous *video noir* milieu, even if anybody had the ambition to try. *Naked City* was not as sensationally violent as *The Untouchables,* and it did not exist in a make-believe Chicago of the past but in an on-location New York of the present, but seeing scenes from it now makes today's crime-time shows look all the more cosmetic, escapist and bland.

Programs of the past that attempted "prosocial" messages even before the term was coined—like *The Defenders* and *East Side/West Side*—don't qualify as *video noir* no matter how cherished a place they occupy in television history. Their "message" intentions disqualify them, for one thing, and their attempts to deal with social issues of their day dates them now in ways that true *video noir* programs do not date—at least, not spiritually.

Perhaps the most timeless *video noir* classic of them all is also one of television's few true auteurist triumphs—Rod Serling's *The Twilight Zone,* now seen nightly in Washington on Channel 20—although, in a gesture typically halfhearted for the station, fewer than half of the 100-plus episodes available for syndication have been bought. Nevertheless, though the station keeps repeating *Twilight* shows from an inventory of only 50, the program is earning bigger ratings at 11 P.M. than did the first-run controversial series *Mary Hartman, Mary Hartman.* Stations in 125 markets around the country have bought *The Twilight Zone,* though it is currently airing in only 27 of them.

Twilight Zone was a milestone that could not be duplicated; when Serling was later recruited to host NBC's tedious and mundane *Night Gallery,* there was no comparison to the original *Twilight Zone* programs he had narrated and often written. Those programs began with Serling growling out a standard enigmatic introduction in his peculiarly punchy, penetrating voice: "There is a sixth dimension beyond that which is known to man. . . ."

Usually the program, an anthology of stories dealing with occult, science-fiction or supernatural themes, successfully entered a seventh dimension beyond that which is known to television. Throughout the series, Serling, the only person who could be called a continuing character, and his collaborators repeatedly and successfully stretched their imaginations when it came to story material and narrative style.

One of the program's most celebrated installments, "The Invaders," written by frequent and invaluable contributor Richard Matheson, had essentially one character and almost no dialogue; Agnes Moorehead played an old woman trapped in a lonely house visited by a tiny but lethal flying saucer from another planet. The confrontation was eloquently skeletal, the setting for it unforgettably bleak and the O. Henry ending a corker.

When Buster Keaton starred in a story about a turn-of-the-century inventor and his herky-jerky time machine—one of the series' few comic installments—the part of the story set in the past was filmed as a silent movie with pit-piano accompaniment. When Keaton propelled himself into the noisy present of the city of '62, the film turned to sound. *Twilight* was forever, perhaps too often, dealing with tales about the defiance, purposeful or accidental, of time. In one mordant tragicomic show, "What's in the Box?," a mercilessly nagged husband played by William Demarest is shocked to see the death of his shrewish wife, played by Joan Blondell, on television before it actually happens.

For one of its five seasons, *The Twilight Zone* was a one-hour instead of a half-hour series, and with "In His Image," written by another frequent contributor, Charles Beaumont, the program proved ahead of its time once again. George Grizzard played a man who seemed to have been stricken with selective amnesia. When also struck by a car on a road near his hometown, he picked himself up to find a fresh long gash in his arm. Pulling back the torn flesh—in one of the most eye-popping moments in the history of the series—he found not veins and arteries but wires and transistors and tubes. Here was television's first bionic man—a manufactured android who'd thought he was really human.

I remember vividly the moment he pulled back that synthetic skin because it knocked me right out of my living-room chair. But that was one of the great things about *The Twilight*

Zone; it dared to be, on occasion, genuinely frightening, not just timidly spooky, like, say, the Boris Karloff *Thriller* series or *Night Gallery* itself. One of the all-time scariest moments in TV annals comes from a *Twilight Zone* episode called "Nightmare at 20,000 feet," also written by Matheson.

In this one, William Shatner plays a man who boards a plane after recovering from a nervous breakdown; he is heading home. Up in the black night sky, he thinks he sees a grotesque little man hopping around on the wing of the plane and tampering with one of the engines. No one sees the man but Shatner, and he is assured the little man isn't really there. He closes the curtain over the window and tries to sleep. But he keeps wondering: Is he there? is he there? Finally, after a prelude of ingeniously sustained suspense, he opens the curtain and *wham*, the creature is not only there, he's staring right in, his gnarled nose pressed against the glass and all of him bigger than life.

The names in the credits of *The Twilight Zone* remain uncommonly impressive. Bernard Herrmann and Jerry Goldsmith were among the participating composers. Mitchell Leisen, Ralph Nelson, Boris Sagal, Lamont Johnson, Christian Nyby, Stuart Rosenberg, Don Siegel and Elliott Silverstein were among the directors. Robert Redford played an eerily handsome choirboy personification of Death on one episode, and Ed Wynn played a veteran pitchman trying to make a deal with another Death specter on another episode.

Most TV series have traditionally presented narrow views of American life, the world and the universe. Indeed, the universe has rarely been mentioned. *The Twilight Zone* may have had its gimmicky or arch chapters, but as a television program, as a work of *video-noir* pop art, it offered an expanded vision, not a limited one, and its dramas were usually set in artificial environments barren of comforting cues or carefully established bearings. It was not the familiar but the unfamiliar that the program celebrated, and it brought routine television to a new level of beguiling adventure for the engageable mind.

July 16, 1978

The *60 Minutes* Decade

IT LOOKED fairly certain that Anwar Sadat and Menachem Begin were not going to make the 10th anniversary party of *60 Minutes*, the hugely successful CBS-TV newsmagazine, even though both were among the leagues of newsmakers who have appeared on the show and thus got invited.

"That's all right," chuckled CBS News President Richard Salant. "At nine we'll move the whole party to Camp David." He was joking. And moving the party to Camp David from the Four Seasons restaurant, where it was held last night, could hardly have made it any more magnificent a media event about a media event than it already was.

True, the list of no-shows among the invited guests was perhaps more impressive than the shows. Woody Allen and Richard M. Nixon were among the many who just didn't manage to drop by for a drink and a shrimp. Rare is the party on the planet Earth, however, that can bring together the likes of William F. Buckley, Jr., and Eugene McCarthy, Ilie Nastase and Kurt Vonnegut; G. Gordon Liddy and New York Mayor Edward Koch; Beverly Sills, E. Y. "Yip" Harburg and Eubie Blake. This one did.

Don Hewitt, the *60 Minutes* producer, told all the guests they were "superstars," but some of them were as much victims of *60 Minutes* as heroes. Norman Lear, who revolutionized television comedy on the same network *60 Minutes* is on, recalled that "Mike Wallace did try to skewer me" when Lear was on the show a few years ago. And designer Emilio Pucci said he was still bitter about the correspondent from a European agency who had interviewed him for the program.

Ah, but the sublime honor of being gored by a maker of superstars that is also a smash hit! It tends to enhance one's celebrity rather than promote one's notoriety. The way *60*

Minutes perpetually sets up ripe adversary situations and the slick, showy way it pokes fingers have helped make it the addictive institution that it is. Whatever its occasional excesses, the program is a triumph of essentially chivalrous and invariably entertaining journalistic manipulation.

And then, of course, there is the sincerest form of flattery. On Sunday night, a rerun of *60 Minutes* did better than new editions of the other networks' magazine shows—the ticky-tacky *20/20* on ABC and the spunky *Weekend* on NBC. As it happens, Salant was among those watching *Weekend*. In fact, Mike Wallace called him up in the middle of the show complaining of a 100-degree temperature and the flu. "I told him, 'Mike, it'll have to wait; I'm watching *Weekend*,'" Salant said. "I think his temperature went up to 102 after that."

Hewitt, a brilliant and volatile producer, said he was not much concerned with the competition from the other networks. "Maybe I shouldn't say this, but I never think about *20/20*," Hewitt said. "*Weekend* could develop into something in time, I think." He was asked to account for the tremendous popularity of his program, which has made more appearances in the top 10 of network ratings than any other news program in television history. Hewitt has it all figured out.

"Look," he said: "On television you've got guys playing cops, you've got guys playing doctors. This show—*60 Minutes*—is about three reporters. And Dan Rather, Mike Wallace and Morley Safer are better, and more fascinating, just being themselves than Redford and Hoffman ever could hope to have been playing Woodward and Bernstein.

"Every Sunday millions of people say to each other, 'Let's see what Dan, Mike and Morley are up to tonight,'" Hewitt said. In other words, people tune in the adventures of the *60 Minutes* team the way they tune in the adventures of *Charlie's Angels*. Except that Wallace, Rather and Safer are never called upon to flounce about in wet swim trunks.

One of the amazing things about *60 Minutes* is that success has not diminished its vitality. This is especially noteworthy in that CBS, far more than the other two networks, is infected from top to bottom with outrageous pietistic self-esteem. Even now that Black Rock, as the network's New York headquarters is called, has become the *Gray Lady Down* of broadcasting. The network that once made Fred Silverman feel unwelcome because he wasn't classy enough is now groveling for audiences with trashy imitations of Silverman successes and a promotional campaign built around the tasteless slogan "Turn Us On, We'll Turn You On."

CBS News remains, however, the shiny sparkle in the CBS eye, and *60 Minutes* represents the news department's greatest and splashiest current success. So it was no surprise that CBS Board Chairman William S. Paley referred to it at the party as "the most successful documentary series in the history of broadcasting," and praised it for its "style, wit and tenacity in the best tradition of CBS News." He said it sent "a ripple of pride and courage" through the company, presumably to the tippy, tippy top.

But Paley, standing behind a huge chocolate cake made to look like a stopwatch, then wished for the program something he probably also wished for himself: "May you live a thousand years."

Despite the TV maxim that you never tinker with a hit, there will be some changes on *60 Minutes* this season, Shana Alexander and James J. Kilpatrick and their weekly childish arguments, "Point–Counterpoint," will be seen less often. Harry Reasoner will join the program later in the season. Correspondent and rustic sage Andrew Rooney will also appear regularly.

Mighty and all-powerful as *60 Minutes* may appear to be, it ran into a stubborn obstacle on one of its reports to be seen on the new-season premiere this Sunday. Of all things, the report is about network television, and among those whom Wallace had hoped to interview but could not get access to was the one and only Freddie Silverman, now president of NBC.

Wallace is not too cheery about being turned down. "That son of a bitch!" he sputtered at the party. "In July, Freddie assured me that he'd do it, and then suddenly he was not available to me. As a matter of fact, we could not get Robert

Daly [of CBS], Anthony Thomopoulos [of ABC] or Freddie Silverman—the three men who program network TV—to talk to us on camera about network TV! It's such horseshit.

"And the irony of it," Wallace noted, looking as though his temperature were rising again, "is that all three of them had said, at one time or another, that 60 *Minutes* is their favorite news show."

One of the program's segment producers said that despite the absence of the executives, the report on network TV programming came out well. In fact, the producer said, "it's ———-ing hilarious!" He said that 60 *Minutes* did what it thought would be the honorable thing—"If anything, we're harder on our own network than we are on the others."

The entrance of Paley turned the already overcrowded room into media bedlam about midway through the party last night. Paley walked through the crowd and up a flight of stairs —which were then immediately roped off, as if to prevent the monarch from having to mingle with his subjects. But it turned out that the velvet ropes were for the protection of the big stopwatch cake, which, when it was wheeled out by waiters, almost sent Dan Rather tumbling backward into a gigantic potted plant.

Poor Shana Alexander, on the other side of the cake, almost got pushed backward onto an even larger cake, this one spelling out "60 MINUTES" in great pink letters. "I nearly sat on it, and I almost bounced," she said of the cake. Paley descended the stairs to address the crowd, cut the stopwatch cake and then sauntered into the throng, where he laughed and chatted with, among others, McCarthy and a bearded, but still palid, David Frost.

And although 60 *Minutes* sometimes seems to be slicing up pieces of sacrificial cake for its enormous national audience each week, the fact that a program with no featured bouncing bosoms or wan punk dreamboats regularly makes it into the top 10 is one of those tiny little redemptive encouragements in American television. "For this season, we've got more good stories in the bank than we've ever had," Hewitt promised. And yet he also said that swelled heads and self-importance are not likely pitfalls for *60 Minutes* no matter how successful it gets.

"I'd just throw out anybody who takes himself too seriously," Hewitt said. "My pet peeve in this world is news guys who think they belong to the priesthood."

But let's face it—if it were the priesthood, Hewitt would have cornered the market on bishops, cardinals and candidates for the papacy. Watching *60 Minutes* has become one of Sunday's religious rituals for the United States of America.
September 13, 1978

The Time Was Prime for a Pause for Peace . . .

"AS WE APPROACH the seventh millennium of time, the human race will at last find peace," declared President "Adar" on the premiere of ABC's space epic *Battlestar Galactica*. Hostilities immediately ensued, but they were interrupted at 10:30 Eastern time—just as the Cylon warships were closing in—by President of the United States Jimmy Carter.

"We're privileged to witness tonight a significant achievement in the cause of peace," said Carter from the East Room of the White House. And because he was saying it in a particularly prime moment of prime time on the biggest viewing night of the week, it is possible that as many as 100 million Americans were watching him in their homes.

Yesterday, as the euphoria over the "framework for peace" agreements signed by Egyptian President Anwar Sadat and Israeli Prime Minister Menachem Begin was seasoned with notes of realistic skepticism, one particularly obvious question arose. Was the signing as big a triumph for world peace as the national telecast was a triumph for the battle-scarred public popularity of President Carter?

Had White House image-maker Gerald Rafshoon scored his greatest media coup yet—by getting all three networks to carry Carter's *Peace Revue* at a time when it would get him maximum exposure to the nation?

Sunday is traditionally the night when more Americans are watching television than on any other. NBC Research estimates that 62.7 percent of all U.S. television sets were turned on during prime time Sunday, and that the total number of viewers could range between 90 and 100 million.

It was also the most heatedly competitive night of the new fall TV season. ABC was showing its much-ballyhooed $3-million *Galactica* premiere, CBS had the live Emmy Awards from Pasadena and NBC was airing the concluding half of the first TV showing of the remake of *King Kong*.

If Carter, Sadat and Begin had come on the air a couple of hours earlier their ratings might not have been so sensational, but by 10:30 viewers were bound to be hooked by one of the three splashy network offerings, and "overnight" figures show that they remained in front of their sets for the White House show.

The glad tidings of peace came on just as King Kong was fording the East River looking for his girlfriend, as the dread Cylons were closing in on the Battlestar *Galactica* for the final confrontation ("Enemy approaching ... ten centons ... ") and Alan Alda was about to hand out the evening's umpteenth Emmy Award.

Yesterday White House sources insisted, though privately and not for the record, that the timing of the Carter announcement was actually dictated by the events at Camp David and not by the shrewd media strategy of Rafshoon, who did not respond to inquiries.

One veteran broadcast journalist, however, said it was "obvious" that the telecast was timed for maximum TV exposure and that even the Sunday deadline set by Carter for conclusion of the negotiations might have been part of the campaign to bolster his image through TV.

But NBC News bureau chief Sid Davis, chairman of network pool coverage for the event, said, "My judgment is that the White House really didn't know the way this was going until late in the day. When the day started out, it looked like nothing major was going to happen."

At 5 P.M., the White House phoned Davis to ask him to arrange a "possible nine P.M. broadcast" from the East Room, where public television was just finishing up a live concert by cellist Mstislav Rostropovich. At 5:45, as Davis tried to round up crews and equipment for the broadcast, the White House called again and Rafshoon aide Anne Edwards told Davis, "You have until ten-thirty now" to put the show on the air.

George Watson, ABC News bureau chief here, said, "There really is no way of knowing for a certainty" whether the timing of the broadcast was the result of Rafshoon's strategy or of the logistics of the negotiations. "Perhaps we were being jerked around," Watson said. "But I think the White House really was concerned about rampant speculation spreading, so they wanted to get out the results of the conference as soon as possible."

Thinking it over, Watson added, "No, I do not think that the end of the summit was orchestrated with *Galactica* or *King Kong* in mind."

Ed Fouhy, CBS News bureau chief, expressed a similar sentiment but had at least a glimmer of doubt. "No, I'm sure yesterday [Sunday] was dead honest," Fouhy said. Then: "Well, not dead honest, but fairly honest."

For nearly two solid weeks, network news teams had been standing vigil at Camp David waiting for a break in the story or in the secrecy that surrounded the negotiations. Most network sources conceded yesterday that the reason for the secrecy was partly to avoid the bedlam of "media diplomacy" that marked earlier hopes of a Mideast agreement late last year.

Nevertheless, the three networks dispatched their superstars—Walter Cronkite of CBS, Barbara Walters of ABC and John Chancellor of NBC—to corral Sadat and Begin yesterday and begin an undoubtedly long round of postnegotiation negotiations for TV viewers to see for themselves.

As if to further emphasize the importance of TV exposure

in affecting public opinion on Carter's performance as prince of peace negotiations, his address to a joint session of Congress, originally scheduled by the White House for 9 P.M. yesterday, was moved ahead to 8 P.M. so as not to interfere with the telecast of the Monday-night football game.

The three network evening newscasts resembled duplicate newsmagazine covers last night as they devoted large shares of broadcast time to interviews with Sadat and Begin, who must have had little time to do anything yesterday but be interviewed by networks. CBS and ABC evening newscasts are seen at the same time in Washington, and one TV set tuned to each revealed interviews of Anwar and Menachem by Walter and Barbara running almost in unison.

Earlier in the week, Cronkite bowed out of a scheduled appearance on the *Emmy Awards* because he wanted to stay with the story; thus it was Cronkite himself who appeared on screen when CBS interrupted the *Emmy* show Sunday night.

"Walter, in our eyes, has been part of the Mideast summit from the very beginning," said Sanford Socolow, executive producer of the *CBS Evening News with Walter Cronkite*. "He would have been goddamned disappointed if it weren't him on the air to report the conclusion."

Paul L. Klein, executive vice president for programming at the NBC Television Network, said yesterday from Burbank that he was certain the timing of the Carter telecast had been no accident, but also said he didn't see anything wrong with that.

"This is the age of media," said Klein. "You do what you have to do. You try to settle wars, you want to attract attention. I don't see why people try to find anything negative about that."

September 19, 1978

Forever Howard

How-word Co-*sell*—you heard the bell and you came out talking. You bounced off the wall. You covered left field. You went out on a limb. And in the end, there wasn't only one champ, there were two. What a performer! What a man! What a mouth!

"Ali!" you exclaimed during Round 10. "So purposeful! So sure of himself! What an extraordinary career, and what an extraordinary man he has been in every way!" You could have been talking about yourself, Howard—your courage in contending with constant, corrosive criticism; your intransigent declination to moderate your immutable and inscrutable modus operandi; your refusal to play the Pollyanna in an industry that encourages diffidence—and, if you will, your pugnacious perspicacity and audacious imperturbability in the face of a chorus of the world's cruel boos.

Howard, you are not only the champion. You are the event.

Let them call you a fifth wheel in the booth on *Monday Night Football*. Let them refer to you as "His Royal Heinous" and "old flannel mouth." Let them claim they listen to the audio on radio and turn the television sound all the way down when you are commentating. You are a romantic, and a football game is too prosaic a place for you to be. At the Ali–Spinks fight you proved what few of us had realized: Howard Cosell is not providing the commentary for the sporting event; the sporting event is providing the commentary for Howard Cosell.

Maybe you mangle the language hither and yon; maybe you make an art form of overstatement and maybe you threaten at times to rewrite *Roget's Thesaurus* off the proverbial cuff. What matters is not the words you use but the way you use them—like punches, like jabs, like body blows. We weren't watching the Ali–Spinks fight, Howard. We were watching you watch the Ali–Spinks fight. The sound of your voice was virtually visual—the sensory equal of the picture itself—and more than that, it was a transmogrification into a personal and intimate form, a manageable, living-room form, of the roaring crowd that filled the Super Dome in New Orleans.

You became our own personal roaring crowd. You used your hyperbole and your bombast the way a great pianist uses the fortissimo pedal. Only more so, of course. Howard, you are one of TV's true virtuosos, and you understand the kinetics of television with the insight and instinct of a true media being.

It hasn't been easy learning to love you, Howard. There were times when you seemed to be doing your critics' work for them. Now, at sandlot baseball parks across the length and breadth of this fabled land of ours, kids stand on the sidelines imitating your delivery. You are the brunt of jokes from nightclub comics and Congressmen. You are ridiculed even by colleagues and set upon by the envious.

The night before the fight, Johnny Carson told his audience they could see it "free on television" and then added, "Well, not exactly free. You have to listen to Howard Cosell."

For this, the audience cheered.

It has been a career of trials by fire and by frying pan. At the Sweetwater Tavern in East Denver, Colorado, they took turns throwing bricks through television sets when your visage materialized in the phosphorous. At the 1977 World Series, an angry fan propelled a pair of pliers in your general vicinity. In 1975, a bunch of Minnesota Vikings roared with laughter after dousing you with a garbage pail filled with water and dislodging your legendary toupee.

A 1974 headline tells it like it is: "MAN INDICTED FOR THREATENING COSELL BY MAIL."

When would you strike back; how would you defend your honor as a man, a champion and a very highly paid television personality? Like the true gentleman that you are and scholar you aspire to be, you refused to meet violence with violence. A 1977 battery complaint claiming you slapped a Philadelphia newsman five times on his head was dismissed by a Los Angeles judge for insufficient evidence.

Though not, one might venture to add, for insufficient provocation.

And then the final insult. It is 1977. ABC is televising the World Series. You are clearly out of your element, you are occasionally insufferable and you have to put up with amateurs in the booth. But Howard Cosell, you do not deserve this:

Joe Garagiola calls you "dumb."

It's as if Nixon had questioned your ethics.

Or Dr. Bourne had told you to lay off Tylenol.

And why do they continue to villify and slur, pillory and deride? Is there perchance a strain of I Hate New York backlash to this calumniation; or at least, a quasi-regional prejudice at work, since it has been said that to some you embody, to borrow the phrase of no less a literary solon than Alfred Kazin, the "New York Jew"? It gives one pause to contemplate such a disconsolating contingency.

But there is probably a deeper and less tangible antagonism at work here. Because, Howard, you represent heat in an age of cool, passion in a time of indifference and a thick, gooey slice of what-the-hell cheesecake in a time of tidy frozen yogurt. You will defend to the death the courage of your own pre-conceived notions. Your rough edges haven't been polished into slick acrylic gloss. You are a living, breathing ham amid a chorus of mannerly, yellow blazer-wearers; a rumpled, crumpled cornball at a party for androids and curriers of public favor. You make trouble, Howard. You're up and at 'em. And when it's clear to the whole wide world that you're as full of beans as a windbag can be, you cling to your occasionally erroneous surmisals with the zealousness of Hamlet, Louis Pasteur and Hercule Poirot. This is a form of heroism.

"And now, as this fight nears its end," you roared over the roar in the 14th round, "it occurs to us that Bob Dylan struck the proper note in his great song, 'Forever Young,'" and you began to recite, "'May your hands always be busy, may your feet always be swift, may you have a strong foundation—'" blah blah blahblahblah. . . .

"One round to go and boxing history apparently in the offing!"

The bell sounded. Round 15. Spinks was beaten. "The fight is—over! I am going to try to go into the ring. It may be impossible!"

Chris Schenckel, polite, at ease, a breath of purest Valium, took over while you, Raving Howard, struggled toward the ring, which was now such a mob scene that even the champ, Muhammad Ali himself, had momentarily succumbed to topplement.

"This is as bad a situation as I have ever encountered in a ring," we heard your disembodied voice complain, still punching, punching, punching. "I'm trying to talk to Muhammed Ali! This is an absolutely impossible scene! I believe that my mike has gone out and there's absolutely no way of knowing if I am still on mike! [Pause] *The mike cord has been cut!*"

Only you, Howard Cosell. You thought your cord had been cut and yet you continued to talk into the presumably lifeless microphone. You are still the greatest impersonation of Howard Cosell that ever has been done.

It occurs to me that Cole Porter struck the proper note in his great song "You're the Top": "You're the top; you're a Lindy's waiter. You're the top; you're an alligator...."

Howard, may your mouth always be hasty, may your heart always be stout, may you show the hollow younger men what it really means to shout.

And may you be forever Howard Cosell.

September 24, 1978

Robin Williams Visits Earth

THE MINOR RUMBLE of a delivery truck outside his trailer on the Paramount lot is more than enough to set Robin Williams off. Dropping the conversation like a napkin off a lap, he jumps to his feet and shouts in a cracker twang, "Lola! Lola! Get the baby! It's a quake!"

Then he looks around, remembers who he is, sits down again and asks the futile question "Now, where were we?" It's a bit disorienting to come upon a fellow with the inventiveness of an Albert Einstein and the attention span of a Daffy Duck, but these are among the qualities that have made Robin Williams at 26 the hottest comedian in America.

Network television would seem hardly the medium for such a manic new talent, but *Mork and Mindy*, a situation comedy built entirely around Williams' charms and inspirations, has become the highest-rated new series of the year, ranking fourth—near *60 Minutes* and *Charlie's Angels*—among the top 10 in the season so far.

"It is strange to think if this show is doing well, then twenty-five, thirty million people are watching," Williams says. "Whoa! Ohhh. I think about being in a hall with eight thousand people, or a football stadium with a hundred thousand. But thirty million people? That's like eighty football fields. It's frightening." He looks down, almost sorrowfully. "Very strange."

A momentary calm—but these spells do not last long. Unlike Steve Martin, whose fame he may eventually eclipse, Williams is as rabidly comic off the screen as on; during a single lunch-hour break between rehearsals he bounces through at least a dozen different voices, from Peter Lorre's to the squeak of a Hollywood tot to Quasimodo to a swish teacher at an acting school for fish ("I worked with Flipper when he was *nothing*") to that of his own tight-lipped parrot, who lives at home with Williams' new wife, Valerie, and an iguana that sleeps under the refrigerator.

The parrot says only "hello," a two-word obscenity ending in "off" and "Birds don't talk."

For Williams, the world is an attic filled with an infinite number of unopened old trunks—or a gorilla's cage into which passersby toss an endless stream of marvelous objects. His is jubilant humor with an impulse to anarchy that suggests all three Marx brothers rolled into one.

So he doesn't just play Mork—a prankish sprout who strolled to earth from the planet Ork—but contributes his own lines, bits and new Orkish quirks to each show. "From a quarter to a third" is improvised or invented by him, he estimates, and this helps keep him from going stir-crazy within the confines of a weekly series designed by committee to appeal to everybody.

Like Williams, Mork is a chipper, naive misfit with a kid's-eye view of the world. Conversations are held with potato chips, and baloney sandwiches are fed to hungry plants; a broken egg is considered to have died and is buried at sea. Mork must be recharged on his birthday, has a tendency to talk like a supersonic computer and often enters chairs face first.

The native greeting he has brought from Ork is a twist of the ears and a hearty "Nanno, nanno," a phrase Williams invented and made into a household refrain in one night. "It's the Orkian 'Shalom,'" he explains.

His degree of control over the program is unprecedented for such a relative newcomer. That's because there could be no show without him. "What they gave me was more or less carte blanche to do more or less what I want within the limits of a situation comedy—bordering on complete freedom," Williams says.

"I don't have script approval as such, but I can change things if they don't work. It's not like I'm saying, 'This is shit, write it over.' We just play. I go and hang out with the writers and write with them." Williams gets additional creative kicks by continuing to solo in clubs like the Improvization and the Comedy Store in L.A., although his work with a satirical troupe called Off the Wall may have to end because word of his participation got out and now his fans storm the place.

The kind of thunderbolt fame bestowed by national television does peculiar things to idols and idolators. "The only hassle I had was one time I was playing a softball game for Muscular Dystrophy. It was a benefit, and about four hundred little kids there all came up and mobbed me for autographs at the end. That was a little scary, because they were little kids and you couldn't be nasty, push or shove or anything. But they were pushing each other! There was a little kid in the front going [baby voice], 'Come on, sign it! Don't be an asshole!' Incredible!

"One woman—I guess I didn't sign her kid's autograph, or I couldn't get to him, or something—and the woman said, 'He's not so hot. Someday he'll be doing commercials again.' Whoa! I said: 'I'll sign it, honest! I'll kiss the damn kid!' "

Then there was the guy who came up to him on a New York street during a visit to Manhattan a week ago. "Oh, he was the best," Williams said. "He said, 'Are you him, the guy that's on TV?' I said, 'No, I'm his brother. A lot of people mix us up.' He said, 'No, really, are you him?' And I said, 'No,' and as I walked away he yelled, 'Well, if you are him, get the f—— off TV!' "

It is already Christmas on Stage 28 at Paramount. The prop department has sent over a regulation requisition Christmas tree, and the cast of *Mork and Mindy* is rehearsing its holiday show, to be filmed two days later.

"Where's Mork?" one of the actors asks, and Williams, in his perpetual suspenders and a Keith Jarrett T-shirt, bounds onto the set with a mock-benedictory, "Hare Krishna, everybody." While the director talks with the others, Williams suddenly leaps onto a table and turns into Zorro: "Ah, Sergeant García!" he shouts, thrusting an imaginary sword at Mindy, costar Pam Dawber. "Oh, I've skewed Consuelo!"

Soon he is serenading a tree with "chestnuts roasting on a microwave." Then he spies a rope dangling from the rafters, pretends to hang himself with it and announces, "The series is called *Mindy* now."

He is a windup doll who never seems to wind down. But when Elizabeth Kerr, the little old white-haired lady in the cast, becomes tearful over a line in the script about remembering a long-ago Christmas with her late husband, Williams is very quiet and consoling. He tells the director, "This is a very fragile thing, and if you overrehearse this thing you will wreck it."

To no one's surprise, the director completely agreed.

Being around when Williams gets rolling on one of these impromptu binges—especially during a club appearance like the one recently taped for Home Box Office cable TV—is a little like being inside a nuclear popcorn popper as the kernels start to explode. Clearly, *Mork and Mindy* barely exercises his comedic muscles, and he knows, if not admits, it. "It's getting better, though; the focus is shifting," he says optimistically, and he thinks he could stay with the show three, four or five years—but only "if it goes through transformations, if it grows."

To some, a hit TV series is the answer to all prayers; to others it is a certification of selling out. Williams straddles these extremes. Playing an Orkan may not be what he dreamed of while studying drama on a scholarship at the Juilliard School under John Houseman, but he thinks that if he had stayed in New York after graduating, then "just about now I'd be getting regular work, serious acting jobs. Hopefully. Or, just about now, I'd be taking my life."

Williams spent the very first year of his life in Scotland, then moved with his parents to Detroit and later suburban Chicago. Was he gregarious as a child? "No, only with myself." He becomes Peter Lorre: "I was very outgoing with myself. They didn't understand me."

He was once, briefly, a political science major with the wacky ambition of joining the diplomatic corps—"the fantasy lasted one semester." His father always urged him to do what he wanted, Williams says, "but he told me to have another profession, like welding, to fall back on. My mother—a crazy, wonderful Southern belle. A madwoman. A Christian Scientist and a heavy party lady. It's a weird combination. She doesn't drink, but she loves to party.

"A lot of my early act used some of her jokes. Like 'I love you in blue, I love you in red, but most of all, I love you in blue.' That was one of her poems."

He almost ended up "scooping ice cream in an organic ice cream parlor," but comedy called. It screamed. Comedians may differ widely in style, so that an original upstart like Williams wouldn't appear to have much in common with any other—he hates being called "the new Steve Martin," for instance, because "I don't think I'm anything like him." And yet there are common bonds among all clowns: irreverence; bravery in facing audiences; masochism in facing audiences; and the comic's curse of insecurity.

"It's always been a drive to be liked. Lenny Bruce talked about it—it's nothing new: the like-me-love-me syndrome. You want people to enjoy it. Something inside drives you. Comedians have this imbalance that has to be fulfilled, and that's why they're constantly trying to add the other half, that need to be funny. I guess that's what makes some of them very desperate. I don't think I'm desperate in the sense that I'd go to any lengths to get a laugh. Sometimes if I'm dying in a club I'll just end by saying, 'Thank you. If I haven't been funny, relax. The energy's all right. I'll be back. I'm a Zen comedian. It doesn't matter.' "

He looks around the room and spies a bottle of Perrier. A hillbilly demeanor overcomes him: "Want some more of that frog water? I'd like to see a commercial on television—" He shifts into a Shakespearean respectable voice: "You know, whenever I want to have an enchanting evening, I have this frog water. Perrier. For the tragically hip."

What he wants to do: a movie (he is now writing a script), concerts, more club dates and an album in the works. What he won't do: play Las Vegas or appear on *The Hollywood Squares.*

The choices are all his and he has enough energy to run a Ferris wheel for the next 100 years. Whether TV will burn him out quickly or provide him with a base on which to build remains to be seen. For now he is the freshest, most inspired and industrious human leprechaun since the early days of his hero, Jonathan Winters.

A tape recorder sitting next to him has been a silent, obedient listener. Now he turns to it as if it were a kindred spirit. "*You* understand, though," he tells it. "No, what do you know? You're made by Japanese people! *They* understand you."

He looks up and appears fleetingly sheepish. "That's a lot of tape I've wasted. You'll take it back and say, 'That's not funny! It seemed so funny then.' "

He picks up a lumpy carryall with his props, harmonica, book on meditation and *Zap* comic books inside and ambles back to Stage 28. They are waiting for him near the lighted tree the way kids wait for Santa on Christmas Eve; he is their child and their jester and their captured alien, and his bag of tricks seems bottomless for now.
November 19, 1978

Fast *Feud* with Relish

THEY WALK OFF smiling, this family of five from Wylie, Texas, even though they've just lost a chance at $5,000 in cash. But first, the losing mom hugs Richard Dawson, host of ABC's *Family Feud*, and tells him, "Seeing you was worth the trip."

Even the losers go away happy from *Family Feud*.

The phrase "game show" may conjure gross images of self-degradation in the pursuit of loot; it isn't very inspiring to see how low one's fellow Americans will stoop for a trip to Puerto Vallarta. But *Family Feud* is this indigenous American institution's redemption, and encouragingly enough, it is not only the most humane game show on television but also the most popular. It is a smash hit.

Feud is consistently the top-rated game show in lucrative daytime network television, and frequently, as during the week ending November 17, it's the No. 1 show in all of daytime, beating even the mighty soaps. In a way, *Feud* is a nonfiction soap, because a single family may return for several consecutive days as it attempts to win the big moolah.

But the chief reason for the show's success is Dawson—the fastest, brightest and most beguilingly caustic interlocutor since the late great Groucho bantered and parried on *You Bet Your Life*.

The show's fans include Manhattan satirist Fran Lebowitz,

who always watches if she's up by 11 A.M., and it was accorded the honor of a parody on *Saturday Night Live.*

The game itself, invented by Mark Goodson—whose Goodson-Todman outfit has produced such honorable game-show classics as *What's My Line?* and the soon-to-be-revived *Password* (and such dishonorable binges of cupidity as *The Price Is Right*)—may not be a test of knowledge, but at least it is not a test of tastelessness. Five members from each of two competing families try to guess the most popular answers to questions asked of 100 people in surveys conducted by mail ballot.

Recent questions: "Name the best-tasting cookie." Most popular answer: "Chocolate-chip." Or, "Name a famous fairy." No. 1 answer: Tinker Bell."

The winner of the preliminary rounds goes on to "fast money" competition, and this involves coming up with five quick answers to survey questions within 15 seconds. "Name something that keeps you up at night," Dawson asked one harried contestant. "Werewolves," she replied. Wrong!

Dawson has succeeded by breaking the rules for game-show hosts. He is not just another face full of teeth. When contestants give dopey answers, he tells them so, sometimes recommending that they go away for long rest cures.

Occasionally even Dawson, known for his lightning retorts, is floored by the answers given by families on the show. One burly family was asked to name "crimes that each of us has thought of committing at one time or another." The survey results included things like shoplifting and even, in the more figurative sense of the word, murder.

But the family had different answers. First a woman said, "Prostitution." Then a man said, "Grand theft, auto." Finally, for the family's third and final strike, the papa ventured, "Hit-and-run?"

A Japanese-American family lost its chance at the big money because it couldn't think of one more "food that you have to boil." The crucial answer: "Rice."

Dawson asked another man to name an animal with three letters in its name. The man said, "Frog." Dawson broke into laughter, then asked the man's brother the same question. The brother said, "Alligator."

"They sent me silver tie clips later," Dawson recalls. "One sent me a frog and one sent me an alligator."

Among the biggest laughs he can remember was one recorded during the opening of the show, when he meets and interviews family members. "One girl said she worked for Panasonic. I asked her what she did, and she said she worked on TV sets on the assembly line. She said, 'I spot-weld them and hand them on,' so I went on to her sister and I said, 'And what do you do?' and she said, 'I screw 'em.' And I turned to the camera and said, 'Panasonic—just slightly ahead of our time.' "

Another time Dawson asked a contestant, "Name a part of the mouth." The man said, "Tail." Dawson said, "You are weird. Did you think I said 'mouse'?" The man nodded. "So I said, 'Let's give him another chance. Okay, name a part of the mouth.' And he said, 'Nose.' I think it got the biggest single laugh we've ever had on the air."

One contestant was asked to name "a famous place where an annual sporting event is held." His answer: "Forest Lawn." A little girl listened to her fellow family members answer "Toothbrush," "Towel" and "Bathing suit" to the question "Name something that gets wet when you use it," and after a moment's thought she blurted out the only answer she could think of: "Toilet paper."

"ABC wanted to cut that out and we *forced* them to leave it in," says the show's producer, Howard Felsher, a game-show vet of nearly 25 years. "It's a perfectly legitimate answer."

The jokes aside, Dawson communicates a sense of compassion and concern that also makes him unlike any of the goading ciphers running other games. Also, he kisses all the women contestants. On the lips.

"Well, we got into that about the second or third week," Dawson recalls in his *Feud* dressing room, at the bottom of a spiral staircase beneath the studio. "I got to the end of the line and here was this rather darling lady about fifty or so and she was so nervous, she was a basket case. She didn't want to let her family down, but she had no idea at all what to say, and I said, 'I'll do what my mom used to do,' and I kissed her on the cheek, and she gave an answer and it was there on the board. Then I went over to the other family and a woman said, 'Don't I get a kiss too?' and after that there was no stopping it."

ABC tried to stop it, however. "They came up and said, 'Well, we've had a lot of complaints, a lot of complaints.' See, twelve letters they figure are worth thirteen million people. I said, 'You're out of your mind. We're not *Starsky and Hutch*. We don't open the first minute of the show with a head in a garbage can.'"

To settle the kissing issue, Dawson went straight to his constituency and asked viewers to write in votes on postcards —to kiss or not to kiss, that was the question.

"I don't remember the exact totals," says Felsher, "but it was something like fourteen thousand who said, 'Kiss' and three hundred or four hundred who said, 'Don't kiss.' It was that lopsided."

One of Dawson's favorite words is "testy," and his own testiness threshold is pretty low. When a participating sponsor of *Feud* complained to ABC that Dawson was making too many anti-Nixon jokes, and ABC brass told Felsher to tell Dawson to stop, Dawson leaped onto the air and told the unnamed company that if they didn't like his Nixon jokes, they could take their business elsewhere—a safe threat, since *Family Feud* has sponsors waiting in line. When ABC demanded that Dawson's outburst be edited out of the tape, he threatened to quit. It stayed in.

Dawson wasn't afraid of losing a sponsor. "I know advertisers," he says. "They'd sponsor Eichmann if he could move Rust-Off, or whatever." He smiles. "And may I say something? I'd do his warm-up. No, but it's the truth."

Even a family feud with producer Felsher got on the air; Dawson got spleeny over a decision Felsher—as the official arbiter of answers—made, and told a family, "Either you'll be back on this show tomorrow or I won't." But on the next show he apologized for making the threat. "Now tell me anybody who's ever done anything like that on the air," says an admiring Felsher.

Basically, theirs is a backgammon kind of relationship. All five *Family Feud* shows for each week are taped on a single night at ABC studios in a dank nook of L.A., and Dawson sprints down to his dressing room between shows and resumes a marathon backgammon match with Felsher before changing suits for the next show. Dawson virtually never wins but he loves to play.

Just a hair past 46, the British-born Dawson has the slightly astonished look of a man who might once have been married to Diana Dors. Indeed he was, and he has two teen-age sons by that marriage. Dawson spent six years as a prisoner on the *Hogan's Heroes* sit-com, then became by far the most popular panelist on Goodson-Todman's *Match Game* show on CBS.

"What makes Richard so good," theorizes executive Goodson, "is that he generally says the unexpected, is open to his instantaneous feelings, yet can deal with a highly formatted and highly structured program. This also means that occasionally he's a little naughty and occasionally he's a little dangerous."

The trick is in making it look easy when it isn't, Goodson says; "We've made a fortune because people have always underestimated what we do."

Felsher, whose past productions included the rigged '50s game show *Tic Tac Dough*—"I hasten to point out that I'm not hiding that, but it's an old-hat story," he says—thinks Dawson's success is greatly due to his knowledge. "There are damn few knowledgeable emcees. Richard reads, 'cause he's an insomniac, a couple of books a day. Here's a guy who didn't go to high school—he was out on a freighter at fourteen years of age."

"When contestants doze off, that's the thing that really ticks me off," says Dawson testily, "and I tell them about it. But [Bob] Barker [of *The Price Is Right*] or those other guys won't do it because they all want to be Charlie Charming. They never really listen anyway. All those hosts. They'll say, 'Name a country in South America,' and the guy will say, 'Asia,' and they'll say, 'Very good try, but not correct.' Well, you've got to lock the man up, don't you?

"I'll do sarcastic lines just to make the contestants angry enough so they'll forget they're on television and say, 'I'll show this son of a bitch,' and come up with an answer."

Felsher and Dawson are both proud that they've pioneered in having minority, elderly and handicapped contestants on the show. "In the old days, it was always 'no' to handicapped people," Felsher recalls.

An upcoming *Feud* show will be the first to have two black families competing. Which gave Dawson the chance to say, when the first two contestants came up to the podium and stood on either side of him, "I feel like an Oreo cookie."

A blind contestant recently on the show made it to the final fast-money round. Traditionally, Dawson then turns the contestant around, with his back to the studio audience, to watch the answers pop up on the board at the back of the set. "And the blind guy says to me, 'What the hell are you turning *me* around for?' " This breaks Dawson up. "I said, 'I'm turning you around so that I can see the answers.' "

Before he bolts upstairs to tape another show, Dawson is asked, "How do you keep from feeling sorry for the losers?" His answer is indicative of why *Family Feud* is one of the warmest ritual programs in all of TV:

"I don't."

November 29, 1978

Oh, to Click Nixon Around Again . . .

I miss Nixon. I want him back on TV.

How is it that in five minutes of telling us about an earth-rattling change in American policy toward China, Jimmy Carter can be paralyzingly dull—can even make John Chancellor look like the King of the Mardi Gras by comparison—but a whole hour with Nixon at Oxford on public television proved not only as fascinating as the birth of a baby but entirely too brief?

Something is wrong somewhere.

Of course, no one is advocating that Richard M. Nixon be restored to a position of power or influence in the Government of the United States. Whoa, boy! Hey-oh! But we need him on televison. TV made him, and he is still one of the camera's favorite subjects.

Watching the show recorded at the Oxford Union, with Nixon making like Phil Donahue as he roamed the hall fielding, rephrasing and dodging questions (in news photos of the event, he is standing with his arms out as if he were singing; he looks like the new Jolson)—while outside roared the chants of protesters, as continuous and regular as the shoosh-shoosh of the surf at Malibu—this was heaven on air. Whatever else you say about Nixon, you have to admit he is the most Nixonian person who ever lived.

Nixon at Oxford was soapier than the dopiest soap opera, happier than the happiest *Happy Days,* dripping with pathos and bathos and Old Warrior hootchy-kootchy. Peck's Bad Boys have always made for extremely watchable television, from Joe Pine to Joe McCarthy to Elmer the Elephant, a personal favorite of mine when I was growing up with TV near Chicago.

Actually, Nixon's career has from the beginning been inescapably linked with the growth of television. From the Checkers speech to the kitchen debate with Khrushchev to "I am not a crook" to "Crack 'em in the puss"—the immortal advice Nixon gave David Frost on dealing with the press—Nixon has been television's and television has been Nixon's. It is a symbiotic relationship.

This TV Nixon was chronicled and celebrated in a one-hour videotape, *Richard Nixon: 1968–1974,* assembled by video gadflies John Margolies and Billy Adler and shown at the Whitney Museum in New York. The tape was a portrait of Nixon through his own television appearances, without any commentary from outside.

It was just the kind of thing that should be shown on public television, but CBS News has seen to it that it will not be shown anywhere. Because some of the material had been recorded off-the-air unauthorized, CBS News, the biggest bunch of party-pooping stuffed shirts you'll find outside the Federal Government, sued to prevent further screenings of the tape. Thus is the public being deprived of a fresh perspective on an old pal.

The literature of Nixon television includes not only his many, many wet-lipped speeches and press conferences and one-man vaudeville shows; there is also a privately circulated collector's-item tape of Nixon attempting to be buddy-buddy with a TV crew as he prepared to deliver the great speech of his career, his resignation via television on August 8, 1974.

During this little prelude to history, Nixon labored through a few half-hearted jokes with photographers, got suspicious about there being too many people in the room, seemed not to recognize some of his Secret Service men and shuffled his papers. The scene was recorded because a CBS technician accidentally opened the line to the network pool—and most of the nation's TV stations—before the appointed hour of the telecast, and a few engineers had the presence of mind to turn on their tape machines. Every American has the right to see this tape, but few ever will.

Without question there is a place for Nixon in the future of television. McLuhan has said that cartoonish humans come across best on TV, and Nixon, like Tom Snyder, Farrah Fawcett-Majors and Gene Shalit, proves the thesis correct; no wonder Nixon has inspired our best political cartoonists to their grandest and most passionate moments, and no wonder Danny Aykroyd's two best impressions, of equal irresistibility, are of Nixon and Snyder.

The thought of Nixon joining the list of circulating talk-show drop-ins, however, does sound like a compromise of his beleaguered tragic dignity. One hates to think of him trundling out to hobnob with Merv—what if he had to sit between Hermione Gingold and Jill St. John?—or having to humor Mike Douglas by dredging up some limp excuse for a bon mot.

This sort of thing could even lead Nixon to a humiliating cubicle on that living rest home for overexposed celebs, *The Hollywood Squares.* Can you see him crowded into the lower right-hand corner with a big X in front of him? And some little old white-haired lady from Wichita would say, "I'll take Nixon to block."

And Peter Marshall would reach for "a Nixon question" after the dutiful plug: "Richard, as you all know, is opening this weekend at Harrah's in Lake Tahoe."

"Well thanks for mentioning that, Peter."

"That's okay, Dick, and—hey, how about those memoirs! I couldn't put 'em down. But now here's your question. According to Dear Abby, should a girl 'go all the way' on the first date?"

"Well, Peter, I'm glad you asked me that question . . ."

A series would be nice—*I Love Dickie,* about a wacky redhead who marries a president who resigned in disgrace. She keeps trying to break into politics, and they have this perfectly ghastly son-in-law. Or *Eight Months Is Enough,* which each week follows the exploits of a convicted co-conspirator after he is released from the slammer. *Laverne and Nixon* has a nice ring to it, but it probably wouldn't work, and *Grandpa Goes to Washington* has already been tried once without success. *Nixon Days,* however, could take us all back to those wild and wacky '50s—cloth coats in the closet and microfilm in pumpkin patches. We were young, we were innocent and we must have also been pretty damn stupid.

Nixon's years of "public service"—that ultimate in euphemisms—may be over, but Nixon's years in television may be just beginning. I for one would never stop tuning in. At the very least, the following two developments strike me as deliciously compulsory:

First, American Express should pay Nixon $1 million to make a commercial in which he is discovered sitting in the first-class section of an airplane and says into the camera, as plaintively as possible, "Do you know me? I used to be President of the United States."

And then McDonald's should pay Nixon $2 million to film a commercial in which he walks into a fast-food restaurant

136 / ON THE AIR!

intending to order an Egg McMuffin but is surprised by a chorus of workers behind the counter who jump up, point at him and sing out to beat the band, "You—you're the one!"
December 21, 1978

The Great Clichés of 1978

IT TAKES A VERY special year to help you forget a very special year. Therefore, it won't take diddly to help anyone forget 1978.

"Nineteen Seventy-*what?*"

See, you're forgetting it already.

Every year has its clichés, but 1978 *was* a cliché. It was a test-tube clone of an instant replay live-on-tape. It borrowed a little from everybody else and contributed nothing of its own but "Nanno, nanno" and "Push-push, in the bush."

What can you say about a year in which "Grease" was "the word"?

It was a good year for giving up on everything.

People spoke of "meaningful relationships" with "very special people." They cloned the word "parenting" to mean being a parent, but haven't yet come to talk of infanting, childing or just kidding. There was an insufferable excess of Perriering, or drinking of Perrier, and white wining, or drinking of white wine. We complained about property taxes, asked strangers to put out their cigarettes no matter how much they seemed to be enjoying them, watched synthetic Elvises and artificial Beatles.

Youth gangs in the Bronx were big. Arson in the Bronx was big. Street crime in the Bronx was big. Clichés in the Bronx were very, very big. TV-documentary producers were tripping over one another to get in there.

Women took blue-collar lovers. Men discovered The Older

Woman. There was no wisdom like Street Wisdom, and there was much much talk of "caring," especially from gigantic corporations who mysteriously cared more about us than they did about profits. That's what they said, anyway.

Big favor of 1978: "I have something I want to share with you."

To sue or not to sue—that was the question. The answer was usually to sue. Doctors sued patients. Marlon Brando sued Warner Brothers. Women sued men they'd been living with. Men sued women they'd been living with. And everybody and his brother sued Alex Haley.

Big excuse of 1978: "I've had a lot on my mind lately."

Prices inflated, costs escalated, women on "t&a" TV shows "jiggled." College kids became nostalgic for the boredom of the past, finding it preferable to the boredom of the present, and paid numberless repeat visits to the '50s and '60s at Toga Parties inspired by *National Lampoon's Animal House*. People sought death without guilt, sex without guilt and even guilt without guilt. They played racquetball till their sweatbands were drippy, and they trampled hill and dale in mad orgies of mob jogging.

And we all sat around reading books about running and waiting for *Apocalypse Now*.

Apocalypse? Not yet.

Maybe next year.

Nineteen Seventy-eight was such a very special year that people actually became lonely for 1968. The tenth anniversary of 1968 was celebrated with television programs, magazine articles and solemn newspaper columns. Perhaps we longed for the reassuring roar of the riot squad—a sign that something is actually happening in the land. In 1979 there will no doubt be anniversary celebrations commemorating that wonderful year 1929—imagine, the 50th anniversary of the stock-market crash! Lube up your tear ducts and prepare to wax wistful.

There will be other great clichés of '79, of course. In Atlanta, VideoDiscs are already selling like hot cakes—in fact, they even look a little like hot cakes—and in California, they're cranking out "Pardon Patty" bumper stickers by the gross.

When did 1978 reach rock bottom? It was on April 3, when *Time*, a weekly "newsmagazine," featured as its cover story the mopey specter of the year, John Travolta himself, in a story headlined TRAVOLTA FEVER—something for which even the government couldn't invent a vaccine. At the eye of this saturnine hurricane, *Time* put it all together in a few very special and *very* unique paragraphs that unwittingly captured the poor excuse for Angst that is 1978.

Remember, somebody got paid for writing this, and a national magazine that passes itself off as serious printed it as its cover story:

> Check it out! Man walks down that street so fine. Strides easy. Long, looking right. Left then. Then ahead, then left ... snap! ... again, follows that little sister in the tight pants a ways, then back on the beam. Arms arc. Could be some old trainman, swinging an imaginary lantern in the night. Smiling.
>
> Stepping so smart. Rolls, almost. Swings his butt like he's shifting gears in a swivel chair. Weight stays, sways, in his hips. Shoulders, straight, shift with the strut. High and light.
>
> Street's all his, past doubt. And more, if he wants. Could be he might step off that concrete. Just start flying away.
>
> It's all there, in the walk that John Travolta takes through the opening credits of *Saturday Night Fever* ....

Had enough? Here's the bottom line. There's only one more year of the '70s left. Oh, but here's still another bottom line: That means there's only one more chance for the decade to get worse.

And now you have come to the very bottom line itself.

December 31, 1978

The Last of the Media Monarchs

> "*You know, Mr. Bernstein, if I hadn't been very rich, I might have been a really great man.*"
> —*Citizen Kane*

AN IRREVERENT HOLLYWOOD producer, unable to come up with a title for his new CBS comedy show, was asked if the network really cared what the name of the program was. "Not really," he replied; but then he added, "just as long as we don't call it *The Late Bill Paley*."

Around CBS, Inc., the communications empire he founded and has run to suit himself for more than 50 years, it is said of William S. Paley, 78, that he literally never wants to leave, that he can't imagine CBS or the world, in that order, going on without him.

But the last of the first-generation media barons—a founder not only of an empire but, for better or worse, of the American way of broadcasting—says one of the reasons he got around to writing *As It Happened,* his autobiography, is that "finally it dawned on me that I'm not immortal, and if I was to do a book about broadcasting—I'm one of the few people still around who were here at the beginning—then I ought to get on with it.

"So I got serious about it about three years ago, not as something I wanted to write as my final bow-out, but just as something I had an obligation to do."

The book will be published by Doubleday on March 16, and for that reason "The Chairman," which is the only thing approaching a nickname that Paley has at CBS, is willing to sit and chat for a spell. This is all arranged quite presidentially, however—if not papally. William S. Paley is someone on whom one does not drop in. We're talking megamillionaire here, we're talking American media monarchy. Here is a man who has buddied around with Nelson Rockefeller, Dwight Eisenhower, Randolph Churchill, David O. Selznick and Jack Benny, among others.

It is said that the importance of an executive can be gauged by how barren the top of his desk is. *William S. Paley doesn't even have a desk;* he has an ornate round table. The tastefulness of this room, with its very correct paintings and its collection of old microphones, is overwhelming. And tastefulness, even in the firing of underlings, is what Paley has tried to stand for over five decades of brilliant brinksmanship, salesmanship, statesmanship and showmanship.

The sad thing is, there are signs now that the empire has grown too big for the emperor, that the thunderbolts Zeus sends down from the mountaintop have lost their zappiness, that the day of the Gentleman Broadcaster whom Paley embodies is over.

Gone, you might even say, with the wind.

"Listen," says Paley, squirming in a chair and folding his hands over his stomach, "I'm only hanging around here as a shmoozer and kibitzer and adviser." He admits, though, that he cannot imagine himself ever retiring. "If by 'retiring' you mean doing nothing—no. I'd rather stick at what I'm doing because it's what I've always enjoyed the most."

Paley stepped down as chief executive officer in early 1977. He remains chairman of the board and he will probably always be, in the corporate folklore of CBS, "The Chairman."

Paley does not think television has failed the American people, of course. That would be like Alexander Graham Bell conceding that the telephone is a darn nuisance.

"I'm not ashamed of what we've done at all. I think, conditions being what they are, we've served the American people very well. I don't know of any other system in any other country where the public seems to enjoy the medium as much as they do here. I'm proud of it."

He is asked if he can say he is proud of most of the programs now on CBS.

"I'm proud of what we've done for the audience that we're

serving, yes," he says. "I think it's a well-balanced schedule. People are enjoying it. And are benefiting from it."

He points to such alleged *succès d'estime* as *The Paper Chase*, a weekly drama that has won high praise and low ratings. Some say it has been kept on the air only because it is a personal favorite of Paley's. And that it is a personal favorite of Paley's because the hero is an old man, a venerable professor, with whom Paley identifies.

"Oh, no," he says, with a crusty sort of chuckle. "I'm not in that category at all. I think he happens to be an outstanding actor, John Houseman; I think it's a high-quality show, and I wasn't the only one here who thought we ought to go with it. A lot of arguments took place about it."

It has been said that some of the very CBS programs Paley points to with pride—*60 Minutes* and *All in the Family*, to name two—would flop today because the network couldn't afford to keep them on the air until they built up audiences. Neither started as anything even approaching a smash hit.

"No," Paley declares. "I think we're just as apt today, if we see something that we have conviction about or we think represents a new trend and might eventually have a very special appeal to a mass audience, to go with it and stick with it and have patience and courage.

"You've got to do that. Sometimes you do it until you're sick and you have to give up. We did it with a show a couple of years ago called *Beacon Hill*. Remember that? I almost cried. It was one of the best shows we ever did. And we kept it on and on and on. And each week it was lower and lower and lower. We wanted a show that would be equal to some of the things turned out by the BBC. I'd like to turn it around and send some of our shows abroad. Although a lot of our shows do go abroad—but mostly the popular shows.

"But when it comes to the high-quality shows which are used mostly by the educational stations, the BBC have done an outstanding job. They really have. I'm quite envious when I see it. I don't see why we shouldn't do the same thing. We could. We have the talent. And the resources. I hope we have the courage."

William S. Paley has not just set the tone at CBS. He has

also set the melody, the rhythm and the lyrics. There is a CBS style and it is Paley's style, and the people who didn't whistle his happy tune were *out*—out, you might almost say, with the wind.

"I don't give orders, to take things off or put things on," Paley says. "I never did, as a matter of fact. This has been a kind of consensus approach. I have to admit that my voice probably sounded louder than the others, that maybe I'm more persuasive or maybe my authority gave greater weight to what I had to say, but I always encouraged the fullest reaction from everybody."

James T. Aubrey, one of the true legends of broadcasting, was the fair-haired genius during the early '60s at CBS, but then his personal life began embarrassing Paley and CBS. Aubrey was not august. And soon Aubrey was *out*.

"Now, there was a guy who had it right in the palm of his hand; who had it made," says Paley. "He was going to be my successor. There was no question about it. But he just blew it.

"But then, he was absolutely magnificent in defeat. He came in to see me. He said, 'You know, I deserve it all. I'm sorry. I wish to hell you'd give me another chance, but I know you won't. And I'll tell you one thing: I'll never say one bad word about CBS or you.' And he stuck to that word.

"He just got carried away and got into a bad period where he was doing a lot of silly things."

Now, Paley says, after several tries, he has at last settled on someone worthy of succeeding him: John D. Backe, the chief executive officer. Paley speaks admiringly of "this fellow Backe," and of Robert Daly, president of CBS Entertainment. The words he uses to describe Daly reflect Paley's own strict personal values: "Very strong, very decisive; low-key, not the least bit flashy."

It is said that executives who do not personify such qualities are expelled from membership in the Paley club. Fred Silverman got his start in network television at CBS, but they still talk about him around there as not having been Paley stock; in other words, he wasn't a mirror image of Paley.

"There's no snobbery here of any kind," Paley states flatly, contradicting innumerable stories about him and CBS. "There's nothing against the guy who doesn't go to Brooks Brothers or didn't come from the right school or doesn't come from the right side of the tracks. There's none of that here. Never has been, never will be.

"There is a certain standard of taste, I think, that we became known for, and I had a lot to do with. Frank Stanton had a lot to do with it too, and when those things come from the top, they permeate the organization. We just won't produce anything that doesn't have the look of quality about it. I've got a pretty good eye, you know."

CBS has a pretty good eye too—the unmistakable company logo designed by the brilliant art director William Golden in 1951 and now the province of CBS art director Lou Dorfsman. Everything that comes out of CBS is supposed to look CBS and does, from the letterhead to the paychecks to the mobile-unit trucks that crawl around Washington and other cities. And, of course, Black Rock, which epitomizes CBS understatement and class in white, black and gray.

"Putting up this building was a great triumph," says Paley. "I feel good about it every time I walk in.

"You know, I sometimes say, 'What in the hell's going to happen twenty-five years from now, when someone's around who doesn't care about these things?' And they're unnecessary. I know a lot of businesses that pay no attention to details of that kind who are just as successful as we are. They probably make more money; maybe they get as much fun out of it.

"But one's personality has to be felt."

Paley is worried about his book. He thinks it's "too bland," that he should have put in a few more "humorous anecdotes." It is on the austere side, though Paley does recall such moments from his life as the time he got accidentally hooked on Seconal and how he had to excuse himself to go to the bathroom during a dinner party presided over by Winston Churchill.

The book is dedicated to his fabulous wife Babe, who died in 1978. There are few revealing details about their life together, however; Paley announces early in the book that he isn't going to tell all, that "I am not a very demonstrative person. I am not good at flattering people or even complimenting them" and that "I have had few intimates."

This cannot prevent others, of course, from trying to dissect the man and the mythology. CBS has been the subject of more books and articles than any other network, from the lacerating *Reflections in a Bloodshot Eye* by Robert Metz to the forthcoming *The Powers That Be*, David Halberstam's analysis of modern-day media giants, which includes a large chapter on CBS. Paley, ever conscious of his image and his company's image, managed to secure galleys in advance. He was not pleased. "It goes along pretty well, and then all of a sudden he jabs the knife in and turns it and turns it," Paley says. He confesses to being "rankled."

More rankling to him still are forays into his private life. Paley is now said to be the most eligible rich bachelor in New York, and *Esquire* magazine even published a list of the women who were allegedly chasing him the most breathlessly.

"Oh, that's ridiculous, really," says Paley of rumors that have seen him romantically linked with or pursued by Jacqueline Onassis, among others. "I don't know who started it. It was a cheap shot. These were women I have known for years, who were friends of mine, who were friends of my wife and there's not one of them I have a romantic interest in. There's nothing I can do except—you know, nothing."

He does not feel he is being chased by any of the women said to be chasing him. "Listen, if they are, they're chasing someone else and calling him Bill Paley. I know them all too well. You get to know someone too well and sometimes it interferes with any sort of romantic possibility. I've known Jackie for I don't know how many years; I haven't seen her even once since my wife died. Her sister I see more—Princess Lee [Radziwell]."

Recently, Paley said, another publication linked him with the wife of a friend. "That's the cheapest thing I ever came across in my life. I was so upset I could hardly stand it. That's taking journalism and making really a nasty thing out of it.

"Oh, my God—imagine mentioning a man and a wife and saying, 'This is the girl that's going to win out!' She has a really good sense of humor, though; she called me up and said, 'Am I really Number One?' She's an old friend. There's no romance within fifty miles of us. There's nothing to that at all.

"I'm trying to reorganize my life, develop a new life-style. I've had a very happy life, married to quite a wonderful woman. And it's not easy."

Paley read Horatio Alger novels as a boy, but he is not a poor kid who became rich. He is a rich kid who became richer. Asked how a man of his incredible wealth and social prominence can identify with the mass audience CBS tries to woo, Paley says he continues to rely on his instincts. They haven't always been infallible. He tells in his book how he fought Lucille Ball over her insistence that her new TV series, *I Love Lucy*, costar her husband Desi Arnaz.

"I said, 'He's just a good Cuban bandleader, and that's all he can do,' " says Paley, smiling.

He also notes in the book that although Ed Sullivan's variety show, *The Toast of the Town*, looked good when it first went on the air, "We planned to replace Sullivan" as soon as possible.

Of current programs, Paley says he is especially fond of *M*A*S*H* and *60 Minutes* and acknowledges that Mary Tyler Moore's latest attempt at a variety hour is not exactly boffo. "She's doing a very different kind of show now—very much against my advice," he says sternly.

Paley has been adamant about his company's mandatory retirement policy when people as prominent as Eric Sevareid reached the age of 65 and even longtime president and CBS ambassador to Washington Frank Stanton was sent packing. Paley remains the single exception. One assumes, of course, that Walter Cronkite will also be exempt. "I don't know whether he will be or not," Paley says. "It's something I probably won't be deciding. But Walter is the best of the best, and I adore him. He's Mister America. And I'd like to have him around here forever."

Again it sounds as though Paley will be around forever to see this through. You can hardly blame him for hating to leave the world he made in his own image, a conglomerate he estimates will do in excess of $3.5 billion in business this year. It includes such prime holdings as Columbia Records and the royalties from *My Fair Lady,* but it is broadcasting that has been Paley's love and life.

There are many possible ways of interpreting the growth of broadcasting—radio and television—in America, and many possible ways to look at the wily pioneers like Paley, who took the first chances and made the big bundles. But there is no way of encountering William S. Paley and not seeing some kind of greatness there, even if it is a greatness past its time.

And there is no way of looking at Paley in his rarefied lair, in his neat striped shirt and suspenders and dark blue suit and white hair, and noting the slightly menacing trailblazer's glint in his eyes, and not thinking, there will never be such men running television again.

"I love the medium. I always will. I just feel I'm damn lucky that I stumbled into it, which is what I did."

One chapter of his book is called "Triumph."

"I'll tell you what most of it was: hard work. I never knew people who worked harder than we did. A sixteen-hour day was nothing! I was young then, and I could do it. There was a drive, there was an aspiration to succeed.

"It never has been the same," Paley says.

"Those were my happiest days."

March 11, 1979

Watching *The Teng Show*

WE WERE BORED. We were lonely. We lusted for a new superstar, and the media, especially television, were ready to supply one.

Teng went the strings of our hearts.

Now that the vice premier of China has gone home, it can't hurt to wonder if what we saw of Teng Hsiaoping's visit to America on American television was reportage or the sale of a bill of goods. Network coverage of the visit—wags have dubbed it *The Teng Show*—seemed delicately deferential for the most part and unquestioning in a way that must have pleased the White House far too much.

More disturbing, in a subtler but perhaps more insidious way, was the treatment given Teng by federally funded public television on *America Entertains Vice Chairman Teng*, a live special from the Kennedy Center that gave new meaning to the cliché "all smiles." Host Dick Cavett was all smiles, Jimmy Carter was of course all smiles and public television was smiling itself into a dither.

George Stevens, Jr., who produced the after-dinner entertainment, is certainly not to be faulted for the way he rushed together a presentable and eclectic smorgasbord of Americana —although highlights like the Joffrey Ballet and the Harlem Globetrotters were somewhat beclouded by the bumbling giggles of John Denver and the near-surgical heart-tugging of the cloying Shirley MacLaine.

Public television's handling of the event, however, leaned toward obsequious reverence; public TV became a tool in the Carter Administration's campaign to put Teng, and normalization, over with the American people (the tool apparently needs sharpening, because a recent poll showed Americans divided over the President's decision to embrace China and forsake Taiwan).

It is true that an oil company coughed up the $500,000 to put the program on television, but there are still federal funds involved in any national public-TV transmission. When we add the fact to the public relations nature of the event, to the way public TV handled it and to the political interests it served, the whole project takes on a distressingly propagandistic tinge.

It suggests that public television risks becoming, on such occasions of official ceremony, State Television, or Political Television, or, in this case, the People's Republic of Television. It might be healthier for the nation if the White House and public television were at each other's throats—as in Nixon days of yore—rather than have them bosom buddies scratching each other's backs.

At the opening of the broadcast, Cavett, ill suited for such a role, narrated, to fill time, a taped replay of Teng's first day in the United States. Carter's repeated goofs in identifying the vice premier by title ("Mr. Prime Minister, Mr. Prime, Mr. Vice Premier . . .") were edited out of the tape, and so were the appearances made by two pro-Taiwan demonstrators on the White House lawn. Nor was there any mention of the larger and noisier demonstrations that occurred on the other side of the White House and in Lafayette Park.

Instead, Cavett dismissed such events in a manner reminiscent of Marie Antoinette; "one or two inevitable hecklers were escorted away" was his only suggestion that discord had dared to intrude on nirvana. Was this because he didn't want to offend the vice premier, who could not possibly have been watching, or because he didn't want to upset the White House, which currently looks favorably on increased funding for public TV and might not look favorably on the exposure of a single wrinkle in the day's scenario?

As television, except for the lengthy translations of wordy introductions, this was not at all a bad show. Director Don Mischer caught a few privileged shots, like one of Carter escorting his guests into the presidential box of the opera house, another of Teng, preparing to speak from the stage, removing a little piece of crumpled paper from his pocket and unfolding it, as he had done earlier in the day. On it was his speech.

But then Cavett, whose eagerness to please bordered on *idée fixe*, committed his supremo blooper of the evening, identifying for the home audience a shot of "the distinguished Robert O. Anderson," president of the Atlantic Richfield Company, which had funded the broadcast. Considering the number of other dignitaries Cavett had failed to identify (including Kennedy Center chairman Roger L. Stevens), this was an especially unfortunate mistake.

When it came to bowing and scraping before Teng and his

allegedly charismatic presence, however, the commercial networks weren't exactly caught napping. Frank Reynolds ended an ABC News broadcast with a gush of flowery futurology about the wonderful new era beginning; it sounded not only premature, but also an expression less of Reynolds' awe at the grandeur of events at hand than of his desire to give TV viewers a cheerful little earful, no matter how wind-filled and fanciful.

Over on *NBC Nightly News,* Teng was bidden farewell with a montage of happy images from the trip, while—though NBC News refused to credit the source—the Kennedy Center orchestra heard on the PBS broadcast played repeated chipper choruses of Rodgers and Hammerstein's "Getting to Know You." Again, discouraging words, or images, were verboten; none of the week's demonstrations or foul-ups were shown, nor did we see the fall, at a Houston rodeo, of a horse whose rider carried the American flag.

It was at times as if television had decided to accept without debate precisely the symbolism that the White House wanted all the activities to have.

The American networks went out of their way to assist the Chinese television personnel traveling with Teng. Much manpower and equipment was lent at no cost. But Burton Benjamin, director of news for CBS News, said this week that the effort was not an attempt to curry favor with an eye toward future Chinese–network relations but rather reciprocity for help the Chinese gave American television when presidents Nixon and Ford visited China.

"No matter how hard we insisted, they charged us virtually nothing," Benjamin said. "So we offered to reciprocate. We supplied them a camera crew and producers. They paid for travel and living expenses and for satellite and transmission costs, by far the largest nut of the deal."

Benjamin said the CBS donation to the Chinese amounted to about $39,000.

He denied that "we gave this guy a free ride" and pointed to a piece done by correspondent Bernard Kalb on the Monday *CBS Morning News* telecast after Teng went home. Kalb expressed what many TV viewers may have been thinking—that there was a considerable disparity between the cuddly, charming man the correspondents kept describing and the actual figure of Teng we saw on the screen.

"Teng Hsiaoping really is a feisty, tough, essentially ruthless political figure on the Chinese Communist scene," said Kalb. "And apparently, in some sort of hunger on the part of the media to establish an extraordinary personality, he has been endowed with attributes that I have not yet found."

Kalb didn't say it, but the thought has to arise: how much were the networks and public television used by the White House to communicate a point of view through the availability of staged events so terribly adorable that no news director would ever consider throwing them onto the cutting-room floor?

"I don't think that people were really listening precisely to what Teng Hsiaoping was saying," said Kalb. "It was a 'spectacular' that we were watching this week; but what we in fact were seeing was simply the packaging, the public packaging, for strategic self-interest."

February 11, 1979

Videoplomacy: Peace According to the Networks

PEACE ON CBS was brought to you by General Motors. Peace on ABC starred Barbara Walters as herself. And at NBC, David Brinkley wasn't so certain there was peace in the first place.

No one from any of the network news departments was asked actually to sign the Middle East peace treaties between Egypt and Israel on Monday, but in a way the networks were parties to them. The live telecast of solemn rites from a windblown White House lawn could be considered just as significant and symbolic as the event itself. Indeed, the event might not have taken place without it. We are living in an age of video diplomacy—videoplomacy—and this baby has been in the works for a long time.

And so it is not being the least bit snide or disrespectful to suggest that after the signing Monday afternoon, the participants could have thrown the treaties into the rubbish. All they really need to save is the videotape of the ceremony. The tape is the document. The live telecast was the event.

The treaties themselves were mere props in an impressively staged theatrical production.

For maintaining a tone of seasoned skepticism in the face of the religious spectacular tossed by the White House, NBC News deserves especially high marks, since in television it is often much more inviting to tell viewers what they'd like to hear than it is to deal with the grimmer realities. Not that the other networks trotted out the party hats and noisemakers—at least, not until the evening celebration at the White House—but NBC showed the most intelligent restraint.

While all three networks aired late-night specials on the treaties Monday, NBC called its report *The Treaty: A Cautious Celebration,* whereas CBS—its broadcast fully sponsored by GM—preferred the more pretentious and optimistic *An Act of Peace,* and ABC the slightly more trite *Middle East Peace: Signing at the Summit.*

The signing ceremony, covered live by all three networks, found ABC News in particularly good and aggressive form. ABC stayed with live pictures from the White House longer than CBS or NBC did. So only ABC had a live shot of Jimmy and Rosalynn Carter walking back into the White House hand in hand after bidding bye-byes to their guests. Corny, maybe, but real.

"Jimmy's wave at the door was priceless," said ABC News vice president Jeff Gralnick yesterday. Gralnick produced the telecast for ABC and is glad now he lingered at the White House rather than going off the air, as NBC was the first to do, or going back to the studio for a confab of correspondents, as CBS is wont to do and did.

ABC News was also the first to show pictures of demonstrators shouting and chanting in Lafayette Park during the ceremony. Like it or not, this was part of the story, and since viewers could plainly hear the chants, at least until the band drowned them out, it only made sense to tell and show us who was chanting. But on CBS, Walter Cronkite seemed more concerned with describing the table on which the treaty was signed and the leather binding around it.

Walter tends to take these breaches of decorum personally.

NBC produced the pool coverage of the event, and it was NBC's version that was beamed back live to Egypt and Israel, where ebullient celebrations, seen on the networks' late-night reports, were taking place. But pool director Charles Jones relied too much on long, wide shots of the White House grounds. "For some reason," Gralnick says, "NBC was in love with that God's-eye shot from across the street."

This was a story of faces, hands, pens and flags, however, and not of crowds. So Gralnick at ABC estimates that about 30 percent of his pictures were from ABC's five supplementary cameras.

Some of the shots, pooled or otherwise, were striking, particularly a triple profile of Sadat, Carter and Begin facing forward motionless as they listened to national anthems. They seemed to be posing for a commemorative coin; it was a beautiful picture. Later, at least once, Jimmy Carter could be seen accidentally applauding a reference to himself. At least, one assumes this was accidental.

At the beginning of the ceremony, the men were three shaded figures from within a dark White House doorway until Carter signaled his guests that it was time to march out and face the nation. Indeed—the world!

Naturally, there were some instances of excessive zeal on the part of correspondents—except in Brinkley's case, since excessive zeal has never been his problem. Over at ABC, Barbara Walters kept up an embrace watch during the ceremony —the three men had shaken hands, she noted, but had yet to "embrace" as they had at Camp David. She found this very, very interesting and promised to keep us informed. Oh, Barbara, you old embraceable you.

Walters, Cronkite and Brinkley were all invited as guests to the party thrown that night at the White House. Brinkley did not attend because he had work to do at the studio. But Cronkite and Walters went both as guests and reporters, signing on from the White House grounds in their evening finery, while other reporters, not yet among the guest-list set, did the nuts-and-bolts work.

Gralnick, for one, sees no conflict in a reporter like Walters also being part of such an event. "It's damned helpful," he says.

Again, NBC was showing the keenest news sense in stressing the tentative nature of the treaty and the possible perils that might lie ahead—particularly in an excellent report filed by John Hart from the West Bank of the Jordan. It may not have been what we most wanted to hear, but it helped give a sense of balance and offset the glamour of the James Earl Carter production *Peace '79*—a great little television show, and perhaps even a pilot for a series.

March 28, 1979

Carol Burnett

CAROL BURNETT'S HAIR does not look the way it looked for 11 auburn years of *The Carol Burnett Show* on CBS. "It's my own," Burnett declares, leaning forward and parting it with her fingers. "See the gray? Look, there it is! I'm proud of it."

It was a dark night for television when Carol Burnett left the air last year, but not quite so dark for her. She expanded her range in movie roles (*A Wedding*), discovered activism in behalf of the Equal Rights Amendment and let her hair return to its original brown. And gray. "Twenty years ago they dyed it orange for the musical *Once Upon a Mattress,* she says, "and it's been various shades of red ever since."

Now Burnett makes her most daring leap yet; she plays the part of Peg Mullen, whose son was killed in Vietnam, in *Friendly Fire,* a three-hour ABC movie from the book and *New Yorker* articles by C. D. B. Bryan. This film, written by Fay Kanin—who has joined Burnett on a stopover in Washington—is perhaps the most straightforward and heartbreaking dramatic work on the Vietnam war made available to a mass audience.

There have been significant books about Vietnam—perhaps none more brilliant and troubling than Bryan's; there have been films, and there have been such shattering theatrical works as the David Rabe trilogy, one play of which, *Sticks and Bones,* was shown on CBS, after weeks of clumsy corporate hemming and hawing, in 1973—much closer to the war than *Friendly Fire* is now.

And yet the national telecast of *Friendly Fire* may have a more devastating and purgative effect on the country than any of the previous works on the war, because watching it is like ending years of tearless, numbed mourning with one great cry.

It is better than *The Deer Hunter* and *Coming Home* put together, and it could have a far greater effect on the country, since 50 or 60 million Americans may tune in to watch it on the same night. *Friendly Fire* has the impact of a death in the family. And Burnett completely transcends her old image as the knock-kneed zany who fell into potted plants after Harvey Korman opened a door in her face.

Burnett, 44 now, looks anything but gangly or whacky. She looks smart and serene—even though her husband, producer Joe Hamilton, is upstairs in his hotel room with a bad back, and the two of them plan to take their 5-year-old daughter, Carrie, to Europe on Friday to shop for schools. And, Carol Burnett looks pretty—pretty in a satisfied and uncomplicated and comfortable sort of way. Pretty? She's beautiful.

Yet she may not be the first person who would pop into all

readers' minds as the perfect Peg Mullen after they've read *Friendly Fire*. How surprised they will be by her performance, probably the best of her career. Burnett herself is not worried that people will be confused by this change of image.

"I think they're just going to be carried away by the story, I really do," she says. "As far as I know, this is the first film about the war from the point of view of the people at home, which I think is going to touch people. And one of the last lines is something nobody can argue with, when Peg says, 'When it's your son, there's only one side,' whatever you may think about war games or politics or who's right and who's wrong.

"There's no question about my 'image' in my mind. I don't believe in limiting oneself, and it's sort of a pet peeve of mine the way American show business mucky-mucks in business suits categorize people. I love comedy, but why not do other things too? I like the British attitude. Glenda Jackson does a play for three months, then she'll do television, then she'll do a nightclub act, and then if she joins the circus, no one thinks a thing about it."

Burnett has not met the woman she plays in the film, Peg Mullen, who refused to accept the Army's version of what happened to her son. The Mullens' campaign to learn the truth about their son's death turned into one of the first antiwar protests to arise from within the so-called "silent majority." In fact, the Mullens are known to have been displeased with the Bryan book and reluctant about having it turned into a television show.

Kanin says, though, that "they have made their peace" and that "they were ecstatic about Carol" playing the part. The role of Mr. Mullen is played by Ned Beatty, who is brilliant as all get out.

"Peg just wrote me a note," Kanin says. "It's a beautiful letter, saying they made their peace with the fact that it's going to be on television and as a matter of fact, they even offered us the use of their farm in Iowa to shoot in. Pat, the oldest daughter, read the script and made some comments which were very helpful. Peg said they didn't want to go through all that pain again, but they see what's going on in the country, and think they see a kind of rise of militarism again, and that maybe the movie can say something."

For Burnett, the change of pace is more than a switch from comedy to drama. She has not been associated before with material of such social consequence. She would sometimes end her TV show with a "save-a-tree" ecological remark, but she was an apolitical public personality.

"I was never outspoken politically because I felt I wasn't intelligent enough in that area to come out and start doing that," she says. "In my own way I would vote for the people who felt the way I did. As a performer, I was always nervous that, well, suppose I made a wrong choice and I might sway a couple of votes the wrong way? Then I would be responsible. I didn't think we should use our show as a soapbox.

"Now, with certain things, I feel differently. Like ERA. I have come out because to me, that's not political. It's a moral issue. If I had three sons, I'd be out screaming about it. As it is, I have three daughters, and I owe it to women who aren't in show business and can't go to a bank and get a loan and not be discriminated against to speak up. I'm not the same person I was fifteen years ago. I don't think any of us are."

She would like to meet Phyllis Schlafly, the obsessed ERA foe. "I might even pick up the check," she says. "I would ask her why she is doing this, because evidently she's supposed to be intelligent, and an intelligent person has to be for equality. So there must be an underlying motive she has—which makes her a very tough opponent. Like McCarthy.

"The dumb ones don't worry me because they just don't know what the amendment is, they haven't read it, and they just hear all this stuff about abortion, gay rights and blah blah, and they'll say, 'Oh! I don't want to go to the same bathroom with so-and-so!' And who does? And who will? I think Mrs. Schlafly probably does not go to the bathroom when she flies because they all use the same lavatories up there. Those long flights must be murder for her. She's got to take the Concorde. And no liquids before she goes on board, either.

"I mean—for her to throw that out as an argument, is so ludicrous. It's evil. I mean, it's so dumb!"

Burnett's performance in *Friendly Fire* is effective partly because she has come to represent on television an earthy, middle-class normality. In fact she is not, of course, middle-class and, though born in San Antonio, Texas, grew up in nothing more normal than Hollywood, California—in a house one block from Hollywood Boulevard, at the corner of Wilcox and Yucca.

"I worked on the corner," she says, and then laughs a loud Carol Burnett laugh. "Hey, that's an exclusive! No, I mean, my first job was at the corner of Wilcox and Hollywood, at the Warner Brothers Theater, which is now called something else. I was an usherette. I saw *Strangers on a Train* fifty-seven times. In fact, I was fired because of it. This young couple wanted to go in five minutes before it was over and I said, 'Look, it's coming on again in ten minutes, it's a Hitchcock thriller, please don't go in.' The manager fired me on the spot. Sixty-five cents an hour down the drain."

"I'll bet the male ushers got eighty-five cents," says Kanin.

"Seventy-five, eighty-five, something like that," says Burnett, not very bitterly.

Burnett wore a uniform with epaulets, and when the manager fired her, he ripped one off. "Really. I'm not kidding," she laughs.

"So recently, about two years ago, three years ago—whenever it was—the Hollywood Chamber of Commerce calls and asks me if I would like to have a star on Hollywood Boulevard. And what's really funny is they ask you to pay for it; 'We want to honor you; give us a thousand dollars.' But it goes to the Hollywood Chamber of Commerce, so I thought, Okay, but only on one condition. I want it right in front of that theater where I got fired. And they did. It's right there."

There is a shameless gloat of victory. Burnett has bobbed to the surface again. In another moment she is posing for photographs and complaining about the ones ABC has used to advertise Sunday night's showing of *Friendly Fire*.

"I saw that ad," she says. "Oh, does that stink! Ned and I

knew it when they were taking those pictures. We said, 'Don't do this. It really looks like something right out of a movie from the '30s.' We said, 'This is really like Expression Number Forty-Two.'"

In the ad, Burnett is posed dramatically with a folded flag, and Beatty stands behind her. It does look corny. The program is not. When Burnett saw the film for the first time, she cried, she says, especially when Beatty, as the father, came down a ladder outside his farmhouse and put on his hearing aid so he could hear the news that his son had been killed. Burnett's eyes tear as she describes it. This happens one other time, when she is recalling some of the characters she played on *The Carol Burnett Show,* and I take it upon myself to interrupt her.

"You're reminding me how much you miss that show," I tell her.

"Thank you," she says, her violet eyes glistening, and we all but melt into puddles right there.

April 19, 1979

The Best Theys of Your Life

HIS LITTLE FRIENDS in the box talk to him. They talk to him incessantly. And they tell him things. They tell him who he is. They tell him what to think about himself, and they tell him to think of himself all the time.

Sometimes they address him as "America." He likes that. "Take off your coat, America," a voice says. "Come on, America—get on the Honda Express." But sometimes this is confusing. "America is turning 7-Up," he hears—but he doesn't feel at all like turning 7-Up. And Sears is "Where America Shops," they say, but he hasn't been to Sears in months; years, maybe. Does this mean he isn't part of America?

He begins to feel alienated. "Women of America, are you in charge?" a voice on behalf of Master Charge asks. He is not a woman of America, and at the moment there are no women of America in the room with him. Just himself and the set. He wonders if he really is a part of the great audience, if the voices he hears perpetually are actually talking to him.

And then they start with the questions. Questions, questions, questions. "Do you hate your hair?" he is asked. He hadn't thought about it. Hate my hair? Well, I—he is told he should "love" his hair. Love my hair? Well, I—but it is time for another question: "Who do you share the power with—the power of the pump?" This sounds to him like a sinister secret group plotting the takeover of the country by force or violence. But no, it is by aerosol: "Vitalis Super Hold—Get the Pump and Share the Power!"

"How do your teeth feel?" a pretty girls asks. "Do this," she says, and she flicks her tongue across her teeth. He does it too. "Mmmmm," she purrs. Yecch, he thinks. "Mine feel great," she says. His feel just sort of, well, toothy. She explains patiently but rapidly that if he only had the brains to use Pearl Drops Tooth Polish, he could twirl himself into ecstasy over his teeth too. This is a source of pleasure that had never occurred to him before.

"Which one keeps you drier?" the pretty lady asks; he already knows it's Tickle—why does she keep asking? "What does extra strength mean to you?" the handsome man asks; but he knows it as well as his own name: "Extra Strength Means Excedrin."

"Which costs more," the man asks, "canned dog food or Gainesburgers? The answer may surprise you." It won't surprise him; he's heard this a thousand times.

And then there's that fellow with the eggplant nose who seems to represent either the voice of the Almighty or a Jewish mother to the world: "What *will* you do?" he asks again and again. "What *will* you do?"

That voice has a point. What *will* he do? Something wells up from deep within his soul and tells him what he will do. He will stay tuned, like 50 million other dummies.

At least he knows how to spell "Relief." He would know how to spell 'phenomenology" if he had been asked a hundred thousand times.

Of course, the grilling he gets is nothing compared with the grilling some people get. People in the little box are forever being confronted in supermarkets and on what appear to be old *Star Trek* sets and interrogated in a heartless style not seen since Richard Loo brutalized Yankee Dogs in World War II movies.

A married couple have already promised to start using Ivory Liquid, but that isn't enough for the man with the threatening microphone. "What happened?" he asks them after they have dutifully done their dishes—and he knows the answer as well as they do. "So what do you think now?" he persists. "Do you want to stay with your brand? So what did you learn?" It's a wonder they aren't sitting under a bare light bulb.

The poor souls who stick their hands through holes in curtains to feel one another's hair are also subjected to a merciless drill. "What do you believe?" the man asks impertinently. "So what are you going to do?" he continues. If they give the wrong answer, will they be hauled out in front of an ivied wall and shot, or will they just spend eternity in the purgatory of disobedient consumers? Does Orwell write the dialogue for these inquisitions?

Sitting there alone in his room, he likes it better when his little friends in the box talk to *him*. But they keep giving him orders; they keep telling him what to do. He gets perplexed. He feels picked-on. Sometimes he just doesn't know which way to turn.

"Reach out and touch someone," he is told one minute, but as he goes toward the telephone as instructed, he hears, "Let yourself go—to Pizza Hut." As he is looking for his car keys he hears, "Get your body in beautiful shape from head to toe with Body Tender—new from Gillette." That sounds reasonable until Roy Rogers appears with hamburger in hand telling him, "And you thought you couldn't get food this good and this quick." As a matter of fact, that is exactly what he thought; where are those car keys?

Somehow, "they" always seem to know what he wants. "TWA knows how you like to fly to California," they say—but how did they find out? He is told he wants fast-fast-fast relief when he has a headache, which is a fair-enough assumption, but he also is told he should enroll at once in a school that will teach him to become a computer programmer, and that a tire company ominously predicts, "sooner or later, you'll own Generals." Then, *"The Mike Douglas Show!"* trumpets an all-knowing unseen voice, declaring, "More than ever before, Mike knows what *you* want and *he's* got it all!" And one of those ragtag local TV stations looks into his mind and pledges he will get "just the news you want" and get it in fact from "people like you." When he gets a gander at the people like him, he is amused to see that they are nothing like him at all. They have steel hair.

"Kool-Aid—you loved it as a kid, you trust it as a mother," says a voice. "Isn't that you behind those Foster Grants?" asks a voice. "Maxwell House is coffee you can count on," soothes a voice. "Gravy Train satisfies *your* hungry dog," insists a voice. "Squeeze—and go from flat to fluffy," orders a voice. "Come on, come on and have a Pepsi Day," implores a singing chorus. "Come fly with me in my '79 Thunderbird," coos a sexy vamp. "Fill your cup to the rim with the rich taste of Brim," commands a man.

"Take your lips as far as they can go," says yet another voice, "with Maxi Moist Lipstick. Take your lips to the Maxi!"

Now he is knocked for a loop. How far his lips could go had never before struck him as a topic for consideration. He is trapped in the room at this point, rendered immobile by all the conflicting directives. "We do it all for you," the little friends in the box reassure him. "Because you have an appetite for life," some other little friends chime in. "Whatever you do, that look just comes through—it's confidence, confidence," they sing with a genuinely inspiring conviction. "Pamper yourself," "Indulge yourself" and "Treat yourself," they say in succession.

"Roman Meal thought you'd like to know."

How do they know all about him? Why do they keep telling

him what to do? When will they ever give him a moment's peace? "Stress!" screams a man from ABC News. "What you don't know can kill you!" Oh, no! He panics. He looks for the nearest exit. It happens to be a window on the seventh floor. He opens it. He looks down. It's an abyss, all right, but such a blessedly quiet one.

And yet something stops him just before he leaps. Another voice, this one from inside himself, is telling him something. And to satisfy an instinct he does not really understand, he runs his tongue across his teeth again. *Mmmmmm!* It *does* feel great!

His little friends have got him where they want him.

May 6, 1979

The Garner Files: Marshmallow Macho

JAMES GARNER LOOKS uncomfortable sitting on a banquette at the Beverly Hills Brown Derby. Good. You would want James Garner to look uncomfortable sitting on a banquette at the Beverly Hills Brown Derby. Bret Maverick would look uncomfortable there. Jim Rockford would look uncomfortable there. "I can't read this menu and I'm not hungry," Garner grumbles to a waiter.

You'd want Garner to grumble, too. For several of the past 25 years of television, first with *Maverick* and now with NBC's *The Rockford Files*—just renewed for a sixth season—James Garner has embodied a crusty, sardonic and self-effacing strain of American masculinity. He is the spirit of laconic macho, resigned to a world of Sunday drivers and doing his best to avoid fender benders. Jim Rockford is a paragon of skepticism, the kind of character Garner plays best; a barker, not a biter.

Occasionally, however, Garner has bitten. "For some reason, everybody seems to think I'm just a wonderful guy," Garner says. "Nobody'll say anything bad about me. And there are things bad about me. A lot of things bad about me. I smoke too much. I open my mouth at the wrong times. And when I lose my temper, I deck people." He means he hits them. "Right below the mouth if I can get a good shot in. If they deserve it.

"There was a producer who shall remain nameless who I did that to," Garner says matter-of-factly. It was after a dispute over some scripts, for which, Garner says, the Writers Guild fined the producer. But then there was a dispute over some music. That brought out Garner's decking instinct. "If the Writers Guild fine didn't teach him, I will. And I did."

James Garner is a man's man, a woman's man, an actor's actor and nobody's fool.

The kind of man Garner is coincides with the kind of guy he plays, and this is someone who will stand up to mucky-mucks and bureaucrats, be they police captains or studio executives. *The Rockford Files* is as good as any detective show ever on TV, and funnier than many comedies, and one of the reasons for its high standard has to be Garner's own protective instincts toward the program and his struggle to keep it from becoming just another Edsel trundling down the assembly line.

"My company produces it," he says. "What is it with Universal—'in association with'? That's not the way I look at it, but that's what it says on the screen. It's got another name on it, too—Roy Huggins United Public Arts or something. Roy Huggins brought me the script for the pilot. That's his contribution. Made himself somewhere around a million and a quarter dollars on that; never had anything more to do with it. Oh, it's terrible. If we had that money, we could put it working on the screen, where it belongs."

Huggins says his contribution to *Rockford* was more than Garner credits him for. "I wrote all but about four of the screen treatments for the first year, under my pseudonym, John Thomas James," says Huggins. "I don't ever have anything to do with a show after I once get it through the first year. That's the way I work." Huggins says of the cantankerous Garner, "We have a love-hate relationship; I love him and he hates me." Even Huggins says of Garner, "He's really an extremely likable guy."

"I've pretty well changed Universal's production ways with my company, and I had to force it on them," Garner says. "It took a lot of stubborn screaming, ranting, raving and threatening, but finally in the second year we got them off our backs. I don't know if I scared the executives physically or what, but I scared them, and they finally backed down." Universal is the largest supplier of prime time television programs, and the studio has become what Garner calls "a factory" where the object is usually to get it out rather than to make it good. So Garner insisted on picking his own production crews and even owns the location equipment used on the program, because he says Universal's trucks were always breaking down.

Now Garner says he feels a little like breaking down himself, after five years of tiffs and tumbles. He didn't want to do another season of *Rockford Files*, but Universal has a contract with one more year to go, and NBC is not in a position to let a solid hit slip away. "What I need," says Garner, still grumbling and definitely not whining, "is physical rest. Three out of five years now I've spent my time off in the hospital—leg operations, broken ribs from fights, all kinds of things. You stay on the pavement twelve, fourteen hours a day, five days in a row, and see what it does to your feet and legs. It's a killer!"

Of course, we all thought actors were driven up to TV locations in limousines, which chauffeurs kept running so the air conditioning would stay on.

"Hell no, I don't get out of a limousine," Garner persuasively points out. "I drive my pickup truck up there about six-fifteen in the morning and we go to work. I can't do something unless I get all wrapped-up in it. No offense to Jim Arness, because the poor man is in bad shape—I mean, physically—but he used to just phone it in. He'd come in and they'd give him his pages of script and they'd say, 'Now say this and this,' and they'd shoot it and he'd go home. If you noticed, for the last ten years of *Gunsmoke* everyone else carried the show. He just came in and worked a day and a half or something, and rightly so, because the man was in physical pain. He had arthritis, bad knees, whatever. That can get to you after a while.

"David Janssen had I don't know how many operations—three or four. I've had six. David Soul did two years on *Starsky and Hutch* and went into the hospital. It's just pure overwork. It happens to a lot of them. Nobody knows it, and they're all afraid to say it, because they don't want to lose their image as the big hero. The reality is, it's a tough, tough job. Television is a killer."

"How old is Rockford?" Garner is diplomatically asked.

"He's fifty-one," Garner replies.

Garner has been costarring, with actress Mariette Hartley, in commercials for Polaroid's One-Step camera for the past three years. Because they are so funny and comfy on screen together, many people think Garner and Hartley are husband and wife. "That doesn't make my wife too happy," Garner says. He and the real Mrs. Garner live in Brentwood behind a locked gate; they have two daughters—Kim, 30, and Gigi, 21.

Hartley and Garner film about 15 Polaroid commercials a year; these spots are models of genial, no-nag advertising.

"There's no loss of dignity," says Garner; "you don't demean yourself by selling a product. It's not a hard sell, because I can't do that. I tried it when I was younger and selling insurance door-to-door. I just couldn't bear to do it to people. I'd see some poor woman with a child and I'd just say, 'You don't need this, ma'am,' and I'd walk away. I just couldn't do it. I knew she needed the money to feed those kids."

It is Garner's Tootsie-Pop soft center that may be his most attractive attribute; like Burt Reynolds, he comes across as strong and assertive but still accessible and levelheaded. Garner likes racing cars and playing golf, but he hates everything about show biz but acting. He hates cocktail parties. He hates premieres. He hates award shows. He went to last year's Emmys only because he had won the year before.

Garner plays a publicist in *Health*, the Robert Altman film he has just spent six weeks shooting in St. Petersburg, Florida. It is Garner's first film in a decade. He can't even remember the title of the last one *(The Castaway Cowboy)*: "It was a Disney film, I think. 'Hawaiian' something. It was a little picture for Disney in Hawaii." The reason Garner stays in killer television, he says, is that "I hate the shit they're doing in movies." Most of the scripts he is sent are either too violent or too dirty for his taste.

Of the films he has made, there are "only a few that I'm totally proud of": *The Americanization of Emily, The Skin Game, Support Your Local Sheriff"* and another whose title he cannot recall *(Move Over, Darling)*. "What the hell was the name of it? The one with Doris Day. Ummm, the one where we went into the pool with the car."

Garner prefers not to see any of his films, however, or his TV shows, good or bad. He is afraid of being embarrassed by them. "That's the only way you can judge your work, you know—by how embarrassed you are by it. It's the same with *Rockford* or with anything I do.

"Out of a hundred and twelve shows that we've done, I've probably seen twelve *Rockfords*. I don't like to watch them. I don't like to watch me. You take a guy like Dick Cavett—Dick sits and watches his shows all day and all night, over and over and over. Well, I would throw up! A lot! There was a *Maverick* on late one night and I turned it on and watched it for only a minute and then I had to get it off.

"People who watched *Maverick* thought it was adult. Do I think it was adult? Not particularly. It was just a cowboy show that stuck its tongue in its cheek. Naw, it wasn't adult at all."

Garner would be the last man on earth to analyze his appeal. Is he a James Garnery type of person off the screen? "No, I don't think so; but then, I wouldn't know what a James Garnery type of person is. Everyone else knows, but I don't. I don't have any idea."

For one thing, a James Garnery type of person might say what James Garner says when asked how he's feeling. "Don't fly with head colds," he advises. "That's a naughty-naughty." Only Garner could get away with saying "That's a naughty-

naughty" and still retain a tough-guy posture. Only Garner could retain a tough-guy posture while making a confession like this:
"I was bad last night. I got into a bag of Cheetos. Watching TV. Oh, I love 'em—the crunchy kind, crunchy. They really are so good, aren't they? My wife had me go to the market last night, so I just saw them and I grabbed them and when I got home, so that she wouldn't know—because she's trying to diet—I snuck them into my office. And then to keep them away from my wife and my daughter I make the justification, 'Well I'd better eat them all, so they don't have any of them.' See, I was protecting them.
"And I really tried, but I couldn't eat them all. They made me sick." This makes him laugh. Extravagant praise of *The Rockford Files* and, implicitly, of him (he himself has extravagant praise for his fellow actors and the show's writers) makes him wriggle, but only a little.
"At least I can do it with a minimum of violence, and I can hold my head up," he says. "I mean, what we do I'm very proud of. It's a good little hour movie every week. You walk away from it with a smile, anyway."
You walk away from James Garner with a smile too. He roars away in his pickup truck, cutting a swath of no-nonsense through the foof of Beverly Hills.
May 13, 1979
In the fall of 1981, James Garner returned to NBC-TV to star in a revival of Maverick.

Moyers' Superb Study of Job Hunting

ALTHOUGH THE TITLE is deceptive, "How to Get a Job," tonight's edition of *Bill Moyers' Journal,* really does deal with how to get a job. It shows students at an innovative school in San Diego learning the ropes of job hunting and preparing to face the gorgons and Whipsnades of the dreaded personnel department.

But there is another level. The film is also a persuasive, heartening study in resolve and resilience, and on that level it is always engrossing and occasionally quite moving. Several of the students are followed as they progress through the course—a baker who wants to cut records, a reformed alcoholic, a bubbly data processor and a gung-ho woman crane operator among them—and their determination becomes both symbolic and immediate. It is impossible not to pull for them and hope they make good, because they so obviously either want to or try to want to.

From the telltale quiver in a voice, or the revealing look of eyes momentarily stricken with self-doubt, anyone can sense the vulnerability of these people and share their terror of rejection by the system. Producer-director Wayne Ewing, a Washington filmmaker recruited by Moyers for this project, brings us incredibly close not only to these people and their problems but to something within ourselves. Within everyone —the fear of failure.

They cheer each other on, they go through rehearsals and bull sessions and the teachers lavish upon them the clichés of this era of I Can: "feeling good" about oneself, relating on a "one-to-one level," using "feedback" and "body English," "sharing an experience" and having a "positive attitude." But what the film also exposes and illuminates is the positive side of California's pathological positivism. These are people who must learn confidence in their own worth if they are to survive, and how many of us can safely predict we will never find ourselves in the same boat?

If they were fired from a previous job, they are told, they should just feel like "part of Americana." From this film one learns new respect not only for the reluctantly unemployed, and not only for those who have the courage to come back swinging, but also for the embattled and assailed old system itself, because it can still be made to work too,

Moyers learned of Chuck Hoffman's San Diego school from a column by William Raspberry in *The Washington Post*. Hoffman, seen only briefly during the film—which wisely concentrates on the students and teachers—claims an 85-percent placement record, so impressive that the Federal Government, Moyers reports, is going to apply Hoffman's ideas to a pilot project in Baltimore. The film is less an extended plug for the program, however, than an expertly photographed and edited advertisement for the pervasiveness of the rebound impulse. Without clamor or piety, it says something genuinely inspiring about human spirit. "How to Get a Job" is a superb piece of work.
June 4, 1979

Everyman Has a Headache

JOHNNY CARSON LAUGHED so hard during Rodney Dangerfield's most recent appearance on the *Tonight* show—his 61st—that Carson fell off his four-coaster chair and nearly plunged into the sleepy lagoon painted on the wall behind his desk. The studio audience applause lasted through three commercials and a station break.

Clearly, Rodney Dangerfield has tapped a vein, and it is the vein of pure dismay. Now 57 and actually in his second life as a stand-up comic, Dangerfield is not only jester but guru and ombudsman to the abused, downtrodden, put-upon and ignored. In a world long gone mad, that takes in almost everybody.

Dangerfield likes to boast to show-biz cronies that he can do 90 minutes of straight yock-provocation without ever repeating himself, but what makes him the king of all comedians is his masterly consistency as a conceptual monologuist. Almost all his jokes are expressions of a character he created and embodies, a poor soul who, in the catch phrase that now draws cheers of recognition, "don't get no respect."

Onstage, he will say, "You know the trouble with me? I appeal to everyone who can do me absolutely no good." Looking at the audience with not only baggy, bloodshot eyes but also virtually a baggy, bloodshot face, he will say, "At my age, if I don't drink, don't smoke and don't eat certain foods, what can I look forward to? From this point on, if I take excellent care of myself, I'll get very sick and die."

Offstage, in his subminimally furnished, shades-of-gray, East River–view Manhattan apartment, Dangerfield recalls words of advice from Jack Benny. "He was an ace, he was a doll, and he says to me, 'Rodney, I'm cheap and I'm thirty-nine, that's my image, but your "no respect," that's into the soul of everybody; everybody can identify with that.' Everyone gets cut off in traffic, everyone gets stood up by a girl, kids are rude to them, whatever. He says to me, 'Every day something happens where people feel they didn't get respect.'"

And perhaps because seldom in history have so many felt they get so little respect from so many so often, Dangerfield's career has never been zoomier. He is a top, top draw in Vegas; his appearances on the Carson show are avidly taped by fans all over the country; he is about to cut his first comedy album in 12 years and costar with Chevy Chase and Bill Murray in *Caddy Shack,* a film comedy expected to be next summer's *Animal House.*

And Dangerfield's, the New York nightclub he founded and which experts predicted would close within two weeks, will celebrate its 10th anniversary next month.

Most amazing of all—at least to Rodney—is his huge following among the young and the hip. They consider him the contemporary not of the Buddy Hacketts and Henny Youngmans but of Robin Williams, Steve Martin, Richard Pryor and Andy Kaufman. Dangerfield spoke at Harvard last year and came out first in a survey of college students' favorite comics. Why? Because to them he personifies the ultimate victim of the system that conspires against us all. He fights back, and becomes the audience champion, by making his victimization hilarious.

This is a man who will go to any length to get no respect.

This is a man who goes into a store to buy rat poison only to have the girl behind the counter ask, "Should I wrap it, or do you want to eat it here?"

This is a man who will suddenly be asked to leave a bar because "they want to start the happy hour."

This is a man who was arrested for jaywalking only to hear a crowd of onlookers yelling, "Don't take him alive!"

No respect. No respect at all. "Same thing when I was a kid—no respect. I was lost at the beach once and a cop helped me look for my parents. I said to him, 'You think we'll find them?' He said, 'I don't know, kid, there's so many places they could hide.'

"I tell you, since I was a kid, women always gave me a hard time. My mother never breast-fed me. She told me she liked me as a friend."

Ka-boom-boom.

"My mother had morning sickness *after* I was born."

Ka-boom-boom.

"My old man didn't help, either. One time I was kidnapped. They sent back a piece of my finger. He said he wanted more proof."

Ka-boom.

"Hey, I tell you, when I was a kid I went through plenty. My uncle's dying wish—he wanted me on his lap. He was in the electric chair!"

It is hard to recall a stand-up comic with such dark, absurdist material (all written by him) becoming so enormously and cross-generationally popular. The audiences at Dangerfield's club include double-knitters from the Jersey 'burbs and such hip young rock stars as Billy Joel and Led Zeppelin. Do they all identify with dumpy old Rodney and his bill of particulars against an uncaring world? Apparently. If Rodney Dangerfield is Everyman, Everyman has never had such a headache.

Is there a sad Hamlet beneath this sad Hamlet exterior—beneath this hangdog body that looks as though it would be most comfortable lying face down on a floor? Not exactly, but Rodney did go through plenty when he was a kid. Born Jacob Cohen, he grew up poor in Kew Gardens, Long Island, and still remembers how teachers made anti-Semitic remarks about him in front of the class at P.S. 99.

Before school he made a buck a week minding a newsstand, and after school he delivered groceries—to the homes of the kids he'd been in class with during the day. "That puts you a little outside, makes you feel below them, socially. So I grew up thinking I was not as good as other people. I was also put down because my parents were separated and I didn't have a father. And I experienced a great deal of anti-Semitism. I was an unhappy kid, and what happens is, you try to escape from reality by writing jokes."

At 15 he was writing jokes and at 17 performing them at amateur nights in Queens for "eight quarters a show." Later he'd earn $5 a night as a singing waiter at a club called the Polish Falcon in Brooklyn—"That's where I met Lenny Bruce's mother"—and did his material anywhere else he could. By this time his name had been changed professionally to Jack Roy, and legally, it still is.

"My first job actually for money was when I was nineteen. I got twelve dollars a week, room and board in the Catskill Mountains. I can't say they were the good old days. When people say 'the good old days,' they mean their youth. You have better days when you're older, but you don't have the same head for it. Youth is what makes them the good old days, you know?"

Rodney is sitting on a couch in his bathrobe with his yippy poodle, Keno—after the game of chance—on his lap. He could have named the dog "Stop it, Keno," because that's what he repeatedly says as the pooch interrupts him with barks or kisses.

"I worked in all kinds of dumps," Rodney recalls, looking as if he were waiting for ether. "I worked 'em all. I worked on a bar once, three shows a night, seven nights a week, and the manager asks me to take a cut in salary! Then when I didn't, he gets drunk and wants to do some damage to me. You get humble from things like that; you know, you learn humility.

"A strange animal, a comedian. You walk out when you're a kid, and you're going to be terrible naturally, so you're completely humiliated, right? To the point, at places I worked, where they want to pick a fight with you. You walk off the floor and somebody says, 'I think you stink—what are you gonna do about it?' They think you're bad and they want to beat you up. If a guy heckles you and you top him, he'll want to beat you up too. Tough joints. Tough.

"Dustin Hoffman, when he was making *Lenny*, hung out in my club for a few weeks. He says to me, 'Why not quit? Who needs that humiliation?' But instead, you go out the next day looking for another job and get humiliated all over again. So it's a strange need, I guess, to want to be a comedian."

Somehow Dangerfield lost the need, however, and ended his career as Jack Roy at the age of 28, to go into the construction business. He did it for 12 years, still writing jokes in his spare time, and then, even though his relatives told him he was crazy, decided to go back on the proverbial boards. Rechristened Rodney Dangerfield arbitrarily by a nightclub manager, he took to working Greenwich Village clubs at no pay, just to perfect his material.

"First I came back as a lark," he says. "I'd do weekends in dumps, whatever it was—I used to go out and get a hundred dollars for two nights and my bar tab was more than that. They would anticipate a fight in those places. I remember one place after a fight they figured I owed them ninety-six dollars. So they said, 'Here's your salary—four bucks.'"

Even now, at the top—the Picasso of stand-up comedians and one of the few keeping the actual telling of jokes, as opposed to more avant-garde, free-form comedy, alive—Dangerfield finds he really does have trouble getting respect sometimes.

"This is a true story," he says. "One night I'm waiting to go on at my own club and a guy says to me, 'Hey Rodney, do me a favor, will you? Can I have an autograph and some more butter?' People will talk to me just before I go out to do a television show. I'm waiting backstage to go on the Sullivan show years ago and Sullivan is introducing me and a guy yells over, 'Hey, Rodney—any girls in that joint over there, your club?' I can be leaving the club and a guy will say to me, 'Hey, Rodney, give me a lift uptown, will you?' And the guy's a complete stranger!"

Rodney says, "Keno, stop it" and then, "They identify with you, I guess, like one of the guys—you know?"

As Rodney reminisces, another man in a bathrobe appears in his apartment, walking from the kitchen to the bathroom. Rodney explains that this is his neighbor, who has a wife and kids across the street but has "domestic problems" which occasionally cause him to move in with Rodney. Dangerfield also calls him "the funniest guy in the whole world." He's in the construction business.

Dangerfield has had his own domestic problems. The wife he divorced years ago subsequently died, so he is now raising an 18-year-old son and a 15-year-old daughter himself. He wants them to go to college and not to become comedians. On TV, Dangerfield will make jokes at the expense of his kids and his wife; but these are characters he has invented to supplement the character of himself, and it is the character of himself most of the jokes deride.

It is the man who is getting so old that "my last birthday cake looked like a prairie fire."

It is the man who tells his doctor he doesn't know what's the matter, but every morning he gets up and looks in the mirror and wants to die, and the doctor replies. "Well, one thing we know—your vision is perfect."

"Hey," this man says, "I know I'm ugly. I went to a freak show and they let me in for nothing.

"I remember one date I had; we ran into some guy she knew and she introduced us. She said, 'Steve, this is Rodney. Rodney, this is goodbye.' "

In his club, is Dangerfield's material more risqué than on TV? "Much," Rodney says. "I'm an old-fashioned guy, but then I see what people are accepting. Like in my nightclub, I'll really let go, and on my way out I'll meet a man and wife with two daughters sixteen and they say, 'Rodney, we came from North Carolina, can we have your autograph, we all think you're great.' I think to myself, They should be saying to me, 'Hey, how come you're so dirty?' but they say, 'Oh, no, that's great.' Everyone seems to accept it today. If they're laughing at it, I guess you do it."

Dangerfield estimates he has turned down parts in 15 different network comedy series over the past few years. Now there is talk at ABC and CBS of starring him in a series, one perhaps to be "cocreated" with Steve Martin. But Dangerfield says, "I wouldn't want to do thirteen weeks of a lousy show. That's not very gratifying. You do things for money and you do things for art. We all love money, of course, but my thing in life is not to see how much money I can die with."

Dangerfield, who drops homilies like names at Elaine's ("Life plays many tricks on you" . . . "Everyone has their story"), has the perpetual pallor of a worried man. "I'm a downer myself, I would say. I'm not joyful at all. I'm a downer." But as long as elevator doors shut in people's faces, as long as credit-card companies mess up bills beyond all hope, as long as there are people around to tell other people to get lost, Rodney Dangerfield will never have to wonder where his next laugh is coming from.

The pseudo-bohemian *SoHo News,* in a cover story, dubbed Dangerfield's art "the comedy of angst."

"The comedy of who?" Dangerfield asks.

"Angst," he is told.

"What does that mean?" he asks.

"Despair," he is told.

"Oh," he says. "Keno! Stop it!"

August 28, 1979

The Glories of Gin: John Cheever's Spirit

TONIGHT THE DRIEST martini in America turns up where one might least expect it: on public television, which begins a series of three adaptations of John Cheever stories with "The Sorrows of Gin" on *Great Performances*.

Granted that few evils equal the evils of liquor, it's a pleasure nonetheless to encounter a good stiff drink in what is usually a quaint little tea shop. This production is accomplished and well crafted in every way that counts; it is bracing, clever, smart, wise, pungently funny and deliciously sad.

It's the veritable happy hour on the veritable 5:10 to Shady Hill, the New York suburb where Cheever's people scramble, squander and piece out their lives.

"The Sorrows of Gin" sees this daft stab at living through the eyes of 8-year-old Amy Lawton, who watches her parents fight and drink and try to hang on to cooks. If it isn't one thing, it's two things. And one night, there is such a fight over a missing bottle of hootch that the noise carries upstairs to Amy's room.

"The voices woke Amy," Cheever wrote, "and lying in her bed, she perceived vaguely the pitiful corruption of the adult world; how crude and frail it was, like a piece of worn burlap, patched with stupidities and mistakes, useless and ugly, and yet they never saw its worthlessness, and when you pointed it out to them, they were indignant."

To the ineradicable credit of writer Wendy Wasserstein and director Jack Hofsiss, they have preserved the spirit and the intent of such softly lilting passages. They have extended the life of Cheever's work, enhancing it rather than just illustrating it. It's a victory for everybody.

The actors are purely extraordinary, even as a list: Edward Herrmann as the father, Sigourney Weaver as the mother, Eileen Heckart as a sot cook and Rachel Roberts as the embattled Mrs. Henlein, who takes magnificent umbrage at being accused of guzzling booze on the sly.

Herrmann's deftest moment is a tiny one: he has marched into the living room with one of his many nightly drinks and suddenly can't remember where he has put it. He looks as if he were lost in space, as if everything had for a split second dropped out from under him.

But for all the formidability of the big-name cast, young

Mara Hobel as Amy is quite rightly the most fascinating presence on the premises, whether mimicking her parents in the sanctuary of her own room (which naturally has its own television set), dutifully following the advice of a cook and pouring Daddy's gin—"filthy stuff"—nimbly down the drain or listening politely as her father mourns, "Amy, you know what happens when you grow up? You stop looking out the windows of airplanes."

This child is an angel. This production, crisp and bright on videotape, leans toward the heavenly.

Two more Cheever stories will follow on succeeding Wednesdays: "O Youth and Beauty!" next week and "The Five Forty-Eight" on November 7. Some of the characters—including the Lawtons—pop up in more than one play, because all three are set in the Cheeveresque world of the lamentably, but not scandalously, overprivileged.

It is a world of Lacoste shirts and commuter trains and Little League tryouts and fear of crow's-feet and station wagons and gin and rum and vodka and Scotch. If it is not precisely in every detail a real world, it is a reality as filtered through the eyes and heart of an artist, which is just the sort of perception television lacks more than any other.

October 24, 1979

Operators Are Standing By

RETURN WITH US NOW to that bustling little hamlet known as Disposable Income, N.J., nestled precariously at the intersection of Interstate 101 and Highway Clutter, just south of the Piggly Wiggly, north of the K-Mart, east of the Sun and west of the Star.

It's Christmas morning again at the home of Mr. and Mrs. John Q. Public and their 2.3 children, Johnny, Joanie and

Point Three. Which house is theirs? Why it's that natty little tract number right down there—the one where the sound of the malfunctioning smoke alarm is drowning out the sound of the malfunctioning trash compactor. The Publics have been good consumers all year long and, ipso facto, good TV viewers.

They watched and watched and watched. They bought and bought and bought. Especially they watched their local TV station, where commercials are occasionally interrupted by old movies and where no commercial is shown fewer than four times per hour.

And now they are to divvy up the bounty in the shade of their Miami Pink Christmas tree.

"Oh, joy, oh, rapture, oh, recession-proof economy!" exclaims little Joanie as she opens her first present. "It's just what I wanted—my very own plastic ice molds, one in the likeness of a carp and one in the likeness of a mackerel! This will certainly add new excitement to every occasion!"

"Just think," says Mom. "No more dull dinner parties!"

"Why," exults Dad, "I can't begin to imagine all the boring, miserable, backbreaking drags that will turn into gay, wild, tempestuous fiestas thanks to your new ice molds! You'll be the envy of the entire neighborhood."

"But the entire neighborhood bought them too," notes an acerbic young Johnny. No one pays the slightest attention, for now Dad has torn into just what he's always wanted—the amazing Conko Drink-O-Matic.

"Why, now I'll be able to drink coffee, tea, soups, salads, borscht, Gelusil or whiskey sours on my way to work in the car, without ever spilling so much as a single drop on one of my unspeakably hideous ties!" he proclaims. "It makes the perfect Christmas gift!"

"And only nine ninety-eight," says Mom.

"Nine ninety-eight for a lousy thermos with a trapdoor?" interjects an irreverent young Johnny.

No one pays the slightest attention.

Besides, young Johnny is thrilled to the point of delirium over his own gift—Clunko's Mike-O-Matic, the revolutionary toy microphone that can be plugged into any radio so that he can shout and squeal in stereo all over the house.

Mom just loves her own personal, lavishly illustrated copy of the heartwarming new book *Dead Movie Stars*, all about people who are no longer with us.

"Not available in stores," notes Dad.

"We just rushed nine ninety-eight to Book, Box UHF, Light Industry, N.J.," says Joanie.

"We could have simply dialed 201-555-4545, and saved C.O.D. and handling charges," notes Johnny. "Operators were standing by, ready to receive our call."

"Not available in stores," murmurs Dad again.

"A keepsake you'll treasure for years and years to come!" says Joanie.

"But look, the pages are starting to fall out already," demurs a jaded young Johnny.

Elated though Mom is with her book, she is still more uncontrollably delighted with her very own set of 14 Ginsu knives, guaranteed to last for 9,432 years, through famine or flood, through triple-digit inflation or neutron bombings, or her money back. Mom can't wait to take a whack at a baloney.

"Me next, me next," sings out Papa. And you should see the look on his face when he opens his individually wrapped gift and discovers his very own Kill-O-Matic, the revolutionary way to strafe and maim roaches, ants, caterpillars, tarantulas, black widow spiders, water moccasins, killer bees, arachnids, palmetto bugs, agoutis, horseshoe crabs, eelpouts, Clydesdales, the neighbors' cat or the neighbors.

And Mom simply adores her new Pluck-O-Matic, the revolutionary way to remove unwanted hair from lashes, shoulders, kneecaps, agoutis, horseshoe crabs, eelpouts and the neighbors' cat. "So simple, a child could do it!" she sings out merrily.

"In point of fact, too simple for a child to do it," retorts the disgruntled young Johnny.

But all this excitement has been but the buildup for the present of presents, the perfect Christmas gift of perfect Christmas gifts, to come.

"First, though, could someone please turn off that gulldang smoke alarm?" asks young Johnny.

"Now, young Johnny," cautions Dad. "That smoke alarm is for our protection. Remember the poor people we saw burned to a turn in that commercial the other night."

By now the big package has very nearly opened itself, and hey, is Mom ever surprised. "Land o' Goshen!" she exclaims. "My very own Meal-O-Matic was thrill enough last year, but now, to think of little me getting my very own All-New Super Meal-O-Matic this year! Why, it's the perfect Christmas gift!" she exclaims with mad abandon.

"Chops, shreds, grates, grinds," says Johnny.

"Gnarls, mauls, roots, routs," says Joanie.

"Slices, dices, minces, prances," adds Dad.

"Stews, brews, roasts, toasts, bastes, wastes, creams, crams, cracks, breaks, streaks, creaks, bakes, flakes, flocks, shakes, splays, spays!" shouts Mom.

"No more dull dinner parties," the children chime.

"And the worst job of all—ugh!—polishing the silver," Mom trills.

"God bless us, every one," says Johnny at last.

"And God bless television, for reminding us how desperately we need all the things we can't possibly use."

December 16, 1979

Terrorvision

CBS NEWS CORRESPONDENT Tom Fenton was finishing his stand-up report near the American Embassy in Teheran when demonstrators began crowding around the camera crew. He thought things might get out of hand when suddenly a demonstrator rushed forward to ask him, "CIA?"

"No," Fenton replied quickly. "CBS!" He and the demonstrator, and many in the crowd, broke up laughing.

It was another irony in a situation riddled with paradox. The capture of American hostages in Iran has moved well into its second month and become television's first, live, Global Crisis Mini-Series. Depending on its outcome, it may be anything but the last.

NBC News president Bill Small says one of his producers recently moaned, "I look forward to the day when our lead is not Iran," but no one knows how far off that day is. The sight of chanting, fist-waving mobs has become part of the fabric of everyday lives for millions of Americans through TV, and one can't be blamed for wondering if some dank new age has now been ushered in—an age of Terrorvision, in which the term "air power" takes on an entirely different meaning.

Last night's NBC News interview with Marine Corporal William Gallegos of Pueblo, Colorado, taped earlier in the day at the U.S. Embassy, may have been the most powerful broadcast yet out of the heavily televised trouble spot. It was the first chance for American viewers to see one of the hostages in captivity, and it made an uncommonly compelling 18 minutes of grim-reality television.

Although Gallegos did not appear visibly traumatized, the sight of him suddenly personalized the story as it had not been previously. "The students here have been really good to us; it's hard to believe, I know," Gallegos told two NBC reporters in an embassy room dominated by a poster of the ubiquitous Ayatollah Khomeini.

The Iranians were operating the cameras, which occasionally panned to lingering shots of anti-Shah posters, particularly during a five-minute harangue by a spokeswoman identified only as "Mary."

NBC News could have edited the interview, a spokesman insisted last night, but chose, on the advice of correspondents in Teheran, to run it in its entirety. This left the natural tense rhythms of the session intact and made the broadcast all the more gripping, if all the more bizarre, a spectacle.

The network had planned to air the interview at 9 P.M., and promoted it heavily with the sensationalistic title "Hostage! The First TV Interview." But at the appointed hour, the specter of debacle loomed: correspondent John Chancellor told viewers the satellite feed from Iran was "delayed because of technical difficulties."

He also said the difficulties might be "not technical but political"—that Iranian authorities might have decided they didn't want the interview seen. But it finally came on the air at 9:46.

An NBC News spokesman said immediately after the broadcast ended at 10:14 that there was no evidence of sabotage and that it was being assumed the problems were accidental. Chancellor was quick to point out to viewers, following the interview, that it left many questions unanswered and contained contradictions and inconsistencies with what had previously been learned about the hostages and their treatment.

But as is so often the case with television, it was not so much what was said as what was seen and perceived that gave the interview its impact.

NBC News officials defended concessions they had made to the Iranians, in order to get the interview, with remarkable consistency. An NBC News spokesman said yesterday that the statement made by "Mary" helped demonstrate the "intensity and depth" of Iranian feeling. Later, Small said the statement would show the "intensity and depth" of Iranian feeling.

And finally, on the telecast itself, Chancellor spoke of the "intensity and depth" evident in the statement.

Newspapers are certainly represented in Iran as well, but television and its dramatic pictures have brought the living story into the American living room. The White House and State Department aren't seeing a lot of this stuff even one instant before it is made available to millions of American viewers.

What viewers often see is huge crowds of Iranians demonstrating their hatred for the United States; and yet if there weren't official Iranian cooperation with U.S. TV networks, those pictures might never cross the Atlantic. And network news personnel stationed in Iran have, for the most part, felt little threat to their own safety.

"I wouldn't rate it as a very dangerous story," says Fenton, now in London after three weeks in Iran. "It's a problem of the cultural gap. Americans don't realize it's just Persian hyperbole when the crowds chant 'Death to Carter.' They're not ready to slit the throats of Americans by any means.

"At the same time, the Iranians don't understand Americans. They have absolutely no idea how furious Americans get when they see their flag burned or their president hanged in effigy."

The Iranians are, literally, sending out a signal, one that literally goes over the heads of official diplomats—by satellite. Each day the networks get 2½ hours of satellite time via the state-controlled VBIR, "Revolutionary Broadcast Center." With some exceptions, this operation has been running along swimmingly.

"They have been edgy and shoved some people around," says Ernest Leiser, CBS News vice president, "but they are dying to get their message across." In this age of instant communication, exposure is power and access is politics.

The Iranian television show isn't being produced purely for the consternation of Americans, either. Demonstrations are also covered by Iranian TV. Not for nothing was Sadegh Ghotbzadeh promoted from head of the Iranian television authority to foreign minister—a move roughly comparable to a U.S. president's naming Fred Silverman secretary of state.

Yesterday in Tabriz, pro- and anti-Khomeini forces battled for control of a central power source: the television station.

Meanwhile, how do the American networks know they aren't being used by the media-hip Iranians? "We don't want to be used by them, but we still want to get every tidbit we can about everybody," says Robert Siegenthaler, director of special events for ABC News.

"These people are tremendously media-conscious," Siegenthaler says. "The Revolutionary Council are like cheerleaders with bullhorns, and they bring out the demonstrators —truck drivers one day, ladies and self-flagellators the next— and so we try to keep using words like 'orchestrated' and 'well organized' so that we're not being a kind of mindless mirror. We are trying not to be victimized."

The object all sublime is to get on television, to make that direct entry into American—and Iranian—homes and minds. No one in TV journalism quarrels with the idea that the Iranians are trying to use the press—only with the suggestion that they are succeeding. Some of the attempts at manipulation are as crude as this: ABC News personnel have been approached by strangers claiming to have secret tapes of the hostages taken inside the embassy and offering them for sale. It's on a level with the porno trade, and "No one has bought the Brooklyn Bridge yet," says Siegenthaler.

Fenton says the students are getting so "savvy" about TV exposure that they have offered him "secret government documents" in exchange for "five minutes of unedited air time." Time may be money, but Air Time is power.

Finally, this weekend, after two more offers the networks all felt they could refuse, NBC News came up with a counter-offer; it got the Gallegos interview in return for giving a militant Iranian a few minutes to state her case on prime-time television. At CBS News, NBC's move was looked down upon as a capitulation to manipulation.

But NBC's Small said, "If I were at one of the other networks, I would like to have this myself. We think it is a terribly important public service to present the first interview with a hostage in the embassy. I'd hate to think someone got so righteous as to say we shouldn't do this. We need all the insights into this situation that we can possibly get."

Small said that although Iranian representatives were present when the tape was edited in Teheran, they had no say over how it was edited. The *Tonight* show was canceled and a one-hour late-night analysis scheduled, Small said, to make it clear what the circumstances of the broadcast were. "I don't think our viewers are going to be fooled," he said.

As usual, pro-Khomeini Iranians in the United States were undoubtedly monitoring the NBC newscasts and reporting their reactions to the folks back home. Let's say the Iranians are very image-conscious—so much so that CBS News was briefly denied access to the satellite on Friday because Iranians here took offense at remarks made earlier in the week by writer Carl Rowan on WDVM-TV, the CBS affiliate in Washington.

CBS was about to send back a report on anti-Khomeini demonstrations in Tabriz when the Iranians pulled the plug on the satellite. It took "hours" of haggling to get back the bird, a CBS News source says.

By insider's estimates, each network has already spent between $500,000 and $750,000 covering the Iranian crisis. Expenses in Teheran alone amount to $75,000 a week for each network. Unanimously, network news executives say the public is rewarding this effort with lavish attention. ABC News, which has been the leader in the amount of Iranian coverage broadcast, has found that its late-night reports have on occasion outrated entertainment programs on other networks, including NBC's *Tonight Show*.

Even if State Department spokesman Hodding Carter III hadn't brought it up—and infuriated the networks—with his recent remarks, the question of where coverage ends and participation begins would naturally have arisen during this story. No one complained much when it appeared that Barbara Walters had helped talk Sadat and Begin into a powwow for peace during the media blitz on the Mideast in 1978.

But in a situation as fraught with potential calamity as the Iranian crisis, there is natural concern that TV's penchant for participatory journalism could endanger lives or prolong the ordeal.

Ed Fouhy, Washington bureau chief for CBS News, thinks such talk is just idle steam. "That 'TV diplomacy' stuff is nonsense," Fouhy says. "It's untrue. It's a base canard. I'm inclined to use the old Fred Friendly answer: Colonials threw tea into Boston Harbor, and there weren't any cameras there."

"We are not negotiating—far from it," says Fenton of CBS. "But we are looking for anything that might be an opening. You couldn't help feeling that if there was anything that looked like a possible compromise, it was worth promoting."

ABC's Siegenthaler rejects Hodding Carter's notion about the Ayatollah's allegedly hardening his line during the network interviews; "I don't go for that at all." But Siegenthaler did say that covering a situation in which hostages have been taken does bring up its own set of problems—a set of problems the world may see a great deal more of in the electronic '80s.

"In the mid-'70s, when we had the Moluccans and the Hanafis, we went through a whole set of jazz about how do you deal with a hostage situation," Siegenthaler says. "Deejays were calling the Hanafis inside the buildings they'd taken over, and all that. The thing is, no general set of rules applies to every situation.

"We can't consider suppressing the news, or lying doggo, or only reporting what the police tell you. It's a terrible, thin line to walk, and sometimes, I guess, we stray."

"One of the most disturbing things to the press over there is when correspondents are accused of trying to negotiate," says Walt Garrity, an NBC News unit manager who has just returned after 15 days in Iran. "It's an injustice. Because they ask a question doesn't mean they're negotiating. The government emissaries couldn't get in, anyway."

This line, however, leads inevitably to other conjecture: Would the tactics being used by the Iranians ever have been considered if television's global link-up weren't there to beam the message back to Americans? If TV strategy is part of the Iranian plan, isn't television a participant no matter how hard it tries not to be?

"The funny thing is, we had so much trouble getting into Iran a year ago, and you couldn't even get near that TV station," says Burton Benjamin, director of news for CBS News. "But now there's no trouble. Obviously they want their message to get out."

And NBC's Garrity says, "We had a nice relationship with Iranians. They like Americans over there. The people feel wronged by the United States and various administrations, and they'll shake their fists and shout 'Death to Carter' at you, and then they'll smile and tap you on the shoulder. They have an honest liking for the American people, and some of them are damn decent to talk to."

News executives will not talk on the record about how this

attitude might change should worse, as has happened throughout world history, come to worst. There is talk of a civil war in Iran which might endanger the press along with every other American. Privately, government sources note that even if there were a way to free the hostages, that would still leave 100 American journalists now headquartered at the Inter-Continental Hotel, which militant students roam at will.

"No one wants to think what would happen if there were a rescue attempt or some kind of punitive action taken," Siegenthaler says.

It's ABC that has played this story the most heavily, with more hours of special reports than the other two networks combined. ABC has even prepared a fancy electronic logo for each report; *America Held Hostage,* the program is called. All three networks are now ballyhooing their coverage with promotional announcements, each implicitly claiming that the bad news is better on one network than on the others.

In addition to the overseas crews, network news departments are maintaining 12-hour shifts of crews at the White House, the State Department and now, at the temporary residence of the Shah in Texas.

There is no sign that the American people are tiring of the coverage. "The only way we have to measure that is audiences," says Leiser of CBS, "and ours and ABC's are huge. We're getting a thirteen rating at eleven-thirty at night, and that's only a couple of points behind the *Evening News.*"

ABC has promised nightly reports as long as the situation in Iran "remains critical." At the other networks, this is quietly considered more a matter of showmanship than of journalism.

"There's not a story to do every night, no," says Fouhy of CBS News. "To commit in advance, not knowing what the news will be, is obviously overkill."

If ABC's approach may be unprecedented, so is the news story. Even if there were no other positive side to the crisis, Americans are learning more about the temperaments, politics and geography of the Islamic world than they have ever had a chance to learn before.

"We're getting very good feedback," says ABC's Siegenthaler. "There's a technical crew in Detroit that stays on after the local news at the affiliate there just to watch our Iran shows. To know as much as possible can only be good for people. If they see the situation reported with all its nuances, I think there is less tendency toward jingoism and xenophobia."

And Iranians on the streets of Teheran seem determined that Americans will know "as much as possible" about their side of the stalemate. Fenton says it was not uncommon for Iranian passersby to offer him and his crew advice on camera angles, help set up the tripods, even help plug in the video cameras. "We are part," he says, "of their game."

December 11, 1979

TV in the '70s

ON TELEVISION, the 1970s were the decade of sex and violence, t&a, Mork and Mindy, Laverne and Shirley, Archie and Edith, Begin and Sadat, Farrah Fawcett, Deng Xiaoping, Kermit the Frog, Mr. Cholesterol, Pope John Paul II, Mike Wallace, Kunta Kinte, Mary Hartman, Richard Nixon, Ayatollah Khomeini and Fred Silverman.

It was Down Time. It was Primal Time. It was a time of video synthesizers, video beams, video discs and video games —all in the vanguard, we were persistently told, of a video revolution that will liberate us from the grips of *Happy Days*, Sheriff Lobo, Geraldo Rivera and the Incredible Hulk.

Like all decades, this one was cyclical. Cop shows came in a wave and left in a hail of bullets. Jiggle girlie shows bounced their way into America's lap. At the beginning of the 1970 prime-time network TV season, there were 15 hours of musical-variety programming in the schedule each week. At the beginning of the 1979 season, there were none.

In some senses, the decade was full-circular. As it began, public TV's imported serial *The Forsyte Saga* was just making its impact. Soon a new TV form, the miniseries, was being hailed as the medium's salvation, a respite from humdrum weekly shows. Programs like *Roots, Rich Man, Poor Man* and *Holocaust* lured as many as 130 million viewers.

But by the decade's end, miniseries flops like *The Dain Curse* and *Blind Ambition* had producers and networks convinced the format was too costly and risky, and it was back to the ostensible sustenance of meat-and-potatoes weekly shows.

Beyond the usual mercurial trends in programming, the '70s may represent a much larger cycle nearing its end—the era of network domination of television. Technological breakthroughs involving cable TV, pay TV and national cable networks linked by satellite became so clearly a threat to the networks that ABC started advertising its prime-time movies with the legend "ANOTHER OUTSTANDING MOVIE ON FREE TELEVISION."

In 1970, there were only 2,490 cable-TV systems in the United States, serving 4.5 million subscribers. By the end of the decade, the number of systems had risen to 4,150 and the number of subscribers to 15.5 million. There could be 30 million by 1984, and in addition to the viewers siphoned off by cable, network audiences will be offered such other diversions as the VideoDisc, videocassette recorders, home computer terminals and over-the-air pay TV.

No one knows exactly which kind of television will dominate the '80s. But it is very unlikely the networks will retain as much of the pie as they have profitably enjoyed during TV's first three gold-mine decades.

At the same time, the networks showed during the '70s the ability to expand their audiences to take in new, converted constituencies. NBC's *Saturday Night Live* staked out fresh territory in TV demographics, luring back to TV members of a generation that had largely abandoned it. Advertisers found their socioeconomic profile irresistible, and products rarely advertised on TV previously—stereo systems, wines, sports cars, motor oil, Perrier water, pregnancy tests—were added to the list of TV conquests.

Television permeated American society as never before, with broadcasting terms like "feedback," "interface" and "input" finding their way into secular vocabularies. Rock groups with names like Television and The Tubes made albums with titles like *Remote Control*. Some incorporated TV into their stage appearances: The Tubes with six TV sets displaying pictures on stage, the Electric Light Orchestra performing the ritual act of smashing TV sets to smithereens at the conclusion of its performances.

Although Nielsen reported a 3-percent decline in primetime viewing in 1977, and although a *Washington Post* poll in late 1978 found a greater percentage of viewers than ever expressing dissatisfaction with TV, the industry as a whole suffered no economic aches whatsoever. It appeared to be inflationproof and recessionproof, and nonprofitable hours of the broadcast day had all but disappeared.

TV was blamed for much in the 1970s, especially violence in American society.

Dr. George Gerbner, at the University of Pennsylvania, revealed research that found heavy TV viewers more susceptible than others to what he called the "mean world syndrome" —a TV-warped concept of everyday life as such hostile terrain that one felt lucky to get through a day without assault. Near the decade's end, TV was also labeled a key factor in sharply declining scores registered by high school students on standardized Scholastic Aptitude Tests.

In 1972, a report by the U.S. Surgeon General established for the first time a "causal link" between violence on television and violent behavior in children. Concern over TV violence became so pronounced that in 1975 FCC Chairman Richard E. Wiley and network executives unveiled the allegedly voluntary Family Viewing plan. It restricted televised rapes and murders until after 9 P.M. Eastern time.

The plan was a fiasco from the start—as network censors

bowdlerized scripts into vanilla pudding for fear of public reaction—and a judge later ruled the scheme unconstitutional.

The networks were attacked as well for a relatively new TV format called the docudrama, which ransacked headlines for fact-based fictions. Where the facts ended and the fiction began was an iffy proposition in programs like *King, Helter Skelter,* and *Tail Gunner Joe.* Legal complications eventually doomed the form to near extinction, though a conference of Hollywood producers pleaded that the docudrama be kept alive.

Fear of controversy haunted the TV decade, but occasionally networks showed true grit. Though it nervously postponed a planned telecast of the anti–Vietnam War drama *Sticks and Bones,* CBS was also the network that stood by the revolutionary Norman Lear comedy *All in the Family,* which ABC had previously rejected as too hot. It turned out to be the most significant and best-written TV series of the decade.

And though the so-called Tiffany network saw its 20-year domination of the ratings crumble before tacky competition from ABC, CBS at least had the satisfaction at decade's end of seeing its innovative *60 Minutes,* a nonfiction, informational CBS News magazine, become, frequently, the No. 1 show in the nation.

In programs like *Fernwood 2Night, NBC's Saturday Night* and *Second City Television,* TV showed a new receptiveness to satire and ridicule of itself. Television loosened up considerably in the '70s, and occasionally the subject of TV was allowed a few moments of exposure on the almighty airwaves.

But more potent attacks on television came, as usual, from outside. In 1976, MGM released Paddy Chayefsky's sensational and combustible *Network,* a condemnation of the TV business all the more forceful for being written by a veteran of its golden age—the author, indeed, of the TV classic *Marty.*

We leave the '70s wrapped in the security blanket of American television. A decade in which violence on TV was one of the most-discussed of all communications matters goes out not with a mugging but a hugging.

These were the sensitivity '70s, and on television, as they ended, the thing to do was hug somebody else in order to help "get in touch with your feelings"—one of the decade's gollywhomper clichés—and, presumably, to get in touch with someone else's feelings too. TV has become a hugathon staged to help soothe psyches in an Age of Anxiety that television itself has helped bring about. The hug is now a basic phrase in the vocabulary of television behavior.

And television behavior has a definite influence on viewer behavior. Consciously or not and willingly or not, people learn how to behave from television and the movies. Phrases like "go for it" and "give it your best shot" are popularized and promulgated by TV. The notion that to hug someone else is a triumphal humanist gesture is put across through endless repetition on programs of fact and fiction.

It's just ironic—not necessarily outrageous—that an essentially dehumanizing instrument like television, with its impersonal one-way communication from Them to Us, should be so heavily populated with people telling us how to feel and to be proud of how we feel.

In the '70s, the Prob Drama told viewers how they should deal with intimate problems like impotence, homosexuality, mental retardation, autistic children, deaths in the family, infidelity, child abuse and spouse battering. PBS offered *Footsteps*, a series on how to be a parent while Misterogers continued to tell children how to be children.

Evangelical television experienced a tremendous boom; 24-hour-a-day, all-religious channels emerged, as did global evangelical networks linked by satellite. On these programs, prayers are applauded, confessions are cheered and declarations of repentence get ovations. One faith healer actually tells viewers to place their hands on the television screen in order to receive their own little miracles over the air.

The most dominant theme in commercials during the '70s had to do with the way we should want to feel: "It's nice to feel so good about a meal," "Feelin' good about yourself," "You feel good about serving your family" such-and-such cereal and so on. Why just shave, one ad asked, when you can "get stroked" in the morning?

Television did a lot of stroking in the '70s, and it seemed as if every half-hour the phone company was urging us to "reach out, reach out and touch someone"—not physically, as in the big TV hug-in, but electronically, through the impersonal medium of the telephone.

All this carries the warning label that television's role in our lives is growing and growing more intimate with each passing year. In a public-TV play called "Home," by Megan Terry, a future society was shown as organized into human beehives, with TV the only link from one hive to another and to what remained of the outside world.

As we enter a decade in which fuel shortages may keep more Americans trapped at home than ever before, Terry's fantasy seems less science fiction than a soberly realistic prognosis. Have you hugged your television set today?
December 27, 1979

And Now— The End of the World

OKAY, LET'S RUN THROUGH the end of the world again. Now, where the heck is Walter?

"THIS is WAL-ter CRON-kite."

Oh, hello, Walter. Look, stop the Gypsy dancing a minute, would you please? And tell them to put some more Pancake on your nose or we're going to get an awful glare.

"And the rockets' red glare! The bombs bursting in air . . ."

Walter, would you stop already with the singing? We've only got twenty minutes to rehearse. Now, do you remember how we open the show?

"Yes, I do, and in no uncertain terms. First I come on television screens all over the length and breadth of this great land of ours and I say, 'This is Walter Cronkite and the Armageddon News Team. The United States and the Soviet Union have launched nuclear missiles aimed at each other, and within a matter of minutes, as the crow flies—'"

No, Walter, it's not right. It's too grim. They'll be tuning out in droves. We might as well hand the ratings over to Roone Arledge right now and be done with it.

"But Chief—That's The Way It Is."

Please, don't lay that one on me, old-timer. Let's find a way to lighten up a little—you know, cool it out. How about "This is Walter Cronkite. The price of gold plummeted today, the prime lending rate fell to zero and folks, you won't have to worry about making that car payment next month. That's the good news. And now . . ."

"Well, I don't know, Chief. That compromises my journalistic principles somewhat. By the way, do you think this handmade silk tie looks all right with my six-hundred-and-fifty-dollar suit?"

Yes, Walter, it's fine. Now get your avuncular little tail over there so we can tape the promos. This first one is going to air smack-dab between *The Dukes of Hazzard* and *Dallas,* so let's make it sing, Walter honey.

"THIS is WAL-ter CRON-kite. Join me and the CBS News team tonight for exclusive coverage of the end of the world, live via satellite, at eleven-thirty Eastern, ten-thirty Central, right after all the latest sports scores on your local station."

Fine, sweetie, but could you try it once more and this time put a little more spin on the ball? We don't want to discourage them from tuning in, you know.

"Don't call me sweetie."

Oh, of course. Sorry, Walter. Now, once more, darling, and let's sound just a tad more earth-shaking, shall we? Okay, boys —hit the "Cronkite and Company" disco theme.

"THISSSS is WALLLL-ter . . ."

Walter, you're beautiful. You're gorgeous. Isn't he beautiful? Isn't he gorgeous? You keep taping. Now, where's that guy with the opening graphics?

"Right here, Chief. Let me show you what we've got. We open with a big fat close-up of the CBS Eye, see, and then we bring in the announcer: 'CBS News presents A Special Report —Apocalypse '80: Countdown to Bye-Bye.' Then we dissolve to a big shot of the earth, and we chroma-key Walter's face in, and then we cut to the Amalgamated Oil Company trademark, and that explodes into a zillion pretty little twinkling stars."

Don't like the title. Don't like the title. We need something with oomph. How about "Nuclear Nightmare: Pow, Right in the Kisser"? No, too cute. How about "Missiles to Moscow: A Night to Remember"?

"But Chief, who's going to be around to remember it?"

Let's not get emotionally involved in this, kid; this is news. Okay, I've got it. "Doomsday '80: Final Edition." Terrific. It'll hit 'em right where they live. Now, we open with Walter, we go to Dan Rather at the Pentagon, then we go to Roger Mudd at the White House, then we go to Morley Safer at Strategic Air Command, then we go to Lesley Stahl at Bloomingdale's and then we go to blazes.

"Chief, Chief! Mr. Paley's on the line!"

What the heck does that old buzz—Oh, hello Mr. Paley! Yes, Mr. Paley. Yes, yes, yes, Mr. Paley. I know ABC's putting on Barbara Walters and Geraldo Rivera, Mr. Paley. But we're pulling out the big guns for this one too, Mr. Paley. Oh, yes, it *was* a bad choice of words, Mr. Paley.

"Over in Kilarney, many years ago . . ."

Walter, will you stop singing! Mr. Paley can hear you.

"Too-ra-loo-ra-loo-ral . . . too-ra-loo-ra-lie . . ."

Somebody get Walter some black coffee. We still have another promo to tape.

"But I don't want to tape any more promos. I have to prepare for my broadcast."

Walter, look, it's not like the old days. It's not Edward R. Murrow. We're more competitive now. Do you want ABC to beat us? Do you want NBC to beat us? We've got to catch up with the times, Walter. We've got to grab those suckers by the eyeballs and keep 'em watching. I'm talking big Nielsens, Walter. Otherwise God only knows what the overnights will be."

"But Chief—"
Yeah?
"Only God *will* know. There aren't going to be any overnights."
January 27, 1980

One Woman's Story

NEVER HAS A TV PROGRAM taken more stamina to watch than does *Joan Robinson: One Woman's Story*. That isn't surprising; television has spent 30 years avoiding most of the subjects that this 2½-hour film brings up.

PBS insists on calling the documentary a "real-life drama about survival," but the heroine does not survive. She dies of cancer after 22 months of fear, pain, recrimination and struggle. And when the film arrives on public TV stations, it will do so over and above objections, denunciations and misgivings, even from some of those who helped finance it.

"It has been said to be the most controversial thing ever on television," says Mary Feldhaus-Weber, who directed the film. "Maybe it is. It's a look into the abyss."

Abysses are not popular on television. The subjects of cancer and death by cancer are usually dealt with only as elements in soap-operatic inspirational melodramas. TV movies such as *Brian's Song*, *Eric* and the recent *A Shining Season*, while often emotionally affecting, suggest that cancer strikes only the very nice and the very pretty, and that symptoms rarely get more severe than a few raspy gasps and balletic collapses.

Feldhaus-Weber says public-TV station managers are "very frightened" of the film, which traces Robinson's story step by step from the discovery of her disease to her death. PBS asked that about 30 minutes be cut out, including explicit scenes of

Robinson in agony, and had Feldhaus-Weber and her colleagues produce a half-hour follow-up discussion that tries to see cancer in more hopeful terms.

PBS also insisted on a prologue in which a doctor warns, "This will not be an easy film to watch" and a viewer advisory that runs three times during the broadcast. The program deals with "emotionally powerful material" that "may be disturbing to some," says the disclaimer, with almost laughable understatement. There is no "may be" about it: *One Woman's Story* will disturb everyone who sees it, and many will likely say it is too disturbing to be shown on TV, that they "don't want to see things like that" in their homes.

After all, for three decades we have looked upon television more as a fantasy machine than a reality machine. *One Woman's Story* breaks some long-standing rules of propriety. It does not try to be delicate (or sensational), but it is urgent and traumatic to a degree perhaps possible only with television, which has been taken into the confidence and sanctuary of millions of American homes.

If TV is going to deal with any realities, it ought to be able to deal with all realities. *One Woman's Story* invades some of the darkest and most private aspects of being alive and of dying, in a detail and with a candor unprecedented on the air. It is not what you'd call an encouraging sort of experience, but it is a rewarding one. And there is a victory involved; the victory is that the program is being shown at all.

Some in what might be called the cancer community—groups who deal with cancer patients and disseminate information—would prefer that it not be. The Damon Runyon Cancer Fund of New York contributed production money, but now, says Feldhaus-Weber, "they wish their name wasn't on it. They're very negative and very upset about it."

William Cockrell, executive vice president of the American Cancer Society's Washington office, says the society is not officially disapproving of the film, but has withdrawn an earlier endorsement because it is "too negative." And Irving Rimer, spokesman for the national society, says from New York that the film goes "in a direction I don't think the public has ever been exposed to. Things are shown that are usually shown only to doctors and not to the public."

"There's been a large percentage of extreme hostile reactions," says Feldhaus-Weber. "Some people have said the film will lead to mass suicides, or that we're taking all hope away from fifty million cancer patients. I've spent six and a half years of my life on this film, and I felt bad when I heard those comments. The reason we made the film, and the reason Joan wanted it made, was to be a help to people who had cancer and to their families.

"If people get too wrought up, I can just say, 'I'm sorry.' "

Joan Robinson, a writer and editor in suburban Boston, learned she had terminal ovarian cancer at the age of 41. Later she also developed breast cancer, and at 44 she died. When she realized the severity of her illness and its hopelessness, she asked her friend Mary Feldhaus-Weber if she would like to put on film her last months of life, in order to communicate to others what it was really like.

Robinson lived longer than expected, and her doctors believe that the making of the film had a positive and beneficial effect; it gave the suffering and the terror a purpose. Unlike afflicted characters on fictional TV movies, Joan Robinson and her husband, Eric, who married her knowing of her illness, went through hell—and cameras and microphones were there to record it.

The result is a film not necessarily morbid or merely depressing, but dealing with all facets of the experience—not only of facing death, but of the dehumanizing business of being sick, of being dependent and restricted, of placing impossible burdens on one's friends and relatives, of being subjected to the indignity that goes with medical treatment. Joan Robinson had not only a colostomy but a ureterostomy as well; early in the film, she worries about how the bags and tubes will look under her "expensive new slacks."

Recordings of Robinson's voice and her husband narrate the film, which follows her through cobalt and chemotherapy treatments, moments of remission, visits to a therapist, incredibly painful examinations by her doctors, a cessation of all sexual activity with her husband as the illness worsens, even considerations of suicide and, finally, complete disorientation, her life reduced to sleeping and breathing, and death.

To be sure, topical issues come up along the way, including the process of prolonging life through the use of drugs, in this case antibiotics. At one point Robinson speaks of her illness as part of a "a major social problem" and tells a friend, "The cost of keeping a person like me alive is fantastic."

But the human side of this story is what makes the film incomparably important and perhaps the most intimate document possible on television.

Realizing that "it is very common to die in considerable pain" from her type of cancer, Robinson asks her doctor about using heroin as a painkiller—a relatively common practice in England, but not here. The doctor promises her narcotics every 30 minutes if necessary to control pain, and suggests optimistically that she may eventually drift into uremia, which he says is "one of the gentlest ways of dying that I've ever witnessed."

Her therapist asks with plaintive concern, "What do you feel, Joan?" and "Joan, you know what I sense today?" And Joan says, "I feel like I want to make vichyssoise, and then I think, What a stupid way to spend the little time I have left."

Over still photographs of Robinson on an examining table in the hospital we hear a doctor say, "I am going to probe . . . and you let me know if it hurts," and we hear Joan cry out, "Oh, yes!" before she breaks down weeping.

On November 23, 1974, after discovering a lump in her breast and being held again at the hospital for further examination, Robinson asks the doctor, "Could I be released for, say, seven hours on Thanksgiving Day?"

After her mastectomy, Robinson is visited by a woman in an outreach program who herself had a mastectomy one month before she was married. The woman cheerfully tells Robinson that her new husband is "a leg man, anyway," and drops off a prosthesis catalogue from which Robinson can select a new, artificial breast.

In one of the many moments of anguish and fear, Joan Robinson says she wants a miracle to save her and tells her husband, "Facing death means giving up everything. . . . I don't want to give up everything." Then she begins worrying about the cost of her funeral, and Eric says, "Well, that's very nice of you."

In the spring of 1975, Eric, who has been a model of composure throughout the film, comes downstairs at night to talk with the film crew about his own ordeal, how his wife has become obsessed with the subject of cancer, how all sexual relations for them have ended. "I'm not very good with women anyway," he sobs.

The disease worsens, and we hear Robinson in pain. "Oh, please, God, help me. Oh. Oh. Why doesn't the Demerol help?"

And then, debilitated both by her illness and by the treatments, she says, "This is not living. This is not life. This is not worth it."

At 11 P.M. on August 14, 1975, Joan Robinson dies, and a form is filled out at a hospital desk.

"Basically, no one wanted this film," says Feldhaus-Weber now, but she wanted it, her friend Joan Robinson wanted it and so did the other filmmakers involved. To say the least, it was not easy. Even finding crew members wasn't easy: "One person who filmed natives dying in the jungle of cholera fainted on us."

Money kept running out, and midway through filming, expensive color film was abandoned for cheaper black-and-white videotape. As irreverent as it may sound, the fact that Joan Robinson lived for 22 months, longer than expected, meant that the filmmakers had problems getting renewed funds.

"There was a black-comedy element to it, and no one appreciated it more than Joan and Eric," says Feldhaus-Weber. "Funders would say things like 'What if she lives forever?' or 'What if she dies during the weekend, and you can't get any film stock?' The film was a great blessing to us, and a great curse, because it took over our lives.

"Sometimes we felt we were doing something unnatural, but we knew that Joan wanted it and could see the human value in it. I sometimes cursed myself for getting involved with it. But Joan loved having us there, particularly toward the end, when Eric was away in England and her own doctor was out of town, and we were there. She felt it gave her a reason to live."

The film is one of the few to have a "spiritual adviser" listed in the credits. "That was to keep us on the right path. There was a lot of praying and meditating to keep the film clear, to try to decide what was the humanly correct thing to do. At one point, even though we're not married to each other, some of us working on the film consulted a marriage counselor in order to get the film finished, because we'd become so alienated from one another, just as Joan and Eric had."

To those who would say to her that the film is too realistic, too unflinching, too intimate, Feldhaus-Weber responds, "The film is so much less bad than the experience itself. Eric saw the finished film and he told me it was one one-thousandth as bad as the experience. I feel we have a whole generation now that knows nothing about death. They haven't seen people die. And I feel it's better to know about such things than not to know.

"I think it's a transcendent film. When people ask me what the film is about, I say it's about the strength of the human spirit and transcendence, and that I believe Joan is in heaven now."

Obviously, Feldhaus-Weber's involvement in the project was more than the usual movie director's. Once when the camera was not rolling, Robinson even asked her friend if she would help her commit suicide. During a more lucid moment, before filming began, she and Robinson signed an "indenture of trust" giving Robinson—or, after her death, her lawyer—the right to any deletions she wanted in the finished film. As it turned out, her only major stipulations were that her breasts and pubic hair not be seen. A few people's names and some "raucous, bawdy talk" were also eliminated, Feldhaus-Weber says.

The final defense of the film is Robinson's own. Over shots of her funeral, Eric reads a last statement written by Robinson just before her death. "She wrote that statement at her darkest moment, when she was totally alone, curled up in a fetal position," Feldhaus-Weber says.

In the statement, Robinson deals with her thoughts of suicide and dependency, with the challenges that her illness brought her, and then she says that one compensation will be to have left behind "a film which I hope will be socially useful."

At the beginning of the film, when she first learns of her cancer, Robinson says she turned to the woman in the next bed at the hospital, "and she said, 'Don't talk to me about it. I don't want to hear about it.'"

Television doesn't often talk to us about the things we don't want to hear about. In *One Woman's Story*, we are given a rare opportunity to confront matters of life and death, and to be left limp, and though it is an awesome kind of privilege, no one could be blamed for preferring to look the other way.

January 20, 1980

Petty for Teddy

IT'S HARD ENOUGH running against an incumbent for the presidential nomination. Senator Edward M. Kennedy (D-Mass.) has also had to run against all three television networks. It would take a combination of FDR and Abraham Lincoln on the same ticket to defeat that kind of coalition.

For the past three months the network news departments have had a field day playing Get Teddy. They have turned the election process into the Wide World of Politics and portrayed Kennedy as the creamed skier feasting on the agony of defeat. They supply the viewing electorate only with a daily fix on winners and losers, and they have all but declared Teddy the loser.

The latest sneak attack was committed by the exhibitionistically scrappy Phil Jones, who covers the candidate for CBS News. On Monday night's *Evening News,* Jones described Kennedy's appearance at Georgetown University and cracked, "and with that, Kennedy looked into the TelePrompTer and read a speech." CBS even included a shot of the TelePrompTer. *This* is news?

President Carter planned to use a TelePrompTer too for his State of the Union address; one was installed in the House of Representatives for him. But he changed his mind and relied on a typed text. No one at CBS, however, said, "and with that, President Carter looked down at his script and read a speech."

Even some network newsmen acknowledged—"privately," the way wee small voices at the White House are always being quoted on network newscasts these days—that the anti-Kennedy bias is phenomenal. We turn on the nightly news to find out how badly Teddy is doing today.

"It's the new sociology of news," says one of the most respected TV newsmen in the business. "They forced Teddy to declare for the nomination, and then the minute he declared, they started saying, 'What good is he?'"

Says another longtime newsman at another network: "I don't think it's all television's fault, but television probably thinks less than newspapers—good newspapers—do.

"And all the while TV has been beating up on Kennedy, there's been almost benign neglect of Carter. Here you have a guy who is really a disaster, but the networks have gone right along with his Rose Garden strategy. There is absolutely no innovation in their coverage."

The symbolism that goes with presidential regalia is passed along to viewers by television, and rarely given a critical glance by TV newsmen. But the symbolism that goes with a Kennedy candidacy is subjected to repeated smart-alecky scrutiny, partly because the Kennedy mystique has such historical resonance.

When Roger Mudd decided to prove his manhood on the

air with the landmark Teddy Kennedy profile which CBS televised on November 4, it looked as though Mudd might be opening the door to new, tougher, more rigorous political reporting on television. It's been tougher and more rigorous, all right—but only on Kennedy.

Jones followed up on November 17 with a *CBS Evening News* report in which he deemed it terribly newsworthy that Kennedy had misidentified a railroad, that he was "using his family" to get votes—surely an unheard-of ploy in American politics—and that he stammered in response to a question on racial issues.

"He often appears to be a man without a plan," said Jones.

More recently, Kennedy was subjected to further unprofessional indignities on the ABC News program *Issues and Answers*. In the last minute of the show, reporter Bob Clark suddenly said, almost jokingly, "Senator, if I may interrupt, people are going to think we are derelict if we don't get one Chappaquiddick question into this show."

Kennedy had less than 40 seconds to respond to the question Clark asked. He tried to bring up what he thought were the actual "moral issues" of the campaign, but was cut off in mid-sentence when time ran out.

"We felt very bad about it," said Peggy Whedon, producer of the program, later. "It was miscalculation, purely. The clock did it to us." Senator Kennedy was "a little testy" about the incident, she said, and "his people were angry" as they left the studio. And with good reason.

Meanwhile, on NBC's *Meet the Press*, President Carter held forth with his big born-again grin as reporters pelted him with questions that, but for a few exceptions, had the stinging power of rose petals.

Television loves to give its audience good news. It loves to give them winners. It loves to give them black-and-white comic-strip versions of complex events. So the hair-spray crowd has put on the kid gloves for Carter, who is given great credit for withstanding all the crises he helped bring about, and saved all the knockout punches for Kennedy.

"It's really been savage against Kennedy," says one veteran

political observer active in broadcasting. "I've been shocked by it; absolutely astounded by the coverage. And the double standard is incredible. Carter is full of 'steely resolve,' but Kennedy is 'hustling votes.' "

Why is this happening?

"I think partly because there's been so much garbage about how the press loves the Kennedys in recent years that the reporters feel they all have to establish their neutral credentials by knocking him around. They're leaning way over backwards, that's for sure. They're preparing audition tapes so that nobody will look back someday and say, 'Oh, Phil Jones—that Kennedy whore.' "

Former presidential adviser Bill Moyers, who couldn't stomach the network news circus and this week begins a new season on public television, feels the problem involves more than just the hostility some correspondents feel toward Kennedy.

"Television is unfair to politicians generally, just as it is unfair to thinking people," Moyers says from New York. "Politicians deal in a world of complexity, and television deals in a world of simplicity. Television insists they play by the rules of television and not by the rules of politics.

"The rules of politics are negotiation, weaving, subtlety, nuance, trading, advancing, retreating and so on; these are the things with which you sustain a political process. But television doesn't like nuance. And television doesn't like subtlety."

TV news melodramatizes events to make them good shows cast with cartoon personalities, and this streamlined version of what is happening in the world becomes the TV reality millions see on their screens. Principal offenders like Jones may stand out for their shamelessness, but the three network news departments are pretty much hewing to the same party line on Kennedy.

"A kind of group radar does take over," says Moyers. "One guy sees a blip and seizes on it, then another guy seizes on that and so on. Teddy Kennedy hasn't been judged on whether he's been a good senator, on his grasp of the issues, on his views on Afghanistan, Iran or anything else. Instead, it's been television deciding whether he's a good campaigner or not.

"At the same time, it's all biased in favor of Jimmy Carter. Inflation is not only as bad as it was, it's worse than ever. Americans are still being held hostage in Iran. And Russian troops are still in Afghanistan. But Jimmy Carter is high in the polls because he is able to communicate, through television, the symbols of leadership even when he is not in fact leading."

Broadcasters are continually demanding repeal of the Fairness Doctrine that is supposed to keep them in line on matters of public import. They say they don't need a Fairness Doctrine. They say it inhibits them. They say we should trust them to be fair.

Like hell we should trust them to be fair.
January 30, 1980

Losing the Picture

TELEVISION IS NOT A visual medium. Appearances are deceiving. TV might have turned into a medium of real visual communication; it was pretty darn visual in its early years, when still at the miracle stage. But somewhere it went awry and became illustrated radio, and poorly illustrated radio at that.

In a prime-time entertainment, television rarely offers an eyeful, much less two eyes full. A wan visual sameness pervades programming, almost all of which is shot within a few square miles in and around Hollywood, which is no-man's-land for reality. Seldom is there the opportunity to be visually delighted or engaged by the picture we see on TV—except, of course, during *Charlie's Angels* or commercials.

Commercials often communicate on a more purely visual

level than programs. They're better photographed, edited for maximum impact and often shot on location, so that they show us much more of the world around us than programs do. RCA wants us to see the Grand Canyon in its true colors, says a gorgeous ad for TV sets, and see it we do—for about 10 seconds.

ABC's current coverage of the Winter Olympics has offered innumerable striking sights, perhaps none more spectacular than the opening ceremonies, which had viewers raving in appreciation. But the sporting events themselves are often saddled with so much extraneous, incessant commentary that the audio overwhelms the video and it begins to look as if the schussing and swooping down snowy slopes are accompaniment to the babblings of announcers and not the other way around.

As for TV news, it has become persistently less visual during recent years, even though there have been leaps and strides in the technology of getting pictures on the air. Partly it's a matter of correspondents and anchormen simply refusing to shut up and let pictures talk.

How can the picture be a star when the reporter wants to be a star—and to stand in front of a building delivering pronouncements?

Reuven Frank, the former president of NBC News who originally teamed Chet Huntley and David Brinkley and produced such acclaimed documentaries as *The Tunnel*, says TV news has completely subordinated pictures to talk. What we have in effect is Television for the Blind.

"Television could be a visual medium," Frank says. "But there's no such thing as photojournalism on television now. You'd think it would be the ideal medium for photojournalism, where the picture tells the story. What we have now in TV news is the need for a picture only because the television tube exists; you have a guy standing outside a building telling you what is going on inside a building into which he is not allowed to go. He only knows what's going on in there because someone at the New York desk called him up and told him."

Frank says TV has changed the way it covers news and in the process made pictures not the indispensable essence but virtually frilly; they don't so much tell the story as fill space.

"It used to be in covering news for TV that the writing of the script was the last act," says Frank. "First you went out and showed what was happening. Then you arranged the pictures in the order dictated by the story. Then someone who knew the story wrote the script to go with it.

"Now the standard way of doing it is that the words are written and spoken and then the pictures, such as they are, are hung on the words. Such pictures as do not fit the script are left on the floor. A camera crew won't even film some things unless they know they are going to be talked about in advance. It used to be that we would write contrapuntally to the pictures, but now that's all gone, and most of the time there is no reason to have pictures except that it's TV and you have to put something on the screen."

What's put on the screen is often a lot of spurious and frivolous illustration to reinforce or enhance the dialogue. In a January broadcast of the *NBC Nightly News,* during a story on Scholastic Aptitude Test scores, a reporter compared them to "an accurate roll of the dice." At this point a picture of a pair of dice popped up on the screen.

Frank calls this approach "comic book" and says it ironically gets worse with advances in electronic manipulation of pictures to be put on the screen. There is increased use of drawings, graphs and gimmicks of all kinds, relevance not usually a criterion. "The next thing," says Frank, "will be 'pow!' and 'bam!' and 'sock!' " as in comic strips.

Frank was executive producer of a brave and industrious NBC magazine show called *Weekend,* and he recalls a telltale comment made to him by a student doing a master's thesis in communications. "Well, the trouble with *Weekend,*" the student said, "is that it's too visually oriented." It was television for people who can see.

February 21, 1980

Dan Rather's New Reality

Now, then, Dan Rather. If this were *60 Minutes*, I'd hold up this *Time* magazine cover—the one with your satisfied, victorious grin on it and the huge caption calling you "The $8 Million Man"—and I'd say, "How do you feel when you see something like—"

"All right! All right!" Dan Rather groans, laughing slightly, recoiling at the sight of the cover, trying perhaps to blush but really looking quite pleased. He is sitting in his *60 Minutes* office with its dizzying, rarefied view of the Hudson River and greater Weehawken, and contemplating his future as news pope to the nation.

In one year, or less, he'll replace Walter Cronkite as anchorman and managing editor of *The CBS Evening News*. And how does somebody get a job like that?

Rather got it by wanting it. Wanting it to bits. Dan Rather toughed it out, and Dan Rather won.

"In a way, I guess I've always wanted to do it," Rather says, "in that I want to be the best. And for my professional lifetime, the perception has been that you can't be the best unless you do the job, at least once."

Rather, 48, punctuates conversation with much talk of being The Best; he comes across as compulsively competitive, beset by best-ness, given to sports imagery about hanging in and winning. "I want to play to my own best potential," he says, and "Sometimes my best is pretty good." He stayed at CBS, spurning five-year, $8-million offers from ABC and NBC, because CBS News is still "the best" in town.

"About the job, I feel terrific; why wouldn't I feel terrific?" he says, his sleeves rolled neatly up. "As for the publicity that goes with it, no, I'm not happy about it. First of all, I don't like the focus on the money. But I understand the realities of it. The business has changed. The whole star system is something a lot of us have talked about for a long time, but it's part of the new reality."

There are many in network news who say Rather's victory in landing the Cronkite post over the respected, high-strung Roger Mudd, 52, was a triumph for the star system, for beauty beating brains, for style over substance. Thus it makes a handy harbinger of things to come for network news in the '80s.

Mudd is known to despise the star system and the idea of journalists as celebrities—something he thinks, friends say, Walter Cronkite and the cast of *60 Minutes* have perpetuated to an onerous extreme. Rather does not say he hates the star system. He says it is part of "the new reality."

In person, Rather is open, friendly and as solicitous as the president of the senior class. He's "easy to work with," a colleague says; "he thanks everybody. Sometimes he just won't stop thanking everybody." But on the air, Rather sometimes seems rigid, terse, programmed and anything but the avuncular old soul he's replacing.

In a way, we are going to go from the warmth of Walter to chilly scenes of Rather.

"Some people have told me, 'You're crazy to stay at CBS. The first guy after Walter Cronkite is going to get his head blown off,'" says Rather. "That may be true. I don't plan for that to happen. People said the toughest place to try to do it is at CBS. 'It'd be easier on you, Dan, if you do it at ABC or NBC.' But I look forward to it."

Inhale. Exhale. Deeply thoughtful squint. White smoke floats by in fluffs against the blue, blue sky outside Dan Rather's window on the world. His eyes look just bright enough, just piercing enough, just determined enough. It's the gleam of born success, the ruddy glow of a Marlboro Man with brains —a guy who, in a phrase he cottons to, "paid his dues" and now gets the prize.

Along the way he learned what he needed to know. He became a pressure player.

"Hey, the pressure's gonna be there," Rather says of the new job. "I'm a pressure player. I know I am. But look, anybody who does it at this level—the same would be true of Mudd, the same would be true of anybody who does it at this level—is a pressure player. Because you don't get this far unless you are."

If Jacqueline Susann were alive, she'd write this character into a novel right away. Maybe she already did.

The toughness beneath the manicured, polite exterior comes out in subtle little ways. For instance, even in praising the man he will supplant as Chief News Giver to the Nation, Rather casually suggests that there are chinks in the armor of the "most-trusted man in America."

"Walter can get overbearing sometimes, he can hold on to the microphone too long—all these things—but that's small potatoes compared to the enthusiasm he brings to it," Rather says. As for Cronkite's reputation as the invincible uncle, Rather says, "Walter hasn't always been Number One. We went through the better part of eight years—eight years! In this business, that's an eternity, and beyond—in which he was certainly not clearly Number One."

Those millions of viewers don't just watch Walter, Rather says; they watch CBS News. "The house that Cronkite built had some pretty good carpenters—Roger Mudd, Marvin Kalb, Dan Schorr and yes, Dan Rather—and a long list of other people, some of whom are still there.

"I can remember the days—'64, '65, '66—when we knew we were better; every night we'd sit down and say, 'We're better than those guys.' But the organization was not perceived to be Number One. And Walter wasn't Number One."

And when Rather's fabulous salary is mentioned, he quickly notes, "Cronkite has been making big money for a long time. And Mike Wallace, too—Mike Wallace was very big in radio and television when I was making eighty-five dollars a week."

When asked about that alleged $8-million deal, Rather says, "Don't believe everything you read," but he doesn't blink when it is noted that he will make "around $1 million" a year, or when he is asked whether he can possibly relate to the world of the common man when raking it in at that pitch.

"I think it's possible. I hope it is," he says. "But I don't know. Mind you, I didn't make six figures until fairly recently. It's no complaint; I've been well paid. And I certainly don't feel guilty about it, no, I work hard. I have worked hard a long time."

He can't help thinking back, though, to life in his native Houston, where his father worked on a pipeline and his mother was a waitress.

"I believe the most my father ever made was one year in which he made $11,200. Yes, the year he died he cleared eleven-two. He worked a helluva lot harder than I did. But no, I certainly don't feel guilty. I'm at total peace with myself about that."

The road to total peace didn't start 18 years ago when CBS News hired Rather away from network affiliate KHOU-TV in Houston. It probably goes back to some magical day when Rather decided he would be the best at whatever he did, even if it meant stretching the talents he had beyond their limits—whether playing on the high school football team or going for some of the biggest glamour bucks in broadcasting.

Grit, pluck, drive and determination helped him get what he wanted in the world, just as they are supposed to. "I've never had a job in this business I didn't like, really like," he says in his carefully, softly, look-you-in-the-eye trusty Texas way.

If there are not that many people who consider Rather brilliant as a thinker, he is widely respected at CBS for his tirelessness and teamsmanship. He is also amenable to a fault. "If Dan were a woman," says a former colleague, "he'd be pregnant all the time. He can't say no."

Scenario-by-Consensus—or, how some insiders at CBS News think Dan Rather got the job of jobs:

Rather is "a company man," the story goes, while Mudd is the type to tell management to "go f—— yourself." Mudd felt his years of work, including weeks of subbing for Cronkite, would earn him the job on merit, while Rather and his high-powered agent, Richard Leibner, trusted nothing to luck or justice and actively "went after it" with a vengeance.

Dan Rather stands up suddenly and turns off the Muzaky radio station that has been burbling in the background.

"That is complete, unadulterated and unalloyed bullshit," he says firmly, now sounding more like Dan Rather, anchorman. "Simply not true. Grossly unfair to both Roger and myself. I'm going to have some difficulty talking to you about it candidly. I cannot say it too often: Roger's one of the best reporters I know; he may be the best political reporter I know. He is not only a complete pro, but he is a good and decent person. Roger and I have been and continue to be good friends."

Good and decent though he may consider Mudd, Rather also notes, later, speaking more forcefully now, "I don't think 'going after it' had very much to do with it—and if anybody went after it, Roger damn sure went after it.

"I think it's true that for a very long time, Roger assumed he was the person, and I think he did so with very good reason. Had I been in his shoes, I would have assumed the same thing."

Rather a company man? "No one was saying that in '67, '68, '73, '74. It was more like 'Rather won't stay in line,' " Rather says. "Lyndon Johnson certainly didn't think I was a company man, and Richard Nixon didn't think I was a company man. And I'm proud of that. I think if you talked to enough people around here, you'd hear them say Rather is less of a company man than Mudd.

"I can't think of a single instance in which Roger said, 'Stick it in your ear,' " Rather says.

Then he waxes magnanimous. "I'm very hopeful Roger will stay," he says. Indeed, that's what all the executives at CBS News seem to be saying, and started saying the day Rather was chosen. They say it so often that they are essentially conceding they have no real hope—and perhaps no desire—for Mudd to stay at all.

"The tragedy," Rather says somberly, "is that somebody has to lose."

For Dan Rather—as the narrator of a TV documentary might put it—it was the end of a long journey, a journey that began 10 years earlier when he learned to his dismay that he had been eliminated from the competition to find a new anchor for the Sunday edition of the *Evening News*.

"I was surprised, shocked, amazed when I heard they weren't even going to talk to me about it," Rather says slowly, quietly.

When news vice president Gordon Manning told Rather he wasn't anchor material, "Well, that hit me like a ton, and my attitude was Wait a minute, I don't like that one damn bit."

It was then that he set his sights on the top of the hill.

"Along about that time, I think it was in 1970, I just said to myself, 'If that's where the next level of achievement is, if that's where the attention is, if that's where the money is, if that's the next ticket you have to get punched on the road to being the best, then you, Dan, had better get into that very quickly and you'd better start establishing you can do it.'"

The race was on.

He went to Manning. "I really leaned on him." He got the Sunday news on a trial basis for six weeks. "I did tire of constantly reading that I was in a race with people and didn't stand a chance. The hell with that! I didn't like the sound of that at all."

Rather grins and becomes suddenly, and briefly, self-mocking: "This is a modesty-prone business in which ego plays a very small part," he says.

Even if one scoffs at the head-blown-off theory, the man who follows Walter Cronkite in the *Evening News* throne is going to be watched very closely by network executives. Network news has never been more profitable, and a surfeit of world crises has boosted audiences to new highs. Intense competition put up by heavy-hitter and big-spender Arledge at ABC has made a hectic three-way heat out of what used to be a gentlemanly two-party joust.

In the zest to compete, will good gray CBS News begin to emulate the yappy underdog, adding more hype, glitz and pinball wizardry in the attempt to retain dominance? Associates expect Rather to make considerable changes in the look, tempo, and tone of the broadcast.

Rather won't say what changes he has in mind. But neither will he say a word against the Arledge hit-and-run technique. Arledge courted Rather feverishly during the negotiation period.

"If the danger with the ABCs of the world is that they will go too far with the 'look' of something," Rather says "the danger for the CBSes of the world is that we will succumb to the temptation to believe that in order to be serious, it has to be dull. Any rational person can see that that simply isn't true.

"Arledge has certainly not met the worst expectations of him. He's been good for the business and good for news. And I don't think even ABC believes that the new era is all flash and splash and dash."

Even in casual talk, there is something rehearsed about Rather, something practiced, polished and perfected. He is careful to ask questions of an interviewer so that an illusion of two-way interest is maintained. He has such a straight-shooter, straight-arrow appearance and demeanor that it seems too real to be real.

He'll say square, pinstripey things like "I think your point is well taken" and "But let's get back to serious business."

He speaks admiringly of a son who plays basketball in college and is known as the guy who can be counted on, in those last closing seconds, to make the shot that breaks the tie and wins the game.

Get on the team, get into the game, take the chance, make the shot, break the tie, be the hero, get the trophy. It's the American way. Maybe the best man didn't win the Cronkite job, but the man most obsessed with being the best certainly did.

"I get irritated when somebody else says, 'So-and-so is better than you are.' I don't take the attitude that I'm better than anybody else. But I refuse to take the attitude that I'm not as good as somebody else," Rather says.

"If I bought the idea that the person who went in after Cronkite would get his head blown off, I might do it anyway. I'm probably crazy enough to do it anyway. But I don't plan for that to happen.

"The air is thinner where I'm going than anyplace I've been," Dan Rather says with visionary zeal. "And there's probably no pressure to match that pressure. Having never been at that altitude, I don't know, but I'm eager to get there and eager to see."

Eager, and willing, and ready. Dan Rather is as ready as they come. It's part of the new reality.

March 12, 1980

Auntie Babsy

NEAR THE END of tonight's *Barbara Walters Special* on ABC, Barbara Walters says from behind her invisible pulpit, "We, the public, are very hard on our idols." We certainly are, Babsy. We subject them to being interviewed by you.

No—just kidding. Who would want to bother to try to get along without Barbara Walters? Barbara Walters—manicurist, pedicurist, guru of kitsch, yenta, maven, gadfly, blabbermouth and Mother Confessor to the world.

Tonight Barbara talks with Bo Derek, Farrah Fawcett, Cheryl Ladd and Bette Midler, and each segment is, in its own insane way, insane—and also, quite wonderful.

It's a theme show, and the theme is four blondes, orthodox or reformed, at "crossroads" in their lives. Of course, by the Walters definition, anyone could be deemed to be at a crossroads at any moment, like maybe a crossroads between a lull and a lapse. But glib chatter calls for slender threads.

The Derek piece, first, is the most unintentionally revealing of the group, since Derek's so-called "Svengali," the highly protective John Derek (once an actor), joins Bo and Barbie on a great sea of pillows, with Walters in her Gypsy fortune-teller outfit and Derek *Homme* doing much of the talking.

"Bo is my everything," he says. "I hate work," he says. "I'm not her Svengali," he says. "I haven't used or abused her," he says. He rubs her leg. He dabs a drop of sweat off her nose. And from Bo there is barely a peep.

Then it's off to Farrah's house.

Farrah has a "concealed media wall," Walters points out. It

sounds like something Mike Wallace would hide behind with a film crew.

Walters is more than fair to all her guests. She doesn't ask Ladd about her broken-down marriage to Alan Ladd's son David, and she calls Ladd's so-so TV special "an enormous hit." In the same vein, she neglects to mention that Farrah Fawcett's movies have been such disastrous bombs that she's had to come crawling back to television to remain in the pupil of the public eye.

"I'm lonely," Farrah says. "I want to have a baby." It is suggested she might want to visit a sperm bank. Really. But it turns out Farrah is having an intense spiritual relationship with the deeply cute Ryan O'Neal.

"This part of my life is so special to me," says Farrah into Barbara's bursting-with-understanding eyes. "I have so much growth now that it's like I'm bursting." Farrah looks beautiful, but no one on the show can quite compete, visually, with the opening shot of Bo Derek jogging on the beach in a thin, filmy white smock. So thin. So filmy. So smockkkkkkkk. . . .

Why, you can see right through it, practically!

Walters asks her guests to rate themselves on that banal 1-to-10 scale. Farrah says, "A nine, barely a nine." Cheryl Ladd says. "A good solid eight," but on Fridays, a seven. And Bette Midler, last and lustiest, replies, "Oh, I think I'm about a fifty-five. I don't know. I'm a happening girl."

Midler is probably the toughest nut for Walters to crack since she played ring-around-the-rosy with Richard Pryor. "Get out of my house," says Midler at one point, but the adorable, brassy, sassy actress and singer is only kidding. Too bad. It would have made a great television first.

Midler recalls her tormented teenhood ("I had this set of knockers"), recalls baring her bazooms at the London Palladium, concedes both "I'm sexy" and "I'm an oddball, I'm definitely odd" and gives her house the white-glove test: "That windowsill is perfectly filthy."

Sometimes fluff has a way of seeming substantial, marginalia works itself in past the margins, things you needn't know become fascinating and mindless escapism gets to be totally engrossing. The time has come to admit that it would be unthinkably painful to have to part with Barbara Walters and to propose that every one of her interview specials be earmarked straightaway for the time capsule—dipso facto, lickety-split posthaste and quick like a bunny.

We, the public, are very hard on our Barbara Walters. But she's the only Barbara Walters we have.

April 1, 1980

Gunga Dan

"YOUR ASSIGNMENT, Dan, should you agree to accept it, is to penetrate the Afghanistan border, gain the confidence of resistance fighters there, let your beard grow a few days, wear a funny hat and file a story for *60 Minutes* that will have Roone Arledge absolutely chartreuse with envy...."

We may never know precisely how dauntless Don Hewitt, producer of *60 Minutes,* and daring Dan Rather, crown prince of network news, plotted the slightly sensational Afghanistan war report seen on CBS last night. But the result was in the best and worst ways typical of the program and its enterprise: punchy, crunchy, highly dramatic and essentially uninformative.

Except that, yes, we knew something about the war against the invading Soviet troops before *60 Minutes,* but—and this is important—did we know how the war was affecting Dan Rather?

We certainly did after Rather's report, which took up the space of two regular *60 Minutes* segments and found Dan, among other accomplishments, logging a striking new variation on the editorial "we." Resistance fighters, Rather reported, "disguised us as one of them."

The histrionic highlight of the report was reached when

Rather made it to the mountaintop, a ridge overlooking a Soviet army encampment. The camera stayed on Rather's silhouette against the dark blue sky as he hushed out a whispery narrative that might have been compared—and was probably meant to be compared—to Edward R. Murrow's historic "This is London" reports during World War II.

Rather—over the sounds of gunfire—murmured what was essentially a radio report from the front.

"The resistance fighters have opened up with automatic weapons from the top of the ridge toward the tanks below," he said breathlessly. "Antitank gun goes off. Now, again, silence. Artillery shell. Antitank round. Impossible to know where it hit. Or if it struck home . . . That round hit the ridge just below us."

And then, the ordeal over: "I don't know when anybody's been so glad to see stars."

Of course, the resistance fighters were seeing a star too—a superstar who would greet them with a businesslike "Hello, my name is Rather." The camera repeatedly cut to Rather to show us his reactions (reactions we were expected to share), whether to the condition of shelling victims in a Peshawar hospital or to the recollections of a villager claiming to have been gassed by Soviet aircraft.

Was it all a story about the war in Afghanistan or a story about the courage and gallantry of someone out of *Foreign Correspondent*—Danny Do-Right, ace reporter? Mike Wallace set it up dramatically at the show's opening with ". . . and up on that ridge, Dan Rather found the war he came to cover."

Rather himself tended to emphasize the hardships of the reportage. He made a "three-hour trek" down the mountain, a "two-day walk" from one village to another, and as for getting to the ridge, "the climb was straight up—ten thousand feet."

Rather wore peasant togs that made him look like an extra out of *Doctor Zhivago*. Vanessa Redgrave wearing the same outfit would have been welcomed at any chic party in Europe. Somehow one got the feeling that this was not so much Dan Rather as Stuart Whitman playing Dan Rather. Or Dan Rather playing Stuart Whitman playing Dan Rather. Perhaps it's all part of the New Reality.

There was one other dominant theme to the report, and that was that the gallant, ill-equipped resistance fighters desperately need American arms. "America seems to be asleep," Rather's interpreter told him at one point. At another, he virtually negotiated with a resistance fighter about whether America should send troops and risk getting into another Vietnam.

Repeatedly he portrayed the Afghans as lost, lost unless help arrives soon, perhaps the way it arrived in the form of British cavalry in the movie *Gunga Din*.

"It's over in Afghanistan," Rather said ultrasoberly. "So you think Afghanistan is gone?" he soon asked an interpreter. "My friend, let me ask you a direct question—is Afghanistan lost?" he asked a villager.

There is certainly nothing unjournalistic about donning a disguise—although a $50 haircut still looks like a $50 haircut even when mussed up a little—and using clever ruses to get a story. True, Rather in his white safari suit, trudging through a village, did resemble a soldier of fortune in an Old Spice commercial, but that isn't exactly his fault.

And as usual, *60 Minutes* was effectively personalizing an otherwise abstract, distant story. But the report also smacked of showy one-upmanship and theatricality. Perhaps Barbara Walters is right now wondering how she'll look in mufti or having a designer disguise prepared. Geraldo Rivera may be trying on caftans at this very moment.

The war goes on. We know little more about it than we knew before. But at least, thank God, Dan Rather is safe. "What's that bombing sound in the background?" he asked nervously at one point. "Nothing to bother us. Don't worry," the interpreter replied. And it's hard to decide whether Murrow is smiling down approvingly or spinning in his grave.

April 7, 1980

Live, from Detroit: The Republican Convention

SUPPOSE THEY GAVE a party and everybody came but nobody knew why.

It's happening in Detroit right now, and the television networks are all but blowing their tops in the attempt to make something terribly meaningful out of the Republican National Convention. First night's coverage actually was pretty entertaining—until the "entertainment" started, that is.

Wayne Newton, looking like a used-car salesman you wouldn't even want your daughter to *speak to*, was scarcely into his Las Vegas lounge-lizard version of "The Battle Hymn of the Republic" when NBC's able-brained John Chancellor observed, "The New York delegation watched the beginning of the show, got up and went home."

It was clear Chancellor and other network correspondents wanted to do the same. And as for the American people, they didn't have to get up and go home because they already were home, and early ratings show they were avoiding the Republican National Convention the way they'd avoid a cookout on Mt. St. Helens. New York overnights showed that some 73 percent of those with their sets on chose to watch something other than the "Here's Ronnie" show playing on the three networks.

Apparently there's not much appetite out there in Television Land for bathiosis grandiosis—trumped-up sentimentality on an *Apocalypse Now* scale. There was something vaguely impressive about Gerald Ford finding his second wind (or was it his first) with his "Bah-loney" speech, it's true, especially since its subtext amounted to "You're more miserable now than you were under me." And there was something weirdly self-parodistic, too, about the fact that he almost dropped the "solid gold" medal the Republican pooh-bahs presented him.

Chevy Chase has been replaced. The spoofed has become the spoof.

But the network news departments proved themselves agile to the point of double-jointedness in breathing a little life into what seemed plainly the Olympics of futility, not just an exercise in it. NBC's coverage was great, CBS' was good and ABC's was sloppy and slipshod, just as one might have expected.

NBC News gave the event the benefit of every doubt, staying with official proceedings more often than the other networks, communicating the most effectively the sense of the occasion and devoting 7 hours 17 minutes to the convention on its first day, as opposed to just over 6 hours from CBS and less than 5 hours from ABC. (These totals don't include regularly scheduled newscasts but do include special editions of the magazine shows *60 Minutes* and *20/20*.)

So much was said in advance about the GOP convention's being a sleepwalk that this may have become a self-fulfilling prophecy. But the fact is, watching lots of people bumble around in funny hats and with some of their inhibitions relaxed is still good television, and it's good Americana, too. And NBC had the good sense to put lots of people and lots of funny hats on the screen, to visually remind viewers that there in that hall are, indeed, representatives from nearly every corner of a country that still prides itself on diversity and variety. It was like a real *Real People*.

Meanwhile, on the CBS *60 Minutes* broadcast, the tone of self-satire was clearly established by the undeflatable Mike Wallace, who poked at Governor Reagan with intimidating questions like, on the subject of a running mate, "You mean to say you haven't got your mind made up?" and, on the subject of import quotas, "You mean you don't know this yet? It's pretty important!"

See here, Reagan, what is this—you trying to put something over on MIKE WALLACE?

For another guardian at the gates, venerable Walter Cronkite of CBS, the convention was played as an endurance test. At one point the Gipper of network news seemed to be fumbling the ball; his running commentary degenerated into a series of Porky Pig stammers. One could imagine tremors going through the CBS war machine—Walter stammered! Walter stammered! Have the Cronkite clone ready to go! But then Cronkite recovered; "I'm trying to say . . ." he said, and then he said it.

The real hero of the day was David Brinkley of NBC, who has been anchoring conventions almost as long as Cronkite (Walter goes back to '52, David to '56) and who interjects notes of irreverence just when they are needed most. "The Republicans arriving here are so happy," he said at one point. "They're just delirious with joy. . . . They are so happy it is almost as if there in this hall they were all snuggled down together in a hot tub."

Discussing the career of Joe Louis, after whom the Detroit convention arena was named, Brinkley said that eventually Joe was set upon by the IRS, "which was trying to get the last quarter he had." After a floor interview with John Connally's only delegate, Ada Mills, Brinkley observed that the woman had changed her political allegiances so many times that "she must be an emotional mess by now."

Brinkley is still solid, sharp and succinct. The best.

Of course there were goofs and fluffs; they're part of the reason convention-watching is still fun even when the convention is a charade. Chancellor had a streak of bad luck, beginning one report with the reminiscence that this was the 32nd Republican convention "since 1964—er, 1856." Later he introduced a snippet of Reagan interview with "Now, Governor Reagan on busing," only to be immediately followed by Reagan being asked, "What will you do about inflation?"

He introduced Tom Brokaw, and who pops up on the screen but a grumpy Tom Pettit, standing silently and waiting for a cue. But Chancellor could also be disarmingly direct, as when he stood on NBC's open-air balcony with Senator Howard Baker and asked him, "Why do some of those people down there dislike you so much?"

All three networks seasoned their coverage with little two-or-three-minute nostalgia nuggets—"A Moment of History" on ABC, "Flashbacks" on CBS and "Convention Moments" on NBC. These were gambits obviously dreamed up not in news departments but in sales departments and designed to introduce excitement into the convention even if the excitement was 50 years old.

Floor reporters did their best to inject life into the show, often despite considerable obstacles. Sander Vanocur of ABC News was literally in the dark, and invisible to the camera, as he reported from the North Carolina delegation; the Republicans have the habit of frequently dimming the lights in the hall to encourage the networks to show on the air whatever piece of film is being shown to the delegates.

Cronkite went to Morton Dean on the floor for an interview with Senator Richard Schweiker (Pa.) only to discover Dean cooling his heels while waiting for NBC's Tom Pettit to finish his interview with the Senator. The CBS camera tried to keep the NBC man out of the picture and the NBC camera tried to keep the CBS man out of the picture. It's traditional.

At ABC, anchors Frank Reynolds and Ted Koppel proved about as charismatic a team as Donny and Marie, who flogged a song to death late in the evening. Reynolds continued to indulge his habit for ceremoniously handing out accolades to ABC reporters on the air, as if he were the Supreme Court of TV journalism. After a Barbara Walters interview, Reynolds said, "Thank you, Barbara. Some tough questions, and some very forthright and candid answers."

A convention that had, to put it mildly, been lacking in melodrama produced some late last night when the crowd in Detroit was, as Chancellor predicted it would be, "electrified" by the appearance of Senator Barry M. Goldwater, the Ronald Reagan of his day, which was about 16 years ago.

But when the tumultuous ovation died down and Goldwater's speech rambled on and on about Soviet threats and national strength, an NBC camera caught two gray-haired ladies sitting and chatting together and blissfully ignoring the speech, and a CBS camera spied two people fanning themselves with programs and looking bored, even as Goldwater was predicting doom for all humanity should Reagan not be elected in November.

The camera caught Goldwater, too, perspiring more and more heavily as the speech wore on, until he finally had to ask for "a piece of Kleenex." He appeared to age about a decade from the beginning of the speech to its end. It was really quite touchingly pitiful.

Bruce Morton of CBS was the first reporter to grab Goldwater after he left the podium, and after Morton finished, Walter Cronkite's voice came down from on high—the CBS booth above the hall—and he chatted with Goldwater as if the two were old chums. Walter said he hoped Barry would soon be flying airplanes again, and Barry said if he did he'd buzz Walter's yacht in Chesapeake Bay. We viewers felt like outsiders at a geriatrics smoker.

Conflict was scarce last night, no matter how tirelessly such able reporters as Dan Rather of CBS tried to fan the fires of discontent over ERA, a subject the TV press has managed to beat into silly pulp. There was a tense moment, however, when Sam Donaldson of ABC and Tom Pettit of NBC both latched on to the same delegate for reaction to the Benjamin Hooks speech. The two reporters literally asked their questions simultaneously, and it was up to the delegate to decide which one to answer.

"A little traffic jam there?" chuckled Brinkley from the NBC booth.

ABC stayed with Monday morning's opening session for only about four minutes, rushing off just before the National Anthem so the network could edify viewers with a rerun of *The Love Boat.* CBS filled a "moment of silence" for the hostages in Iran with the logical thing, a commercial. Only NBC carried Reagan's departure from Los Angeles live, and only NBC stayed with the podium during the official start of proceedings Monday night.

Thus NBC was most efficient at communicating the sense of event, or the sense of nonevent, that goes with a story like this. It may well be that the networks will never again devote so much time, money and energy to covering political conventions, their real function in the political system having been considerably reduced, but at least NBC is both going by the book and using imagination during the last flight of the albatross.

It was a little distressing, though, to see that among the sponsors of convention coverage on underdog NBC were the embattled Chrysler Corporation (unveiling its Sinatra-Iacocca spots) and the beleaguered McDonnell-Douglas Aircraft Corporation ("Builders of the DC-10!" an announcer trumpeted). Somehow these touches served to underline just how forced the forced festivity of the whole convention really was.

At least, NBC News appeared to be showing retroactive sense in cutting down on the number of appearances by Representative John B. Anderson (R-Ill.) during the *Today* show, which is live from Detroit this week. Anderson was supposed to appear twice daily, but has so far appeared only once daily —result of an "editorial judgment," says an NBC News spokesman—and no wonder, what with the snappy answers he's been handing out.

Anderson on his advice for Reagan in choosing a running mate: "Well, I suppose it's rather presumptuous of me to offer any advice; it would be wholly gratuitous."

Anderson on reactions of European leaders to a Reagan candidacy: "Well, I wouldn't want to quote any of these men directly because these were off-the-record conversations."

As Carter media adviser Gerald Rafshoon chuckled last week, "I suppose Anderson is just as qualified to be on the *Today* show as Tom Brokaw or Gene Shalit—but maybe not as qualified as Willard Scott."

Walter Cronkite had Henry Kissinger up to the booth for a stony-faced chat; Barbara Walters, on *20/20*, interviewed no less imposing a political figure than Carol Channing for a story on show biz and politics (Carol Channing?); Gerald Ford referred to "The American peeper who suffer in silence" during his roof-raising speech; a montage of scenes from his presidency was hilariously accompanied by the tune "What I Did for Love" from *A Chorus Line* and John Connally put the

endless reporter questions about the Republican platform into perfect perspective when he told Tom Brokaw of NBC News, "A week from now, everyone will forget what's in that platform."
July 16, 1980

The Man Who

WILL THE TV reporters please clear the aisles?

Walter Cronkite: THIS is WAL-ter CRON-kite, coming to you from the Democratic National Convention, an event that will go down in history as the last convention to be covered by me. And if I may, this reporter would like to inject a personal note. I want to thank all the millions and millions of people who've sent flowers, candy and pictures of Dan Rather with mustaches drawn on them. And now let's go to the podium for the invocation.

VOICE FROM PODIUM: The invocation for today's session will be given by his Eminence, Walter Cronkite.

WALTER CRONKITE: Oh, jeepers! I almost forgot. While I go down to the podium, let's go to Dan Rather on the floor. Come in, million-dollar Danny.

DAN RATHER: Thank you, Walter, and if I may inject a personal note here, I would just like to say, that was one of the finest introductions of a floor reporter you have given in your long and distinguished career. Yes, Walter, you've been sitting on your duff in that anchor chair for many years—many, many, many years. Oh, a great, great, great many years!

WALTER CRONKITE: Can it, Dan. Let's hear some of that million-dollar reporting of yours.

DAN: From here, Walter, it looks like this convention is going to be one of the great stories of the century, perhaps the most exciting political event I personally have ever covered, and of course, I've covered many exciting events, from the Vietnam War to the Freedom March to my own personal attack on Mount Whatsis in Afghanistan. Whew, that was a nail-biter, I'll tell you. Back to you, Walter.

WALTER (from podium): . . . forever and ever, Amen. And now, let's go to Phil Jones.

PHIL JONES: Walter, Senator Kennedy has just made a speech conceding the nomination to President Carter. Kennedy said he will support Carter absolutely and will do everything he can to contribute to the ticket. Of course, Walter, this is obviously a thinly veiled attempt to undermine the Carter candidacy and gather more support for Kennedy. And there are questions about Chappaquiddick that remain unanswered. Now over to Harry Reasoner.

HARRY REASONER: Walter, from where I stand, there's an antiseptic look to the proceedings, a blinding fluorescent glow and a lot of quiet standing around.

WALTER: That's because you've locked yourself in the men's room, dummy. And now, here with me in the booth are President Carter, Rosalynn Carter, Senator Kennedy, Bob Hope and My Mother.

BARBARA WALTERS (outside Walter's booth): Walter! You let me in there this minute or I'll hold my breath till I turn blue!

PRESIDENT CARTER: Thank you, Walter, and may I say on behalf of all of us how much we're going to miss you here in the anchor booth you have filled so well. I'm not sure we Democrats are going to be able to hold a convention without you.

WALTER: Thank you, Mr. President. And now let's go down to the podium to see if anything is happening there.

VOICE FROM PODIUM: . . . and so I move that we disband the Democratic Party and make Ronald Reagan our unanimous choice for President of the United—

WALTER: No, nothing happening there. Let's go back to Moneybags Rather on the floor. Dan, does this look like an open convention to you, or are we going to have to create our own conflicts in order to keep the viewers interested?

DAN: Walter, I'll answer that in my own inimitable way in a moment, but first, if I may, I'd like to say that your interview just now with President Carter was one of the finest of your long and distinguished career. Why, in all the dozens and dozens of years you've been—

WALTER: Dan, start earning that cool five mill, will you please?

DAN: Well, Walter, I have a delegate here who has given me one of the great scoops of all my days in journalism. Would you repeat what you told me to the cameras, sir?

DELEGATE: Sure, Mr. Rather. But first, would you autograph this funny hat for my wife and kiddies?

DAN: Yes, yes; please, you're toying with my dignity.

DELEGATE: Oh, okay. Anyway, I have it on good authority that it's going to be Lady Bird Johnson on the first ballot.

DAN: What a scoop! What a story! That's truly one of the most extraordinary things I have ever heard. This is one of the great moments in broadcast journalism! Why, to think that I, Dan Rather, who braved the hellfires of Afghanistan—

WALTER: Dan! Dan!

DAN: Yes, Walter?

WALTER: Ask him where he heard that.

DELEGATE: Oh, I heard it from that guy over there.

DAN: That guy over there?

DELEGATE: Yeah, that guy over there from ABC News.

DAN: Back to you, Walter.

WALTER: Well, let's pop back to the podium and see if anything is happening there.

VOICE FROM PODIUM: . . . and so I put it to you, ladies and gentlemen, that there is one man and only one man who can lead this nation into the greatness of the '80s, and you all know who I mean. Yes, the grandfather of our country, Walter Cronkite!

DELEGATES IN UNISON: We want Walter! We want Walter! Four more years! Four more years!

WALTER: And that's the way it seems to be. For CBS News, this is Walter Cronkite saying Good night and good luck.

August 10, 1980

The Light That Failed

WHEN JOHNNY CARSON preceded a joke in his monologue by noting that the Hollywood actors' strike could delay the start of the new TV season, his studio audience cheered. They could scarcely contain their joy.

"Aw, that only happened once," claims an NBC publicist in Burbank. "For thirty years the American public has looked forward to picnics on Labor Day and new fall television shows."

Right. People are mad with anticipation over the arrivals of programs like *Flamingo Road, Too Close for Comfort* and *Enos*. Really, what is a new TV season anyway but a new crop of bobbing bazooms? Doing without it isn't exactly the ultimate form of deprivation.

In fact, if it didn't have the unfortunate effect of putting thousands of people out of work, it would be sort of nice to forgo a new fall TV season this year. And next year, and the year after that and—wait a minute, we feel a fantasy sequence coming on. Burble, burble, burble. . . .

Jan. 1, 1981—America ended its first year in three decades without a fall TV season yesterday as a strike by the Screen Actors Guild in Hollywood moved into its sixth month.

Networks report having received 122 letters of protest since the season failed to materialize in September, but at least half were the result of a letter-writing campaign organized by Spelling-Goldberg Productions, sources said.

Meanwhile, a rash of severe overcrowding and near-riots tore through the museums, concert halls and libraries in city after city, as a wave of literacy swept the land. *Good Housekeeping* magazine said the sales of macramé materials have spiraled to such an extent that yarn hoarding could reach epidemic proportions, and thousands of married couples were surprised to discover that they'd given birth to three or four children over the past several years.

Toy stores recorded a consumer stampede on Scrabble and Monopoly games, now back-ordered by the millions. Spokesman for the Census Bureau say divorces have increased 89 percent as TV viewing has plummeted; births are up 225 percent, and the sale of aquariums has skyrocketed overnight into the major growth industry of the '80s.

And a 30-year decline in scores on Scholastic Aptitude Tests appears suddenly to have been reversed. . . .

Mar. 31, 1981—The TV season ended today without ever having begun, as striking actors continued to keep production of entertainment programs shut down for the three commercial networks.

The A. C. Nielsen Company, still in business, released its list of the Top 10–rated shows for the year. They were (1) *Crockett's Victory Garden*, PBS; (2) *ABC Monday Night Football;* (3) *ABC Tuesday Night Football;* (4) *ABC Wednesday Night Football;* (5) *ABC Thursday Night Football;* (6) *ABC Friday Night Football;* (7) *ABC Saturday Night Soccer;* (8) *60 Minutes*, CBS; (9) President Reagan's Inauguration and (10) The Impeachment of President Reagan (all networks). . . .

Dec. 7, 1985–Japan declared war on the United States for the second time in this century today following the collapse of the Sony Corporation, a mainstay of its economy and a victim of the American public's continuing lack of interest in television. . . .

Sept. 8, 1990—An uneasy quiet settled over Hollywood today as the nation began its tenth year without a fall TV season.

Stacks of antique television sets were lighted into bonfires in cities throughout the country, in many cases accompanied by the singing and dancing of citizens gone mad with merriment.

Among those hardest hit by the death of television have been psychiatrists, religious cults, fast-food restaurants, the makers of fanny-hugging blue jeans, Mr. Whipple and the police, who report that violent crime has dropped to almost unmeasurable levels.

Marriage counselors have never been in greater demand, and contract bridge instructors now command up to $100 an hour for their coveted services. But television critics have proved unemployable, and most were sent off to homes long ago.

Walter Annenberg has agreed to sell *TV Guide* to Clay Felker for $755.32.

White House press secretary Jodie Foster said today that President Fred Silverman has called upon citizens to remain calm and that plans for converting Los Angeles into a miniature golf course are nearing completion.

But he failed to end more than a decade of national speculation and public curiosity by again refusing to reveal "who shot J.R."

August 28, 1980

January 20, 1981

"IT IS CERTAINLY ONE of the great dramatic days in American history," said Walter Cronkite on CBS, and it was one of the most television-intensive days as well, as networks scrambled to cover the inauguration of Ronald Reagan and the agonizingly overdue finale to the Iranian hostage crisis.

There were so many stunning pictures and dramatic developments that one risked media-intake overload, a deadening and dizzying sensation, just watching it all unfold. Networks bounced from Washington to Frankfurt to Algiers to New York to Plains, Georgia, in the effort to keep up. What resulted was the most global inaugural day ever. Perhaps not since the funeral of John F. Kennedy have Americans kept so diligent a vigil before their television sets.

Much of the imagery was indelible, often sublime:

• Tears streaming down the faces of hostage families who were caught by TV cameras as they learned from their television sets of the hostages' freedom.

• The hostages themselves, finally glimpsed on the rainy runway, as they changed planes in Algiers—one man later toasting the camera with a glass of fruit juice, another flashing the "V for victory" sign, others looking dazed and blank.

• Jimmy Carter choking up as he stepped off a helicopter and spoke to the raincoat-clad citizens of Plains about the end of the hostage crisis, with WELCOME HOME signs flapping in the breeze nearby.

• Reagan's voice going husky when he emotionally recalled the words in the diary of a World War I soldier killed in action, words about duty, sacrifice and higher causes.

• ABC's split screen showing Reagan signing his first presidential act—a federal hiring freeze—and, simultaneously, Carter's jet taxiing on the runway before taking the country boy home.

• Jody Powell's exhausted profile, bleary-eyed but unbowed, in the Oval Office, in the early morning hours, as word came that the last major snag had been cleared.

• Warren Christopher, negotiator for the United States, presiding over a brief ceremony at the Algiers airport, the approximate equivalent of a small-town smoker in the global village.

No one should need proof of the power of television at this point, but if they did, the Iranians may have offered it by delaying the release of the hostages, after delay upon delay, until after Carter was out of the White House and Reagan had finished his inaugural address.

It was enough to make Walter Cronkite's dander hit new heights.

"I try to remain the cool correspondent, impartial and unaffected by events," said Cronkite of the Iranian delay, "but it seems like the most uncivilized final touch to an uncivilized performance that I can imagine. . . . They seem to dangle this in front of us, deliberately making it as difficult as possible." He called the Iranians "diabolical."

CBS correspondent Bruce Morton said of Reagan that because of the hostage crisis, "he's not even the lead story on his own inauguration day."

But what a day and night it turned out to be.

In its final hours the hostage crisis turned into a live, real-life, international thriller. Television coverage became especially gripping when the networks let their technologies lead them by the nose. Last night, all three ran a sensational 90-minute broadcast relayed here by satellite from Algerian television.

On CBS, this installment of the hostage serial began with dimly viewed jets moving about on the runway in Algiers, with correspondent John Blackstone in the dark as to which plane, if any, contained the released hostages. A camera stared for long minutes through flagpoles at a plane that turned out to be the wrong one.

"We do have a plane now," said Blackstone excitedly to anchorman Dan Rather in New York. "Yes, there is a plane at the end of the runway." But that plane took off and flew away. Then, still another appeared in the distance and moved toward the camera. This was it. "Here they come, Dan," Blackstone said.

There were many more nervous minutes of suspense, made all the more nerve-rattling by the noise of jet engines, which came through the space warp of the satellite relay sounding like some weird sci-fi whine. "One never knows whether to keep talking or just let that picture of the aircraft door speak for itself," Rather said. As usual, in television, the choice was made to keep talking.

Rather was seeing the live feed from Algeria at the same time as the rest of the country, and as had happened before during the hostage crisis, journalists and viewers became partners in a communal vigil.

NBC occasionally interrupted shots of the hostages for shots of hostage families watching the hostages. On ABC, Frank Reynolds apologized for the fact that he had no such pictures on his network. He complained that the closed-circuit telecasting of last night's inaugural balls to sites in 41 states tied up telephone lines and made remote pickups impossible for ABC. But that only made ABC's coverage less gimmicky and cluttered than that of the other networks. This was nothing to gripe about.

Undoubtedly scenes from the telecast would be excerpted on later newscasts and soon pass into the popular iconography of the '80s. But nothing ever will be able precisely to equal the exhilarating tension of watching the spectacle as it happened. And that included waiting out 30 minutes of air time in which there was nothing on the screen but a motionless, mysterious airplane.

There was still another story vying for air time—and helping produce what may have been the greatest news bottleneck in the history of electronic journalism—and that was both the retreat from power and the vindication brought by the end of the crisis for former president Jimmy Carter.

Rumors persisted through the morning that Carter would go on the air and make a speech announcing the end of the crisis. But the time for that came and went. Finally all three networks cut away from the Reagan inaugural parade in midafternoon to catch Jimmy Carter's speech to citizens of Plains, the first time he publicly acknowledged that the hostages were out of Iran.

Much earlier, ABC News president Roone Arledge hatched an eleventh-hour brainstorm to record the waning moments of the Carter administration on tape, and got approval first from former press secretary Jody Powell and then from Carter himself, on the condition that nothing be aired without Carter's permission. At 3:25 yesterday afternoon, ABC viewers saw a tape of Carter on a white House phone learning from G. William Miller, former treasury secretary, that the agreement with Iran had at last been finalized.

Viewers also saw former secretary of state Edmund Muskie rush over to congratulate Carter.

The day was filled with high-powered drama and instant history made to order for television, and it can't be said that Reagan was really upstaged by all of this raw TV journalism. His inaugural speech was tailor-made for TV and even included TV directions—which only CBS followed fully—implicitly calling at one point for shots of such nationalist symbols as the Washington Monument, the Jefferson Memorial and Arlington Cemetery. People watching at home saw the speech as Reagan conceived it for TV; people standing there in person at the Capitol saw a mere replica.

After a weekend of overcovering prospects for an end to the hostage crisis, the networks tended to undercover it as Inauguration Day began. In part there may have been a fear of getting burned by overreaction to hints of hope. Throughout the morning, correspondents judiciously hedged on each new tiny millimeter of apparent progress.

The hostages "should be leaving Teheran before too long," said Tom Brokaw on NBC's early-morning *Today* show. Reporter John Palmer said, "Things look very optimistic at this point that the hostages will indeed be free by the time Jimmy Carter leaves office at noon today."

Just after 9 A.M. on ABC, Steve Bell reported, "Well, it could happen any minute—freedom for the American hostages in Iran." Reporter David Ensor offered as proof the fact that Carter was then being made up for a television address.

Moments later, as Reagan left Blair House for a church service, CBS reporter Bill Plante shouted out a question about the hostages. Reagan said he understood that "the plane's at the end of the runway." A few minutes later, Dan Rather reported on CBS—"this just in"—that the plane was at the end of the runway. He didn't know that Reagan had already broken that scoop on Rather's own network.

Then as Reagan returned to Blair House after the prayer service, Plante shouted at him again: "We're told the plane is on the runway." Reagan was the one who'd told him.

When Reagan left Blair House for the White House, there was Plante, again screaming out "Governor!" from behind a police line. To put another perspective on the way information was flowing, Vice Pesident George Bush told reporters that, in effect, all he'd known about the hostage crisis was what he saw on TV. "That's where we got all our information up to now," he said, about a half-hour after the ceremonies had ended at the Capitol.

During the day, television news was shown off at its best and worst. At its worst, there were the inevitable raids on those poor hostage families, who've spent months in a perpetually—and, literally—wired state, with tiny mikes pinned to their clothes and zillions of watts flooding their faces. Dan Rather holds the dubious distinction of getting first to former hostage Richard Queen after the breakthrough became a fact."Richard Queen, what are your feelings at this moment?" he asked. Oh no—not again!

Some members of hostage families pleaded for shelter from the media for a period of time after the hostages return. They'll need all the luck in the world to bring that one about.

Seldom have the wonders of satellite technology been so dazzlingly deployed as during the day, when a network would skip about from Washington to New York to Wiesbaden to Frankfurt to Algiers, sometimes within a matter of moments. And yet Walter Cronkite was unable, twice, to make contact with reporter Phil Jones even though Jones and Cronkite were both at the Capitol—Cronkite in his booth—separated by only about 60 yards, Cronkite estimated.

After the second attempt failed, Cronkite said, "Well, Phil, the only thing I can suggest is to get on that plane with Cyrus Vance and go to Wiesbaden" in order to get on the air. Because of Cronkite's supportive, rallying-point presence, the CBS coverage had the most character. ABC had the most inventiveness and responsiveness and the most alert hostage coverage.

NBC had John Chancellor and Roger Mudd sitting as far apart in an anchor booth as it may be anchorly possible to sit. Immediately after the swearing-in, Chancellor dawdled away precious minutes interviewing, at a deferential distance, Jimmy Stewart, who was not terribly illuminating. This was one of the wackiest news-judgment calls of the day.

But nobody can be right all the time. Because it was involved in the all-important business of commercials, CBS missed much of, and had to join in progress, Carter's emotional departure at Andrews Air Force Base. CBS missed with another commercial Amy's tears and Jimmy's and Rosalynn's final wave goodbye. CBS missed the entrance of Nancy Reagan and Rosalynn Carter onto the Capitol podium before the swearing-in. It was time for a commercial.

238 / ON THE AIR!

Of course, there is no such thing as decorum on television. Coverage of the inauguration was repeatedly interrupted to sell toilet paper, toilet-bowl cleaner, dog food, a legal clinic offering cheap divorces, *People* magazine and other such trash —none of it trashier than promotional ads for NBC and ABC prime-time shows.

And though Cronkite cut his usual stalwart figure, he had some indecorous moments himself when, true to his own tradition, he didn't realize it was time to shut his big avuncular mouth. He was the only network correspondent who chose to keep yammering right through the playing of the hymn "God of Our Fathers" by the Marine Band. He almost spoke over the singing of the National Anthem and drowned out Chief Justice Warren Burger asking Reagan if he was ready for the oath of office and Reagan's response that he was.

Ironically, commentator Bill Moyers raved at one point on CBS about how TV pictures can carry their own commentary and dramatic impact (this was a day overloaded with those). But even though correspondent Bob Schieffer murmured an amen to that, no one put on the brakes when it came to blabbing.

ABC's Frank Reynolds ruined director Chet Forte's beautifully composed montage of Washington sights (during the hymn) by following it with encomiums about how wonderful it was. Reynolds proved one of the least valuable of inaugural guides, limited to such insights as "There's Happy Rockefeller!" and, on the transfer of power, "What a tremendous thing it is." With the crisis apparently over, he said, "What a great burden is lifted."

He even seemed eager to throw platitudinous water over the lively commentaries of George F. Will and Sander Vanocur. Will said the unspeakable delay in releasing the hostage plane was "just the final episode of Iran manipulating the United States through television."

This is an aspect of the crisis that television has been reluctant to investigate all along. Reynolds dropped Will's point with a thud.

A climax of sorts came at 11:38 A.M. when ABC's Ted Koppel

said that UPI had issued a two-word dispatch: "Hostages free." Cronkite soon followed him, attributing it to a UPI "flash." It remained for Ted Turner's fledgling Cable News Network—which had been ahead of the commercial networks several times during the weekend—to wring the ultimate drama out of the event by flashing on the screen "UPI REPORTS HOSTAGES FREED" just as a Marine was singing, from "America the Beautiful," the line "who more than self their country loved."

It was a heart-stopping day of American television.
January 21, 1981

The Late Bloomer

THE MAN MOST RESPONSIBLE for the success of *ABC News Nightline* is the Ayatollah Khomeini.

The man second most responsible is Ted Koppel.

Were it not for the hostage crisis and ABC's commitment to broadcast nightly reports on it, *Nightline* would perhaps never have become a permanent network fixture, as it did last March. This week it expanded from 20 to 30 minutes, and in April goes from four nights a week to five.

This man Koppel—short, pugnacious, cocky, droll, 40—has helped pull off a double garbanzo: first that a news show would give Johnny Carson a run for the late-night ratings (occasionally beating him, never getting creamed by him) and second that ABC News of all Newses would come up with a broadcast this smart, classy and relatively schlockless.

Nightline represents the most successful programming initiative in ABC News history. Executive producer William Lord can take bows, but Koppel gets a medal. He's moved to front and center of network news.

He's a smoothie. He's a pro. He's a rocket. What makes *Nightline* click is Koppel's bull's-eye interviewing style, a verbal and rhetorical combination of Sugar Ray Leonard and Mikhail Baryshnikov—a succession of jabs, rejoinders and judicious-to-delicious interruptions: Koppel a cappella.

Koppel has jousted with Jesse Jackson, deciphered Carl Sagan, jawed with John Ehrlichman, tussled with Ted Turner, harassed Harold Brown and exchanged parries and thrusts with other guests as diverse as Muhammad Ali, Leonard Matlovich and the Imperial Wizard of the KKK.

He confesses, though, that he has an "electronic advantage." All guests, even those in ABC's Washington studios, are wired to Koppel's voice by an earpiece. He can use it to head them off: "When you have that little thing stuck in your ear, it's very difficult to keep talking while I'm trying to interrupt you . . . when I'm droning in your ear, right there in your head."

"The challenge of the live interview every night is what I particularly love about doing *Nightline*," Koppel says. "It can go wrong, and it can go right, and either way it never allows you to get complacent."

Complacency does not seem a likely pitfall for the hard-driven Koppel. Even chatting fairly casually in his office, he keeps eternal vigil for openings and vulnerabilities: "I think you're phrasing that question incorrectly." "I must tell you that I couldn't disagree more with that analysis." "I think that's an outdated question." Koppel does everything but give you a report card.

On the question of giving thanks to Iran for the success, even the existence, of *Nightline*, Koppel admits to being "testy." He was a regular contributor to *America Held Hostage*, the late-night alarmism that grew into *Nightline*, and later took over anchorage from Frank Reynolds. Koppel says, "It is as ludicrous to suggest that we have ridden to success on the backs of the hostages as it would be to say that David Halberstam rode on the back of the Vietnamese people or that anyone who writes about or deals with any tragedy—Ted Sorensen's book about Jack Kennedy—has done that.

"That's nonsense. That really is.

"I don't think that's a worthy question."

Koppel is sitting at his desk in his shirt sleeves and orangey camera makeup, eating a gooey chocolate-chip cookie. A Chinese flag hangs on the wall nearby, a souvenir given him by U.S. Marines at the "Red Ass Bar" in China, where Koppel spent many jade moons on assignment.

Unique in the high-priced world of glamour-boy network anchors, Koppel does not have an agent to wheel and deal for him. And he claims to be embarrassed, when asked, about the enormous amounts of money he and his colleagues are paid.

"It bothers me a great deal." Pause. "I really feel very uncomfortable with these things because it sounds self-serving, and remember, *you* asked the question."

Pause and recoil.

"I think it's outrageous! I think the salaries are outrageous, and I think the kinds of lives that we can lead as a result are outrageous. I feel very guilty about having so much when there are so many people who have so little. It's easy for people to say, 'Well, fine, don't accept a monumental salary,' but this is an industry of perceptions, and it is an industry in which your influence, your clout, the degree of input you have as a newsman depend very much on the perception everyone has of you—how you are perceived to be perceived by the powers that be.

"There are a few ways that kind of thing can be interpreted, and one of the easiest ways is by the salary that they pay you. Therefore it becomes dogma overnight that if CBS pays Dan Rather eight million dollars for a five-year contract, that they therefore have invested not only a great deal of money but a great deal of CBS's future in his future.

"That translates into immediate power."

Does Koppel want immediate power? "I do have a great interest in exercising power—I hope for the good. Therefore, as embarrassed as I am by it—and I genuinely am; it bothers me a lot—*I'm gonna go for every last buck I can get*, and then try to do good with that money."

He says he and his wife give a lot of money to charity.

Koppel is not exactly charming, but he is disarming. He is liable to greet a perfectly amiable TV critic with "How are you, you sleazy bastard?" One night he appeared—almost directly opposite himself—on NBC's taped *Tomorrow* show with the indefatigably incorrigible Tom Snyder.

"This is a very boring interview," Koppel complained to Snyder at one point. "Get obnoxious!" Later: "Can I finish? God! Such an aggressive interviewer!"

And then Koppel turned the tables and started interviewing a flustered Snyder on his feud with Rona Barrett. Snyder said the matter would be settled soon. "Oh," said Koppel, "so poor old Rona's out, eh?"

Koppel also surprised Snyder with an astute impersonation of William F. Buckley, Jr. Impressions are a hobby. "I'm told I do a very good Henry Kissinger," he says. "My wife likes my Cary Grant. There are quite a few others—Adlai Stevenson, but that's dating myself. Oh, and Ronald Colman." (Doing Colman): "Benita, my pet . . ."

Born in Britain, Koppel was not naturalized as an American citizen until 1963, the same year he joined ABC News—which was then considered, he says, "the doormat of the industry." Wizardly Roone Arledge was supposed to change all that; but Koppel was among those repelled by Arledge's early splashes in the pond and the Rooney Tunes approach he brought to the news. Now Koppel sings to the skies the praises of Arledge and ABC News.

"I think I am as conscious of ABC's weaknesses as anyone," he says, "But the perception that you in particular have of ABC as a news organization is outdated."

"Couldn't we say the perception 'some people' have?" he is asked.

"No, I mean you. I don't mean some people, I mean you."

"Was there a time when my perceptions of ABC News were correct?"

"Sure."

Koppel concedes that not all of Arledge's decisions are pips. When he turned over 20 minutes of *World News Tonight* to the Son of Sam case, "I think that was an error in judgment," but he says Arledge has made other decisions since "for which he deserves great praise—Iran being one of them." Also, it was "stupid" of Arledge to insist that a post-presidential-debate report on *Nightline* be extended after Koppel had successfully wrapped it up. "Yeah, it was stupid. That particular instance was stupid.

"But most of the time he makes very good suggestions or will simply say, 'Let it go,' as he did the night after the election." This was the night when *Nightline* and Koppel went from merely good to brilliant; Koppel interviewed the leader of Moral Majority and such electoral victims as former senator George McGovern, and Arledge extended the air time by 45 minutes because it was such a superior show. It may have been the best thing done on the evangelical right, and most of it was impromptu, live and electric.

"I think that show was a milestone in television news broadcasting," says Koppel.

Ted Koppel is a beacon of dignity at ABC News and for some reason a personality that, though sober and sometimes pompous, appeals to those folks at home. "I like him, and I tried to hire him once," says a top producer at another network. "He's a helluva reporter and a bright fellow."

Koppel himself seems slightly mystified at the way he's zoomed. "I did the Saturday news for two years, and it somehow managed to fall short of being a runaway national success. I was diplomatic correspondent for nine years, and I'm amazed at the number of people who come up to me now and say, 'Boy, you're wonderful, you're terrific, you're fantastic, where have you been, where did you work before you went to ABC?' When I tell them I've been with ABC over seventeen years now, they say, 'How come I never saw you?'"

But it's Koppel's year. He'll be plastered all over national magazines in the coming weeks.

Almost all success in television boils down to the wearability of personalities. Would Koppel be upset if he found out that most people watch the show not because of its journalistic content but because they feel comfortable with him? "It would bother me if I thought they were watching because they thought I was devastatingly handsome, but I'm confident that's not the case."

Indeed, many are the viewers who've written or called to

say Koppel reminds them of Howdy Doody, the late great marionette, or *Mad* magazine mascot Alfred E. Neuman (in person, his face doesn't look quite so quirkily asymmetrical). Whatever they think, it's likely that millions and millions of them don't really tune in *ABC News Nightline.* They tune in Ted Koppel.
January 8, 1981

February Creeps

THE NOVEMBER SWEEPS were really the November Peeps. The February Sweeps have turned into the February Creeps. These peak ratings-taking months (the other one is May) don't exactly bring out the best in the networks. In fact, the networks seem more determined than usual to appeal to the worst in viewers.

If it isn't sex, it's violence. Or it's sex and violence, also known in television as bread and butter.

During one particularly yechhy week of previewing shows on videotape in my office, I had to watch a child molester at work in the CBS *Fallen Angel,* see Sally Struthers tortured at length and threatened with rape in the CBS *Gun in the House,* watch a syndicated documentary, *Mom, I Want to Come Home Now,* about teen-age prostitutes and hustlers.

You certainly don't come away from programming like that with a rosy view of life. If television is America's escapism, how much worse could reality be? In fact, most of the programs are not realistic, only sensationalistic. And luckier people don't even have to watch TV to get this impression. They can just check out the way the networks advertise their shows in *TV Guide.*

In these ads you can see clearly which whims, and lusts, the networks appeal to in viewers—what they think we're all dying to see. From this barometer one gets a profile of how the networks regard the viewing audience: as a thrill-seeking mob of insatiable voyeurs. Whether shows deliver what they promise is irrelevant; the ads reflect what networks think will lure the largest audiences.

Mostly, of course, the bait is ooh-la-la. For example: "Stella Rated 'X'! Accused of making porno movies, Stella strikes back with a 'topless' commercial!" (Ad for NBC's *Harper Valley P.T.A.*) "Blackmail in a sex clinic! Lobo, Perkins, Birdie and the ladies expose their sex lives to uncover a vicious criminal!" (*Lobo*, NBC). "Male models who'll sell you the clothes right off their backs!" (*That's My Line*, CBS). "Male Belly Dancing!" (*Real People*, NBC). "Sexy Super Ladies Stack Up!" (*Women Who Rate a "10,"* NBC.)

And, "a gorgeous fashion model who's (are you ready?) 12" (*That's My Line*). Am I ready? No.

The shows may be like harmless titillation taken one at a time, but the month has been inundated with them. Watching prime-time TV is like being trapped in Sleaze City's tackiest honky-tonk. One gets a warped and depressing view of what it means to be alive.

Coy, suggestive "secrets" have been very big in dramas and action shows:

"Lisa is pregnant. She's come to her mother for help. She's about to learn the shocking secret her mother is hiding!" (*The Choice* on CBS). "Mary Ellen finds her husband alive! What terrible secret is he hiding?" (*The Waltons*, CBS). "Magnum uncovers a lovely woman's secret in a dark alley! Her shocking past is closing in on her—and Magnum's in the crusher!" (*Magnum, P.I.*, CBS).

Naturally, there's violence aplenty in these ads, since the networks have to fill in the spaces between the sexy scenes:

"Tucker and Gloria on the run! And guess who's on their trail: The cops and a real live killer!" (*Foul Play*, ABC). "To stop his murder investigation, a gang beats up Sheriff Pusser. When he recovers, Pusser swears revenge... and justice!" (*Walking Tall*, NBC). "Big Red's gunning for revenge. Can J.D. and Will cut him down to size?" (*Concrete Cowboys*, CBS).

For the networks, the object all sublime is to offer what the world needs now, sex and violence in the same show (it's so convenient that way; you don't have to shop around). This holds out the tasty prospect—or so they think—of something for everybody:

"Buck trapped on co-ed 'Devil's Island'!" (*Buck Rogers*, NBC). "Dan cracks down on 'teen-age' sex extortion ring!" (*Vega$*, ABC). "Lady Truckers Behind Bars! BJ sets up a football game to free the seven luscious lady truckers from prison" (*BJ and the Bear*, NBC). "Michael's getting something on his boss—using every trick in the book! Fallon's promiscuous past could destroy her marriage to Jeff" (*Dynasty*, ABC).

The February 13 episode of NBC's *Nero Wolfe* mystery series was entitled "The Mystery of the Beautiful Woman." The February 20 episode is called "The Mystery of the Playboy's Mistress." NBC also ballyhoos of its *Gangster Chronicles* that Charles "Lucky" Luciano "had the dream—and a mistress who was a hooker." But NBC's *Quincy* takes the cake for cramming the largest number of hotsy-totsies into a single smarmy come-on: "Cocaine, a courier and crooked cops! Quincy suspects the murder of a gorgeous stewardess was really 86 percent double-dealing!"

To crown all this with a note of dumb irony, NBC is promoting this month's shows as "February's Finest." Whom are they kidding? The next time network executives boast about how they've enriched American life and how they give people what they want, we really ought to remind them about the February Creeps.

February 19, 1981

Trauma and Instant Replay

THE SHOTS, THE PANIC, the confusion, the anguish, the shock, the gathering of clues, the search for the truth. It was all on television yesterday as the networks covered the assassination attempt on President Reagan.

Suddenly viewers and television were plunged together into a nightmare scene that recalled November 22, 1963, when Walter Cronkite, choking back tears, said that President John F. Kennedy was dead. But if this is still the age of television, it is now also the age of instant replay. And so throughout the afternoon the networks played over and over their tapes of the shooting.

They slowed the tape down. They advanced it frame by frame. They stopped it and discussed angles of trajectory. The camera zoomed in for a close-up of the presidential press secretary, James S. Brady, as he lay stricken and bleeding on the sidewalk, and then, at 5:13 P.M., viewers heard Dan Rather of CBS News say, "It is now confirmed that Jim Brady has died."

Thirteen minutes later a White House spokesman on the air live said the report of Brady's death was "untrue." Rather said, "There is some confusion." Later, Chris Wallace of NBC News reported on the air that the President was undergoing "open-heart surgery"—also untrue; a White House adviser had to deny the report after Wallace repeated it. Again, as in past crises, the viewer was becoming privy to the news-gathering process.

For all the sophistication of the technology, much of the reporting was still confused and tentative. The story unfolded step by step, sometimes contradictorily—like a grim thriller —throughout the afternoon.

You were compelled to remain vigilant at the screen in fear and fascination. No matter how many times the scene at the hotel was replayed—Reagan waving a farewell, shots ringing out, onlookers scattering, the Secret Service agent pushing the President into the back seat of the presidential limousine, the blond hair of the alleged assailant glimpsed within a madding crowd of security men, the machine gun held aloft by a tense agent—it retained its eerie, mordant, chilling power.

An elaborate, globe-shrinking communications system was conveying, as it has before in American history, a primitive act of brutality. At the same time, it became apparent that we can live in a day of instant and total information and still find ourselves maddeningly in the dark.

Thus when Secretary of State Alexander M. Haig was asked at the White House about Brady's condition at 4:14 P.M., he told reporters, live on network television, "I just saw on television what you saw and it sounds serious." Television has to some extent equalized access to information, or to misinformation, as the case may be.

When he first came on the air for CBS News at 2:55 P.M., anchorman Dan Rather assured viewers at least six times within five minutes that President Reagan had not been hit by any of the five shots then believed to have been fired outside the hotel. The President was "unscathed" and "not hit" by the gunfire, Rather told viewers. It was stated as fact.

But at 3:11 P.M., ABC News reported that Reagan had been struck by a bullet but was in "stable" condition. At 3:12, Richard Roth of CBS News reported that the President "was hit in the left side of the chest," by a bullet. Rather, who later laid the blame for the erroneous early report on White House spokesman Karna Small, told viewers that such confusion was "frequently the case in the early stages of a story . . . particularly when you have an attempt on the President's life."

A moment later, Roger Mudd of NBC News said the Associated Press and United Press International "both say the President was shot in the chest." Soon CBS News had a devastating close-up of cracks made by a bullet in a window of the presidential limousine, parked outside George Washington University Hospital. At 4:23, NBC froze a frame of its tape to reveal what appeared to be the handgun used in the shooting of the President of the United States.

For all the abundance of visual detail and electronic documentation of the event, the confusions in reporting and a suspicion that, somehow, darker complications were being withheld combined to evoke troublesome echoes of Dallas and the ensuing years of conspiracy rumors—a sense of dread and déjà vu.

There were conflicting reports throughout the afternoon not

only about the condition of Reagan and Brady but also on the caliber of the bullet in the gun fired (it volleyed back and forth from .22 to .38), the identity of the other men struck by bullets, whether or not the President would undergo surgery, whether or not the bullet remained in his body, the number of shots fired and other details.

After the Haig statement, Mudd told viewers, "There's an awful lot of information being passed hand to hand and being circulated all over Washington." Much of it made it to the air, later to be corrected or amended. This is what happens in a high-density telecommunicative society.

ABC News was first on the air with a bulletin on the shooting at 2:34 P.M., followed by CBS News at 2:37 and NBC News at 2:38. ABC News was also first to report that the President had indeed been hit by a bullet during the incident.

Rather seemed preoccupied during the coverage with keeping calm—he kept repeating that the President had not been hit during the early minutes of coverage—and in showering with praise the Secret Service agent who pushed President Reagan into the shelter of the limousine. "You ask where all the heroes have gone; here's one," Rather said.

Rather's efforts to promote calm became almost a kind of hysteria of their own.

In effect, the nation became a newsroom at this point; newsmakers, reporters and the public were seeing the raw materials of the story at the same time. One saw the President smiling as he left the hotel, heard the shots, saw the melee that followed and heard frantic cries of police, Secret Service agents and presidential aides:

"A handkerchief! A handkerchief!" called a man cradling Brady's bleeding head in his hand. "Get back! Get back!" another man shouted. "Get a patrol car! Get a patrol car in here!" "Let the ambulance in here; come on, back up, please!"

One network camera turned to follow a woman, believed to be Brady's secretary, as she wept, then ran across the street holding a hand over her mouth. These incredible moments were repeated throughout the afternoon and became no less horrible with each replay. It may be that in the age of replay, it takes several showings for something like this to sink in.

During some of the replays, the network anchormen narrated the footage, talking to engineers playing the tape as well as to viewers. "Stop it," said Reynolds to the unseen engineer as the shooting was played back in slow motion and the figure of President Reagan could be seen hunching forward. "Keep going," said Reynolds, and the tape resumed, under examination as if by a national jury looking at evidence.

As the grim afternoon turned to gloomy evening, the mood was unexpectedly changed with the live appearance on all three networks of Dr. Dennis S. O'Leary, George Washington University Hospital spokesman, who fielded reporters' questions on the President's condition and hailed the patient as "a healthy guy." O'Leary was so affable, articulate and reassuring (*People* magazine is certain to write him up) that the briefing became a communal catharsis after an emotionally exhausting day.

O'Leary said the President was out of danger, and went so far as to outline on himself, using his finger, the trajectory of the bullet and the incision made by surgeons. CBS mistakenly cut away from the briefing—to return to Rather and a plastic model of a body with organs spilling out—but the other networks wisely stayed with it.

Of the operation, O'Leary said that the President "certainly sailed through it" and that this was "maybe not medically extraordinary, but just short of that."

Clearly, O'Leary was just what the doctor ordered.

He was followed on ABC by a tape of Maureen Reagan, the President's daughter, reacting to the shooting. Her response was "fury and rage and anger," but just as she became most emotional, ABC cut away, perhaps through a technical fluff. The entire clip was seen later on the Cable News Network. "The American people have got to become angry about the crime in this country," she said.

Ross Simpson, a correspondent for the Mutual Radio Network, managed to sneak into the hospital with Brady's wife,

Sarah, during the afternoon and said later that he was first to report that Brady had suffered "extensive brain damage" and that according to a doctor his chances of survival were "not good." Simpson was finally ejected by the Secret Service and proceeded to brief other reporters on what he had learned. ABC even put him on the air.

Meanwhile, NBC's Chris Wallace reported, completely erroneously, that the President had undergone "open-heart surgery." An NBC News spokesman said later that Wallace had called the report "unconfirmed"; but like the false reports of James Brady's death, it went out over the air to millions and millions of people.

Whether or not the surplus of misinformation doled out yesterday is an inevitable by-product of an information-addicted, ready-access environment remains to be discussed in future days and weeks. There were a few instances of galling tastelessness, a conspicuous one committed by the CBS Television Network, which, in the heat of the developing crucial story, paused for a station break at 3:25.

This gave Washington CBS affiliate WDVM-TV the opportunity to run two jarringly jolly commercials: "Hi-ho, Pimlico!" and "Kenny Rogers' Greatest Hits."

Sam Donaldson of ABC News, under an umbrella outside the hospital, was telling viewers, "So, to recapitulate, it's been one awful afternoon" when the local ABC station, WJLA, crudely cut in for a lengthy report by its own local news crew. It was the most colossal piece of ineptitude evident during the long afternoon.

WDVM also interrupted its network, but only briefly, to relay information the network did not yet have: that President Reagan was "in surgery" at that moment. Three minutes later, Rather gave what he called an "unconfirmed" report that the President was in surgery. Twenty minutes later, Edwin Newman of NBC News said the President already "underwent" surgery. The story on the President's condition continued to vary from moment to moment and from network to network.

Rather could be heard saying to off-camera personnel that he wasn't sure he wanted to report "that" yet, without saying what "that" was. Then he turned to Jed Duvall, who turned in one of the most capable and assured jobs of the day, and said, "Jed, is there anything that you feel confident enough to report?"

There was no choice but to stay tuned—helpless, dazed and, no matter how much information was related, hungry for more.

March 31, 1981

Going Ape

IN *KING KONG*, on the night of Kong's big opening on Broadway, a woman in the audience asks her companion what to expect. He tells her it will be "some kind of gorilla," and she snaps, "Gee, ain't we got enough of them in New York?"

It has been the fate of the noble gorilla to be turned by popular culture into either a synonym for boor or a slobbering lustful monster. But "Gorilla," tonight's *National Geographic Special* on public TV, proves that this private and erudite creature is hardly so low a mammal as once was thought—in contrast to the Hollywood gorilla of *Kong* and other briefly recalled films in which men dressed as gorillas were occupied chiefly with abducting blondes and delivering haymakers to hunters.

The gorilla, with the chimpanzee, is probably "our closest living relative," says narrator E. G. Marshall. Gorillas share with humans such maladies as arthritis, chicken pox, tuberculosis, the common cold and loneliness when separated from their extended families. Gorillas are "shy and gentle" and live in "remarkably stable family groups." They rarely attack people "unless severely provoked," and it is mournfully estimated by some naturalists that they will be extinct in the wild by the end of this century.

What a piece of work is ape. Exceptional footage captures

not only photogenic citizens of the world's declining wild gorilla population, but also some of the gorillas studied in captivity, including the world-famous Koko, who has been taught the sign language of the deaf by Dr. Francine Patterson near San Francisco. Koko holds a child's Viewmaster up to her eyes and changes the picture with the click lever until she loses interest.

The documentary also looks back to Dr. Dian Fossey's stalking of the wild gorilla in Rwanda, Africa, and the cherished companion she found in Digit, a particularly friendly and handsome giant. But Digit was killed in 1977 by poachers; his head was cut off and mounted, and his hands were severed so that they could be turned into decorative ashtrays, all of this netting the poachers about $20.

There is something incomparably sad in seeing the remains of Digit being brought to Fossey on a litter. The Mountain Gorilla Project, which grew out of this tragedy, now finances patrols of the area by armed guards in order to prevent such killings.

Perhaps the most impressive footage was shot at Howletts, a 55-acre British estate turned into an animal sanctuary in 1956 by businessman and nature lover John Aspinall. Twenty gorillas—believed to be the world's largest private collection—romp and cavort in a large enclosed area not only with each other, but also with Aspinall, who can be seen tumbling and roughhousing with a 350-pound male, among others.

Gorillas appear to be intensely social animals. Taken out of captivity and away from contact with a large family unit, a mama gorilla may simply forget how to care for a baby. And so one of the few gorillas to be born in captivity, Toni, dies at the age of 18 days at a Columbus, Ohio, zoo despite the intervention of a human pediatrician.

At a zoo in Basel, Switzerland, Jorg Hess tries experiments designed to alleviate one of the great curses of gorillas isolated in captivity: boredom. The gorilla cage is strewn with strips of paper, the gorillas are allowed back in and they are momentarily diverted by their new toy, one of them wrapping himself up in it like a Christmas present.

Woe unto parents who don't watch this enthralling show with their kids.

Through 15 television seasons, the last six on public TV, the *National Geographic Specials* have been an uncommonly consistent source of illumination and amazement. Since 1976, when the series moved to PBS, Gulf Oil has invested $25 million in the program. Thus it represents a dual rarity: beneficence by an oil company, and a totally successful project initiated by Washington-based bureaucracies.

"Gorillas" is a kind of follow-up to the 1976 "Search for the Great Apes," another of the Geographic's outstanding hours. Barbara Jampel—who wrote, produced and directed "Gorillas"—has kept it from being a provincial view, in that the study of gorillas is not seen merely as a way of learning more about human beings.

Thus the program ends movingly, beautifully even, with a shot of a little boy reaching out for a young gorilla's hand—a sort of cosmic grasp worthy of Stanley Kubrick—while Marshall quotes writer Henry Beston, who wrote of gorillas, "The animal shall not be measured by man. They are not brethren, they are not underlings. They are other nations, caught with ourselves in the net of life and time—fellow prisoners of the splendor and travail of Earth."

April 8, 1981

Jugular Journalism

A BIG FAT SUN is lolling in the morning sky. It isn't even raining. You kiss your spouse, hug your kids, pet your dog and step out the door. And then, suddenly—Whomp! They've got you. Geraldo Rivera has been poised out there—in his Adidas and your bushes—waiting to pounce with a camera crew and half a dozen intimidating questions about your past.

If you think you have an inalienable right not to be thus harassed, some TV journalists would disagree. The "ambush interview," as it's self-explanatorily called, is only one of the so-called "investigative" techniques popular in TV news and themselves investigated last week by *Watching the Watchdog*, a virtually unprecedented one-hour report produced and aired by WBBM-TV, the CBS-owned station in Chicago.

Although it was seen only in the Chicago area, the documentary has precipitated repeated exchanges of accusations between the station and ABC News, whose *20/20* came under the heaviest fire in the report; together these two factions have provided a brand-new journalistic ethical imbroglio—the first in two or three whole days.

"This thing has turned into name-calling, and I don't want to participate," says Scott Craig, executive producer of the WBBM special. "We raised some real issues on that show and they're getting clouded over."

Those real issues, seldom raised on the air, have a lot to do with the way television covers news and the increasing use of sexy, clandestine, hotsy-totsy tactics that may have less to do with getting the story than with turning TV reporters into stars and heroes. Rivera, although the most flagrant example, isn't the only one who seems to have graduated from the Lone Ranger school of communications.

We all feel in our hearts of hearts that nothing pleases Mike Wallace of prestigious CBS News so much as when he and a *60 Minutes* crew get chased out of a suspect's office or have a door dramatically slammed in their faces. It is conceivable in the vast scheme of things that innocent people might want to slam doors in Mike Wallace's puss as much as guilty ones, but in the visual vocabulary of "investigative" TV sleuthing, slamming a door is tantamount to an admission of guilt.

Only this week, austere old NBC relaunched its ever-ailing *NBC Magazine with David Brinkley* with a lengthy piece about a Georgia photographer of young girls who had been convicted, unbeknownst to the girls and their moms, on three counts of child molesting in another county. Reporter Jack

Perkins confronted him with this record on camera, and when the man got up from his desk and bolted out the door, reporter and crew chased him down the street.

It was the most athletic reportorial display since the blue-jeaned Rivera pursued a pimp over hill and dale and through underground garage in an Ohio town.

Naturally, one is reminded of the old story about the dog chasing cars—what do they do if they catch one? Wrestle him to the ground? Drag him off to the hoosegow? This may be not so much gonzo journalism as Bonzo journalism. It may not be journalism at all, and it makes the innocent as well as the guilty susceptible to harassment by a nonconstitutional extension of the long arm of the law.

But gosh, it sure makes for *great* pictures!

On *Watching the Watchdog*, anchorman Bill Kurtis went through two 20/20 stories in which, it was charged, the techniques employed produced almost all heat and not much light. In one, Rivera and producer Peter Lance thought they had broken an arson-for-profit ring operating in Chicago. Rivera at one point ambushed a man suspected of involvement in the scheme as he left his office and tried to get into his Volkswagen. Then came the blitz.

Rivera: "How do you respond to the charges by various uptown groups that you're engaged in an arson-for-profit ring?" . . . "Why did so many of your buildings, such a disproportionate number of your buildings, burn?"

"The technique is designed to show a man declining to talk," said Kurtis. "The danger, of course, is that it is designed for drama, not to elicit the truth." Charles Roberts, the man pursued, told WBBM, "A man with a camera . . . got up against my car, locked my door so I couldn't get in the car, and they started shooting questions: 'I hear you're a slumlord. You burn buildings. You kill people.'"

Former CBS News president Fred W. Friendly is quoted on *Watchdog* on the subject of ambush interviewing: "That's probably the dirtiest-trick department of broadcast journalism. . . . The picture transmitted in our heads, the viewers' heads, is of the honest reporter asking the honest question and the crooked interviewee being unavailable, when exactly the opposite could be the case."

A federal grand jury was subsequently unable to return any indictments against any of those implicated in the arson ring, including Roberts, who is now suing ABC News.

The other 20/20 story scrutinized on the WBBM report had to do with a doctor in Arkansas suspected of performing unnecessary operations, including operations in which patients had died. According to Kurtis, the ABC News crew unlawfully entered a restricted area in the hospital so that it could film an operation in progress through a viewing window in the operating room. The ABC cameraman was later found guilty of criminal trespass.

WBBM aired the *Watchdog* show in prime time—preempting, ironically or not, *Lou Grant*. Tapes of the report were sent to some TV writers on major newspapers, on the condition that ABC News not be phoned for comment until after the program had aired—an unprofessional and unreasonable stipulation that a New York reporter promptly disobeyed. At this point the squabbling began, with ABC, after some delay, issuing a point-by-point rebuttal to the charges and WBBM, after a staff meeting, coming up with a rebuttal to the rebuttal, and so on.

David Burke, ABC News senior vice president (he runs interference for the redoubtable Roone Arledge), says ABC News will also prepare a broadcast rebuttal to the report, probably to air in prime time on the ABC-owned Chicago station, WLS-TV. "We are terribly comfortable with our position," Burke says from New York. "We have so much refutation available to us."

As for the ambush and the invasion of the operating room, "We're angry," Burke says. "What has bothered us all along is that at no time in discussing the two cases did WBBM put them into context so that people would understand the extent of the stories being covered, the depth of them."

From Chicago, executive producer Craig says Burke's suspicions about shady motives on the part of WBBM-TV are "ridiculous." Burke further charges the report grew out of

Craig's own personal disenchantment with Chicago's Better Government Association (BGA), which was ABC's ally in the two investigations. "I just deny it," says Craig. "I'm a person of integrity."

Anchorman Kurtis says he wishes the "boxing match" would end so that the issues brought up in the program can be discussed. "What I hope will happen," he says, "is that we can get the program to a third party, an objective observer, and air not only the merits of this show, but get us into the whole subject of investigative techniques, because they're growing out of control, I think."

As long as there are an ABC News and a Geraldo Rivera and a Roone Arledge, there will be plenty to criticize in broadcast journalism, but Rivera and Arledge may just be the most convenient targets; they're flamboyant, gaudy, fairly shameless and tirelessly self-promoting (in Rivera's case, it gets to be a case of almost pathological messianism). Questionable practices are hardly limited to ABC News; everywhere on the dial, on local stations and on networks, one can find reporters and news personalities who owe less to Woodward and Bernstein than they do to Starsky and Hutch. TV encourages the concept of reporters as stars.

The heart of the matter is contained in the introductory remarks Kurtis makes at the start of *Watching the Watchdogs*. He says, "We feel the time has come to look at ourselves and the techniques we use."

This is something very rarely done by television about television, and considering that it is the nation's chief source for news, it should be done much less rarely. *Watching the Watchdogs* also has an encouraging underdog aspect; here was a local station daring to take on a network and hold it accountable. ABC's objections cast doubt on some of the points in the program, but not on the merits of the attempt. Perhaps the time has come for the viewer to pounce back.

April 26, 1981

Rona

ONCE, ONLY A FEW people knew about The Rona Syndrome. Soon, everyone will know. No one may *care*, but everyone will know.

It doesn't belong in the annals of journalism; it doesn't even belong in the annals of television; but it must belong in the annals of *something*....

Of course, the news hit America like a nuclear accident: Rona Barrett was threatening to stomp off of *Tomorrow Coast-to-Coast* because she didn't like playing second fiddle to Tom Snyder's first bassoon. Johnny Carson soon got on the case and reported in his monologue, "Snyder's already found a replacement for Rona: Charles Manson."

Not since John Davidson replaced Mike Douglas had there been such a momentous video rite of passage. Where did the sweet dream go sour? The dread and woefully common Rona Syndrome set in. It used to be known as biting off more than you could chew no matter how big your mouth was. Miss Rona reached—for the stars! And not just Burt Reynolds, either. She wanted more than glamour, more than fame, more than the best table at Ma Maison, more than daily morning exposure on national TV with her tattered Tinseltown tidbits.

She wanted respect. Spelled m-o-n-e-y, which is the way they spell everything in Hollywood.

Rona. Rona. There ought to be a song. There's a "Laura." There's a "Nola." There's even a "Ramona." There ought to be a "Rona."

Let's see... "Ro-nahhh, *is the face in the misty light*..." No, not quite right. "*Everything nice like sugar and spice is* Ro-na..." Not really. "*Ro-*Rona, *I hear the mission bells above*..." Absolutely not.

Of course, there's always, "*My Sha-*Rona, *oooh, you make my motor run, you make it run*..."

Or, "Rona *Lisa*, Rona *Lisa*, men have named you . . ."

Near the end of a meeting in a leafy hotel lobby, to a reporter she had considered hostile and unappreciative of her talents, Rona Barrett says, as if to a kindergarten student she'd just taught how to finger-paint, "You can write whatever you want, but now at least you know me. You may walk away with the same feelings that you had before, and that's perfectly all right, but now it's not like you're typing in the dark. Hopefully. I mean, you may say exactly what you said before, that's okay now—you understand what I'm trying to say?"

Well, darn it, there is a certain charm to her, this feisty and diminutive crusader in behalf of more respect for herself. Miss Rona made television safe for a certain strain of banality it didn't really have before, and her talent is making viewers think they need it in their lives. In five years of reportage on ABC's *Good Morning America* and now on NBC's *Today* show, Rona has without question blazed a trail. She has made Hollywood poop marketable on national TV. One may question whether this was a trail worth blazing, but not the fact that she did it.

Born in New York City 45 years ago, Miss Rona eventually heard the money-voiced call of Hollywood and by 1960 was syndicated in 125 papers. Metromedia stations aired her Hollywood reports in 1969, and she was picked up by ABC in 1975, the year *after* she published her autobiography, *Miss Rona*, which chronicled her triumph over the childhood illnesses that had left her with a slight limp.

On television, she has a curiously effective way of leaning over the nation's backyard fence (she really does seem to be leaning forward, in official confiding position) and making frivolous piffle sound urgent; *and* she has broken many a legitimate piece of solid entertainment-industry news. For this reason, she shrinks from that onerous appellation, "gossip," as if it were an icky old, smelly old thing.

In her liquid, New-Yawkish, Betty-Boopy voice ("Good mawning David and good mawning Amaiwicka") and being very careful to be achingly precise. Miss Rona explains, "I think of gossip as a word that is used to describe something that is trivial, and trivia, as opposed to its larger context, which is the dissemination of news before, perhaps, the news occurs.

"I don't report on the social scene per se; I don't cover parties and say, 'So-and-So was with So-and-So wearing a Chanel suit.' I don't do that. That's social chitchat. And I don't write one-liners—you know, 'Last night at George Bush's party Senator So-and-So punched So-and-So in the mouth for no reason whatsoever' and then never explain what the fight was all about.

"That is what gossip columns do—one-liners: 'Hot new twosome, whozee woozee woozee.' I just don't do that, and that's how I think people think of the word gossip, and therefore, since I don't do that, why should I be called a gossip columnist?"

Let's grant her the point, or she may go on forever. Whether she is a gossip or not, she has been the subject of some. She left ABC in a great big huff and then, this year, did a similar swan dive off NBC's *Tomorrow* show. Of ABC she says, "ABC, after doing what I did there, never realized what it was that I did. And then they tried to demean it. To me, that hurt more than anything."

As for Snyder, Carson asked Rona about that big feud on his *Tonight* show, and Rona responded with a dippy "No comment." And this was her big chance to call Snyder names, too. "But I wasn't going to go on there to talk about Snyder; Johnny knew that. I was on there to help get a plug for my special." Ah, Rona. She has all the warmth of a self-service gas station at 2 A.M.

"And I decided, why bother to keep fanning a flame that really deserved a long explanation because basically it would be an analytical one as opposed to just saying that 'Tom Snyder is a son of a bitch.' I don't feel that way about Tom Snyder. I do have lots of feelings about Tom Snyder. Some of them are very sad feelings. But now you're going to tape this and say, 'Rona has very sad feelings about Tom Snyder.'"

Yes, Rona, that would certainly make headlines around the world. Does she take any pleasure in the fact that Snyder's ratings are worse than ever? "Well, it's no secret. We all read the Nielsen rating books. I don't know why. Maybe Tom's tired. Maybe Tom's burned out. Maybe things are foisted upon him that he never felt really comfortable with. I don't know. We all have our time."

Rona says she is not bitter about the experience and the very public tiff. And you know why? Because it taught her something about herself. And in L.A., the land of the blond, that's considered higher education.

"I learned more about myself than I did about almost anything," says Miss Rona. "I am grateful for the experience. It taught Rona Barrett a lot. About Rona Barrett. About her profession. About what she could do, and what she couldn't do. And also it taught Rona a lot about liking Rona, and standing up for what Rona believed was right." Say, who is this "Rona"? We'd like to meet her!

All is not inner peace, however. Miss Rona feels she's being ripped off left and right, and before you say, "Who would bother?" take a look at the way show-biz news is inundating television: on early-evening "magazine" shows, on regular newscasts and of course in the fabulously insipid new syndicated series *Entertainment Tonight*.

We are all being told much, much more about Hollywood than any sane person could possibly want to know.

Barrett cleared the way for this epidemic with her distinctive, businesslike reports on network TV; the woman has her own style, it must be admitted (though there's a touch of Gracie Allen in there), and it is very safe to say she is *absolutely* and *without question* the best at what she does. So she has a right to look down her nose at those who imitate her.

Of *Entertainment Tonight,* she says, "I think it's awful. It's a wonderful idea and very horrendously executed. It perpetuates the myth that Hollywood is silly, that Hollywood has no substance—and what's the purpose? There's no point of view on that show."

Another Rona imitator, and one who quickly got Le Boot, was Ruth Batchelor, hired as Rona's replacement when Rona left *Good Morning America* for NBC. "I feel very sorry for her: that's all I want to say about that." says Rona of her successor, although a *TV Guide* article had them sniping at each other.

Rona says she was quoted out of context and that she bears no grudge against Batchelor, who was baldly inadequate as a replacement. The problem may have been that, for better or worse, there is only one Miss Rona. Certainly Miss Rona subscribes to this theory.

"They should try something different," she says of ABC. "I mean everybody should try something different. Johnny Carson is Johnny Carson. Johnny Carson is not Jack Paar. And Jack Paar is not Steve Allen. And Steve Allen is not, going back to the morning show, Dave Garroway. And Dave Garroway is not Hugh Downs. And Hugh Downs is not Tom Brokaw. And Tom Brokaw is not . . ." Rona, *stop, stop*, before we go *mad!!!*

Being ripped off is nothing new to her, either. "For years, I watched *Time* and *Newsweek* rip me off all the time. I'm not talking about their "People" section. I'm talking about major entertainment stories they would do. They would never give credit, or if they did, it was in such a snotty, nasty way. It was very grievous to me. A lot of that has changed, and a lot of it is due to my standing up for myself. I felt I had to stand up."

No one who bothered to give it a thought would deny that Rona is a good reporter, that she often gets stories or facets of stories that elude other reporters on the same beat. After 25 years as a professional tattletale, she has reached the point, she says, at which "I don't feel I have to prove anything anymore. I don't." But there is one more thing she wants. Respect. Rona has the hots for respect.

"I'd like to be respected. That's what means the most to me," she says. "On the *Today* show they treat me with enormous respect." And, "I think Grant Tinker would be the first to tell you he has enormous respect for me."

No Rodney Dangerfield she. Rona may ask for too much respect. Success in television is often interpreted as a license to overreach. Rona's demands for respect sound a little like David Hartman's insistence on being mistaken for a journalist.

There is also the distinct possibility that American TV viewers are getting so overloaded with empty information about the stars and the studios and how much money Gary Coleman is making that information as a commodity is losing its value. Perhaps we have contributed to this ourselves with our attention to Rona Barrett; but then, there's more to life than David Stockman. There's *got* to be.

"Miss Rona, *I just met a girl named* Miss Rona! *And suddenly that name, will never be the same, to me!*" She came, she talked, she talked, she talked and she smit. "If it has no importance, then don't say it—that's my point of view," she lectures in her twinkly-spunky way. And so profoundly, "I say, you have to take it all into perspective." Asked if she feels chummy enough toward Snyder to send him a Christmas card, she tells the once-hostile, now grudgingly resigned young reporter, "I don't send Christmas cards. So don't expect one, Tom."

December 3, 1981

Duncan, the Wonder Horse: or, The Commando Strikes at Dawn

How CHOICE THE VIEW from the catbird seat. How kicky to be courted by three TV networks at once. How sublime to wind up the highest-paid newsman in all, all, *all* of Television Land.

Tom Brokaw, 41, leans forward in his chair and stops tapping the desk with a pencil. "I will spend," he says in his arid baritone, "even with the guarantees in my contract, the next seven years looking over my shoulder, wondering when somebody's gonna pull the rug out, when somebody's gonna turn off the switch on this magic dream that I'm having, in terms of the wealth that is there."

The wealth that is there has been placed in published reports as high as $2 million a year—a golden carrot handed Brokaw for staying with NBC, where he has hosted the *Today* show since 1976, and for teaming up with Roger Mudd to aim at becoming the Huntley and Brinkley of the '80s and revive *NBC Nightly News* starting next spring. Brokaw will not confirm a figure—"I'll take any one that has been printed"—but at the very least, his salary alone, without additional benefits and income, is $1.2 million per.

Why, that's more than Dan Rather makes!

"I never expected this kind of material wealth to come my way as a result of getting into this business," says Brokaw, leaning back in his chair now, looking, in his shirt sleeves and with his hands behind his head, like a motion-picture idea of an ambitious young politico, which he is. "That's just not why I got into it. It was not the top priority in the course of this negotiation. It came along with the deal.

"Look, I started out making a hundred dollars a week at a TV station in Omaha when I was first married. And my dad—well, I don't want to tell how much he makes; I told him I would never do that—but my dad was a hard-hat, blue-collar worker who carried a lunch bucket every day until he retired a year ago. I'm at a stage in my life where I don't think I can be corrupted by money."

Perhaps very few people in any field reach that stage in life, but if they want to, it helps to work in television. Brokaw, who says he won't even tell his own father how much he signed for, isn't naive enough to pretend that his boyish good looks and cute button nose didn't have something to do with his ascent into the superstar constellations, but as he sits and talks about himself and NBC News, he's certainly deadly serious. And he is highly regarded by peers and competitors as an earnest, diligent and virtually inexhaustible reporter.

His personality seems a curious combination of callowness and pompousness; there is about him an off-putting yet respect-commanding air of straight As and first-string varsity and debating club. Like Rather—against whom he briefly competed as White House correspondent and whom he hopes to blow away in the nightly news ratings next year—Brokaw wears his heartland on his sleeve, waxing wistful about his Midwestern roots and the earthiness of his early years.

Say, maybe he should even write a book about all this, like Rather's. "No," Brokaw says quickly to that, *"not* like Rather's."

He grew up in little ol' Yankton, South Dakota, just about 40 miles, he reckons, from where Johnny Carson grew up, in Norfolk, Nebraska. It makes a television kind of sense: America's joke-teller and America's news-giver being soilmates from the same crossroads of the melting pot—and then years later sitting next to each other at Wimbledon. It's so perfect it hurts.

"I tell you something," says Brokaw, on the subject of perfection, *his:* "People write these wonderful things about me. Well, I'm a klutz like everybody else, I *am!* I lose things, forget things, make bad judgments about stuff, am sometimes uncertain about what I'm going to do. And I read all these accounts and I just can't believe that it's me, 'cause I don't feel that much in control all the time. I really don't. I just *don't.* My children could tell you about all my bad habits. I can't sing. I'm flat-footed. I'm not very fast-running. I've played tennis for seven or eight years and I'm still not very good at it. There are lots of things, lots of things!

"I work hard at whatever I do—that much I'll give me."

"But I ain't a poifect person."

Rather chuckles at the idea that Brokaw and Mudd will be the Huntley-Brinkley of the '80s. "I'm supposed to be the Ed Murrow of the '80s," he said. "It appears the '80s are going to be overburdened with talent."

Brokaw says he doesn't know—no one really knows—if the chemistry between him and Mudd will be right on the air, and intoxicating enough to knock Rather off the mountaintop.

He claims to be personally fond of the irascible, mavericky Mudd. "You know what I like about Roger? Somebody described him as 'mischievous.' I'm not sure that's the word, but he's nobody's fool. And after all these years in Washington, and living at the top of his profession, he's never been one who's played the game of all of that.

"And if he's cantankerous, most instances of that have been for the right reason. He's been cantankerous because things weren't done right, or because he was expected to do something that he ought not to have been asked to do."

But it's been speculated that it will take a heap of self-effacement for Mudd not to resent the younger, richer, prettier Brokaw, especially since Mudd stomped away from CBS News after being passed over for Rather as Cronkite's successor. "We're grown-ups," says Brokaw. "We have a common interest, which is to succeed—not just as individuals, because that would be impossible without succeeding as a team. I'm not here to lord over Roger. He's not down there to dictate to me. I think that we'll work it out along the way.

"I really do."

Still, the courtship of Tom Brokaw by three TV networks has to have set his head spinning at least a little. For weeks stories floated out of New York of ABC News president Roone Arledge and CBS News president William Leonard showering Brokaw with temptations. "I knew, obviously, that I was in a great position. People kept saying, 'Isn't it wonderful?' Sure it was wonderful. It was a kind of agony-and-ecstasy, though."

Some things about the *Today* show Brokaw will not miss. He confesses he has been "uncomfortable" with the show more than once since it was speeded up and jazzed up to meet the competition of ABC's *Good Morning, America.*

"There are things I do here that I'm not crazy about," Brokaw says. "Recently I had to interview one of the performers from *Dallas.* It was just something that when I finished, I said to myself, 'Why'd I have to go through *this?*' Charlene Tilton, or Tilden, one or the other—I've tried to put her name out of my mind. *Tilton.* I didn't know who she was, which is a terrible confession. She was really well-meaning and enthusiastic, but my level of interest was not real high."

Careful viewers of *Today* may have noticed that never once has Brokaw done the studio intro for gossipmonger Rona Barrett out of Hollywood. This is "by informal agreement," Brokaw says. Beneath his dignity, Brokaw also recalls that when *GMA* first gave *Today* a serious challenge, "people began to panic around here" and started advocating "things that I was not willing to do," though he won't say what any of them were.

Brokaw also will not miss the rumors, which have persisted through several years and layers of NBC denial, that he and porcelain-doll Jane Pauley, cohost on the program, never got along off camera (and occasionally made persnickety remarks to each other on camera).

"Jane and I have a very, very good relationship, and we have had from Day One. There have been some moments of difficulty, but my God, I can't imagine other people going through the same circumstances and not having the same type of thing. The best of friends are going to have flare-ups."

Brokaw and Pauley and the rest of the *Today* crew are on their way to London for coverage of the royal wedding. Brokaw speaks like a true TV journalist when he says he welcomes rather than fears the possibility of turbulence in the streets. "I think it's going to make it a far better assignment for all of us," he says. "I don't wish ill to the British people, and I certainly don't want them to burn down towns for our sake. But there has been a lot of ferment there for some time, and it just happens to be breaking out now."

Some guys have all the luck.

On a wall of Tom Brokaw's office is a photo he took of a tombstone marking the grave of Christian Sunrise, a Sioux buried on Sunrise Hill near where young Tommy Brokaw used to go fishing in the Missouri River. Brokaw says a part of him has never left South Dakota and that when he goes back there in his jeans, people look at him to see if he has changed, and nosir, he hasn't, not even with $2 million a year in the kitty.

"I've made more money in the past five years than I thought possible, but it hasn't really changed the way I live that much. My interests are still the same. I don't go to the South of France and rent a yacht. I go backpacking in Montana."

All this money and power won't detach him permanently from the mainstream where he was spawned, Brokaw says. "I still go to see my parents in South Dakota, and my brother's a hard-hat worker for the telephone company, and I stay in touch with his life. Because I'm interested and I love him, and also because it keeps reminding me of what else is going on. I don't intend to hole up in some New York ivory tower and not ever come into touch with how most of this country lives."

CBS News is the prestigious industry leader. ABC News is the electric, pizazzy young upstart. NBC News is languishing now, and without a strong identity. Even Brokaw, who turned down glorious offers in order to stay at the network, concedes that the roof is leaking and the plumbing makes noise.

"We have stumbled on a couple of major stories this year, there's no question about that. The Reagan shooting was one of them; there's just no question about that. And the Pope, in the first afternoon. On the other hand, the *Today* program is part of the NBC News organization, and in both those stories, by the next morning we put on a superior product compared to the other two.

"I don't think we're all that far behind," Brokaw says. "*Nightly News* is a vastly improved product over what it was two years ago. This is not a place in which the foundation has been knocked out from under. All the elements are here. All it needs is a kind of commitment, and patience, and a higher level of energy."

Yes, all it needs, all NBC News really, truly needs, is— *Duncan, the Wonder Horse!* That happens to be the nickname *Today* executive producer and longtime Brokaw pal Steve Friedman gave Brokaw after his whirlwind performance during the election year. Brokaw would finish *Today* on a Friday, jet off to a primary state for the weekend and be back on the *Today* set Monday morning.

Asked if he is priming himself to be combative and competitive for the battle with Rather, Brokaw says, "I don't have to prime myself up. I'm always combative and competitive." And, sounding as much like the high-charged Rather as Rather does, Brokaw declares, "Whether it's CBS or ABC or whoever else is around, I want to be on top."

Duncan, the Wonder Horse says some of his drive may be chronic workaholism, but actually, well, he's just kind of high on life. "Mostly what I am is durable. It's real hard to wear me down, and I'll work real hard at almost anything. They asked me last year, 'How can you do all that?' I said, 'It's the ultimate manifestation of my ego. I want to be on the air *all the time*. That's what drives me.'" He laughs a contented laugh.

"The other thing is, corny as this sounds, I can't believe that life has been this good. And I don't want to miss anything. Having grown up in a small town in the middle of South Dakota, I just didn't know that all this would be possible in my life."

A photographer has been taking Brokaw's picture through much of this reverie. He is asked if the picture-taking bothers him. For a moment, at last, he seems truly to relax. "It doesn't bother me," Brokaw says. "I'm on television!"

July 22, 1981

Wedding

LOVELY, LOVELY, *loverly*.

"Lovely shot there," said Dan Rather as a picture of the balcony at Buckingham Palace popped onto the screen. "A lovely costume that the princess is wearing," said Tom Fenton of CBS News.

They all thought it was lovely, and it was—superb, warming, stunning television. But most of the credit for the visual splendor of yesterday's TV coverage of the marriage of Prince Charles to Lady Diana Spencer goes to that stately landmark, the BBC, which supplied all the networks with pictures that were sometimes breathtaking, sometimes merely grand.

ABC News supplemented the BBC pictures with aerial shots from England's commercial ITV network and probably had the most distinctive coverage of the three networks. Pompous Peter Jennings and lady-in-waiting Barbara Walters surrendered the mikes early in the morning to *Good Morning America* host David Hartman, who was turned into a palatable and even engaging presence by the companionship of Robert Morley, by now—after years of entertaining British Airways commercials—as much an English icon as Westminster Abbey.

"The royal family have a habit of appearing to be talking to each other in public," Morley told Hartman, "but in fact, they're not saying *anything*." At one point he admonished Hartman, "Oh, don't be so silly," and later told him that royalty, that endangered species, was able to lend dignity "even to this program." When Hartman objected to that, Morley said, "I don't like dignity; please don't be offended. Popularity is enough for me. And *you*, I think."

All the networks had signed up supplementary expertise—including the unctuous David Frost on CBS and the not-helpful Peter Ustinov on NBC—but nothing could upstage the pictures obtained by BBC camera crews, who have raised electronic photography to a level of art the U.S. commercial networks and their union technicians have not approached.

Shots did not have to be spectacular to be affecting. There was the prince, during the vows, wiping tears from his eyes. As the prince and princess left St. Paul's, Queen Elizabeth II was spied giving them one last maternal once-over, and, later, was glimpsed under an arch at Buckingham Palace waving bossy directions to the privileged pedestrian traffic as the newlyweds prepared to embark in their carriage for Waterloo Station.

Even if one felt satiated by coverage of the wedding before the telecast began, something about this merger of 20th-century technology and age-old tradition was captivating and moving. Vagrant misgivings, even incredulity, at so much fuss and hoopla over something as quaint as royalty were repeatedly dispelled by the beauty and efficiency, and the human poignance, of the festivities as television captured them.

Perhaps sensitive to past complaints about their overeagerness as chatty Kathies and blabby Bobs, the network correspondents seemed to be taken with a newfound, though inadequate, sense of restraint. ABC's Jennings may be pompous on camera, but his understated narration of the ceremony itself was tactful and adroit.

Rather, whose attempts at getting emotionally carried away in the past have sometimes looked facile and fake, seemed genuine enough when he told viewers, as the royal couple's coach left St. Paul's, "Now if I may be so bold—if there's anyone in your household not watching a television set at the moment, back home in the United States, my gentle suggestion is that you get them. You won't see *this* many times in your lifetime. If ever."

Unfortunately, this followed a nasty gaffe during the ceremony. Celebrated soprano Kiri Te Kanawa was singing eloquently when Rather interrupted to say, redundantly, "From St. Paul's Cathedral, London, England," and then, "as singing of Handel's aria continues, we're going to slip away for a pause for station identification."

What idiot called for that clumsy cutaway? To make matters worse, the first commercial shown during the break was an irritating spot for the Smith Barney investment firm, with John Houseman doing his tiresome stern-coot routine and saying, "Being born with a silver spoon in one's mouth is not enough." There was also an ad for diamond-anniversary rings and, later, one for "Royal" copiers.

When Rather returned, he had the nerve to refer to the ceremony as "this fantastic musical spectacle"—so fantastic that CBS rushed away from it to sell things.

NBC News seemed intent on being the snidest network. After airing excerpts from the BBC interview with the prince and Lady Diana Tuesday night, John Chancellor scoffed, "Correspondents tend to tiptoe through interviews with royalty in this country." (Did he think the occasion called for a billy-club drubbing under a bare light bulb?) This was not long after he reported that there had been more violence in Liverpool—"but we don't know how serious it was." Maybe NBC News should have tried harder to find out.

On the morning of the wedding, NBC's Tom Brokaw wisecracked that the British were more adept at organizing weddings than at organizing their economy, and Chancellor grumped that the size of the crowds was "disappointing"—surely only to him.

Over at CBS News, reporter Tom Fenton plunged into the crowd and, incredibly enough, demanded to know of some people why they didn't stay home and watch the ceremony on television, as if television were the real experience and the festivities themselves a replica. A British policeman, however, was particularly eloquent in dealing with one of Fenton's queries.

Fenton: "Sergeant, what kind of crowd have we had here today?"

Sergeant: "Vast."

Some inanity was contributed by the guest commentators as well. After Rather opined that the princess was "certainly no Grace Kelly," Frost gushed in with, "But as in the movie *High Society*, this occasion is also characterized by the phrase 'true love.'"

And Bonnie Angelo of *Time* magazine's London bureau literally held on to her hat as she squealed to Hartman on ABC, "I would even use the word 'majestic' on this one."

Perhaps as long as there is television, commentators and reporters will keep trying to top the pictures with their own word portraits. Almost invariably, they fail. ABC had transmission problems all morning, and when, just after 11:30, its own audio went dead in London, leaving only the BBC pictures and ambient sound, the silencing of wagging tongues was refreshing. Naturally, viewers were not to be afforded such luxury for long, and the broadcast was quickly terminated at that point.

But it had been, for the most part, pretty enchanting fairy-tale stuff. Lovely, lovely, *loverly.*

July 30, 1981

Marty Lives

WE'LL ALL BE DANCING on the rings of Saturn before we see another Golden Age of Television. What made it golden is that for a few fleeting years, television was a writer's medium. Now, of course, it is a committee's medium, evolving into a computer's medium.

Of all the original live dramas the era produced, few remain as trenchant and affecting as *Marty*, to be shown again tonight as part of a continuing "Golden Age" retrospective. The play was scheduled before the recent death of its author, Paddy Chayefsky, so its rebroadcast—the first in 28 years—makes an accidental but apt memorial tribute.

(TV was a producer's medium then, too, and this *Goodyear Playhouse* presentation, like many other live video dramas of its day, was produced by Fred Coe, who later directed the film *A Thousand Clowns* and who died in 1979).

Dated only in superficial ways—many of them having to do with the technical limitations of early TV cameras and studios—*Marty* kept much of a nation enthralled on Sunday night in 1953 with the spare, sketchy account of an incipient romance between a 36-year-old Bronx butcher and the 29-year-old high school teacher he meets at a seedy dance hall.

Some plays are ripped from the headlines and some are ripped from the heart. Chayefsky opened a vein and *Marty* came out, tender and sweet and sad and yet safely in a realm beyond pathos. Chayefsky breathed subtle and stirring dignity into the homely and overweight mama's boy who repeatedly calls himself "a fat, ugly little man," and who always has to be fixed up with a date on New Year's Eve.

Chayefsky had, among other talents, a knack for the vernacular. His barroom dialogue between Marty and another unmarried galoot is familiar to people who've never seen the original play: "Well, whaddayou feel like doin' tonight?" "I don't know. Whaddayou feel like doin?" "Well. We oughta do somethin'. It's Saturday night."

Soon Marty is on the phone trying with pure futility to make a date with a girl he'd met a week earlier. "Come on, now, you remember me," he says into the phone. "I'm the stocky one." Marty's mother tells him the Waverly Ballroom is "loaded with tomatoes," and reluctantly Marty goes there, to stand among the wayward ranks of the unattached. A man offers him five bucks to take a blind date, "a dog," off his hands, and though Marty refuses, he later meets the woman on a balcony, where she is sobbing.

Marty is the story of two lives saved from joylessness because they happen to intersect. As a portrayal of loneliness, it is timeless; it is also a play about the profound necessity of simple companionship. Chayefsky was writing about human needs long before they had been codified into the clichés of the '70s, and what *Marty* has to say in its final act on the topic of misogyny couldn't be said better today even by a consciousness raised to the rafters.

Rod Steiger's performance as Marty is more than a study in despair and alienation; he lets the ugliness of Marty's self-pity show through. Nancy Marchand as the teacher leans toward caricature, at least at first; she's Angst with a purse. But overall, the performances are as shrewdly economical as the script.

In snippets of interviews stitched—very badly—together at the beginning of the hour, some of the surviving principals talk about the play. Marchand, now Mrs. Pynchon on *Lou Grant,* recalls of the era, "It was like going to California in a covered wagon. We were all pioneers." Betsy Palmer says Steiger was so overcome with the play that he wept at rehearsals.

Steiger himself says the role was originally written for Martin Ritt, but Ritt was a victim of the blacklisting of the early '50s, so Steiger got the part. Ritt went on to direct films such as *Norma Rae, Conrack* and *The Front,* a comedy-drama about blacklisting.

And Delbert Mann, the director, remembers getting hold of the script and wondering, along with other members of the team, "Is this as good as we really think it is?" That's something most of the people working in network television today never have to worry about. They only have to worry about getting up the nerve to show their faces in public.

The kinescope of *Marty* transferred to tape for this airing is in poor condition, worse than many movies half a century old; some of the plays of early TV were virtual art compared with today's pale charades, but they were treated like journalism. Maybe nobody thought people in 1981 would care about a play that was televised and then evaporated into electrons in 1953.

August 27, 1981

Sugar Ray and the Media's TKO

HERE IN THE NATION'S capital, where you'd think news bulletins would really have news in them, the local NBC affiliate broke into *The Tonight Show Starring Johnny Carson* three times with a hot flash that Sugar Ray Leonard had won his fight with Thomas Hearns.

One of these needless interruptions came just as a parrot named Poncho was singing "I Left My Heart in San Francisco." Two guys beating each other's brains out you can see any day; a parrot singing "I Left My Heart in San Francisco" is a true treat. Some people have no sense of priorities.

The next night, Carson himself, who in 19 years on the air has almost never spoken out on any of the serious issues of the day, did get serious for a moment—about The Fight. He complained that the judges were off base in the way they scored some of the rounds. For this he stopped the show in its tracks. You see, these big bang-bang boxing things come along and everybody goes crazy; sanity goes right out the window.

Nothing fans the fires of nuttiness so much as a charismatic champion; boxing keeps trying to die as a sport, but colorful or ingratiating figures come along and galvanize people and boxing gets another lease on life. Nothing so popularizes a charismatic champion as television, and Sugar Ray Leonard, whatever his prowess in the ring, can go 15 rounds with a TV camera any time. He's a champ when it comes to wallowing merrily in exposure.

Politicians now have to learn television before they learn statesmanship. Sugar Ray Leonard may have learned television before he learned how to fight; he's that good. Leonard and his promoters were shrewd enough to give just about anybody holding a microphone a chance at interviewing the champ before the fight in order to up the already ungainly ante. In addition to the pay-TV deals, rights to replay the fight on HBO or ABC were apparently being negotiated right up to the start of the first round.

So, no matter how uninterested a person was in the fight, it was almost impossible to avoid it. All the networks did their little pieces, there was a syndicated special playing around the country and HBO, perhaps assuming it would get the replay rights, had a special too. In addition, local stations from many cities dug into their budgets to send their gung-ho sportscasters off to Las Vegas, where Leonard was anything but unavailable.

He spent so much time talking with the press that you began to wonder if he was getting any training. Leonard is considered good TV because he's cute, he's personable—so cute and personable that he stars in a 7-Up commercial—and unlike Muhammad Ali, he never makes controversial remarks.

He really doesn't remark about anything more meaningful than boxing, and less meaningful than that you cannot get.

For one Washington sportscaster, Leonard playfully demonstrated his sparring technique. For another, he explained the brilliant strategy he would employ in fighting Hearns: he would take a poke at him, Leonard said, and then he would step to one side so that Hearns wouldn't be able to poke him. What a great idea! If Hearns had been watching that interview he might have won the fight!

But the fight promoters certainly knew what they were doing. They got more coverage (yes, from newspapers, too) than even they may have dreamed. On fight night we had the dubious privilege of being switched live via satellite to Las Vegas so that our local sportscaster could tell us who won the fight and how big which gash was over whose eye. They couldn't show the fight, but they could stand there and tell us about it.

No matter what anybody says, these accounts always get down to the nitty-gritty of the sport—which is how much damage one guy inflicted on the other. There are lengthy and loving descriptions of cuts and scars and spurts of blood. All this time, all this TV attention, all this profitable hoopla over something as primitive as one guy clobbering another into a pulp.

But it isn't the brutality that makes these big fights so annoying, really; after all, the average day's edition of *The Price Is Right* is probably more violent and hysterical (someday those women are going to turn into a rabid, rioting mob, and let's hope they go straight for host Bob Barker.) What's more irritating is the way everyone hops on the bandwagon, the way the size of the circus grows and grows to take in every Jack and jerk who stands to make another dollar off the spectacle.

We're not talking small change. We're talking multimedia megabucks. The size of the purse becomes part of the fight's hype and increases the size of the purse. Money is hype; hype, money—that is all ye need to know. One might say "only in America" in reference to folly of this magnitude, but

it could happen in other countries too. Better to say "only on the planet earth," then buy the parrot a drink and ask him to sing "Melancholy Baby."
September 19, 1981

The Caution and the Fear

> "We would not want to be in the position of scooping the Egyptian government on the death of their own leader."
>
> —John Scali, ABC News

AFTER NEARLY SEVEN HOURS of supposition, speculation and confirmation from unnamed sources, the American television networks declared Egyptian President Anwar Sadat "officially" dead just before 2 o'clock yesterday afternoon.

For the third time this year, the network news departments swung dramatically into the red alert of Crisis Television to cover the story of an assassination attempt on a world figure—this one, unlike the attempts on the lives of President Reagan and Pope John Paul II, successful. Once more, live, global, reality television unified the nation in horror.

By this time, the mechanics of crisis coverage have become virtually ritualistic—the parade of guest experts, the tentative and heavily qualified nature of early reports, the final confirmation, the worldwide reaction. A horror scenario becoming as familiar as any other video rite.

Said ABC anchor Frank Reynolds to fellow reporter Steve Bell at the end of the afternoon's coverage, "Here we are, Steve; this is the third time in a little more than seven months that we have been such unwelcome messengers of such awful news."

As with the shooting of the Pope in May, pictures—final

validation of any event in the vocabulary of television—were not immediately available. NBC News had a chilling audio tape of screams, shouts and shots that it played several times, at least once as accompaniment to still pictures of prostrate bodies that newsmen could not identify for viewers.

The Egyptian government had closed down the Cairo airport and embargoed all satellite transmissions from the scene of the shooting until after the official announcement was made. Dan Rather announced on the air, however, that CBS News correspondent Mitchell Krauss, wounded by shrapnel during the shooting, had left Cairo for Rome before the airport was closed, with a reel of videotape under his arm.

Then, soon after the announcement from Cairo, while Krauss was still in the air, the first tapes of the incident were transmitted by satellite. They included footage of pandemonium on the reviewing stand from which Sadat had watched the day's military parade—a jungle of toppled chairs and bloodied bodies.

The footage, raw and unedited, contained penetrating images not only of violence and terror but also of panic and social breakdown:

• A man whose arm had been completely shattered by gunfire trying desperately to get to his feet.

• Officials in business suits, some red-spattered, scrambling for cover as shots continued to fly; and a man in ornate military regalia, standing dazed and disbelieving, watching helplessly, blood trickling down his cheek.

• On the reviewing stand, survivors sifting through the toppled bodies and rubble for more casualties.

• And one incredibly dramatic shot of a hand, dripping with blood, reaching up from the floor and trying to grasp the rim of a chair.

These pictures, shot by ABC News cameraman Fabrice Moussos, had a staggering impact, especially after hours of hearsay; they obliterated all the words that had been spoken up to that point.

Still smarting from criticism over hasty reporting during the Reagan shooting—when presidential press secretary James Brady was erroneously declared dead by all three networks—

ABC, CBS and NBC exercised extreme caution as the story painfully and arduously unfolded yesterday. Gradually it grew less and less likely that President Sadat had survived the attack, even though the first network reports described his gunshot wounds as minor and raised the possibility that he would soon be out of surgery.

Walter Cronkite, the former CBS News anchorman, called into service early in the coverage, warned his replacement, Rather, against accepting without question those first reports that the injuries to Sadat were not serious. Trepidation was the order of the day, as network news personnel moved into roles to which they, and the viewing public, have become agonizingly accustomed.

ABC's Reynolds more than any other network newsman let the tragedy of the day's events show in his face and his delivery; as before, he was more than a messenger. He assumed a consoling and commiserating role. His kind of demonstrative involvement with the story—"this dreadful news"—may be increasingly important to viewers as Crisis Television becomes more and more common, and as the possibility that we will all grow numb to these public tragedies grows more likely.

There was some irony in the fact that all three networks kept stressing how unofficial the reports of Sadat's death were —as they did from about 10 A.M. until the actual announcement of the death in Cairo—since it is television that makes anything "official" for most Americans. Sadat's death probably became official here when Rather heard CBS News correspondent Scotti Williston say from Cairo shortly before 10:30 that her sources indicated Sadat had died.

In the scramble to cover the story in the face of what was almost an information blackout, the networks dragged in innumerable correspondents who quoted innumerable unnamed sources as to the condition of Sadat. Some correspondents expressed peevish umbrage at the lack of official statements from Cairo and from the White House, as if these institutions had a mandate to keep the networks informed as a first priority.

On the Cable News Network, correspondent Daniel Schorr

called the White House "ham-handed" for the way it was dealing with news of the assassination and the way Vice President George Bush had instructed Senate Majority Leader Howard Baker to announce Sadat's death on the Senate floor long before confirmation had come out of Cairo. This helped increase the confusion quotient on the air.

Again, as with the past two 1981 assassination attempts, conflicting reports were aired within moments of each other and the nation became firsthand witness to the newsgathering process—in a way, part of the newsgathering process. These monumental crises tend to divide the world into newsgatherers and newsmakers.

Reynolds was especially—and somehow comfortingly—unguarded. When the Bush-Baker story broke, and after a White House denial reported by Sam Donaldson, Reynolds decided to consult Capitol Hill reporter Brit Hume. "Get Brit for me," he said on the air, "I'd like to get more information on that. Hold on, Sam, let me talk to Brit." Reynolds began talking into a telephone on camera. "Hello, Brit? Brit . . ." Viewers heard only Reynolds' side of the conversation but could watch the concerned look on his face as he spoke. "Brit, go to your camera position, will you?" Reynolds said finally. "Get in a better position where we can talk to you."

Bell remained on the air with Reynolds throughout the day's coverage. An ABC News spokesman denied that Bell was there to keep Reynolds under control; during the Reagan shooting coverage, Reynolds had exploded on the air because he was getting conflicting reports on Brady's condition. Reynolds never lost his composure yesterday, although over footage of crowds in Libya apparently cheering the attack on Sadat, Reynolds said sadly, as two little boys waved into the camera lens, "Look at this—children expressing their joy at the death of a man by violence." One might call this emotional grandstanding, yet it did not seem inappropriate or forced.

Occasionally, the scramble for sources who would say anything became ludicrous. ABC's Barbara Walters appeared on camera at one point to say, "Three minutes ago I received a call from an Egyptian who said that he wished not to give his name but that he had some information for me." Earlier, Walters dutifully reported that a press secretary in Cairo had refused to confirm that Sadat had died but that he sounded to her "like a man deeply grieved." Former president Jimmy Carter was enlisted as a correspondent for CBS News; Carter assured Rather by telephone from Plains, Georgia, in midmorning, that according to his sources in Cairo, Sadat had not been seriously wounded.

Former secretary of state Henry Kissinger, a free-lance expert on international affairs, was trotted from network to network during the day. He began in the early morning on NBC's *Today* show, where he was being interviewed when the first news of the shooting broke. Later Kissinger talked with Rather, on CBS.

Late last night, he showed up on an expanded, 75-minute edition of ABC's *Nightline*. Much of the mourning out of the way by this time, the program opted instead for exceptionally lucid and practical analysis of wider ramifications. Carter, interviewed by anchor Ted Koppel, strongly suggested he suspected the Libyans of complicity in the Sadat murder and called Libyan dictator Muammar Qaddafi "an animal who has no morals of his own."

Carl Bernstein reported that America had sent AWACS, the radar-equipped airplanes now at the heart of the controversy involving Saudi Arabia, to escort and safeguard Sadat's plane as it flew him around the Mideast earlier this year. Barbara Walters narrated a montage of highlights from Sadat's participation in the quest for a Mideast peace—a memoir far more effective than the pompous oration Walter Cronkite delivered earlier on the *CBS Evening News* while waiting at JFK airport for a jet to take him to Cairo.

Cronkite blustered about the times he had spent with Sadat "in the shadow of the Pyramids" or on the banks of the Nile. It was not the sort of thing Walter should have put in his pipe and smoked.

The day also marked the first appearance on ABC of David Brinkley, for the previous 38 years an institution at NBC

News. Brinkley played the part of sage, expressing regret that his first assignment at ABC News was keyed to a tragedy ("but we don't make the news") and congratulating "the guys" at ABC for the job they had done so far. On *Nightline,* Brinkley said of Sadat and the day's "strenuous" eulogies, "All of the praise he deserved."

All during the day reporters scoured the landscape for clues to Sadat's condition, finding them wherever they could—as in the fact that Cairo television had gone abruptly off the air, returning later with prayer readings from the Koran. The position of the flag outside the Egyptian Embassy here was also studied; it changed at least twice during the morning.

Reynolds frankly conceded the iffiness of available reportage to viewers: "So once again we are in one of those terrible dilemmas where we have seemingly reliable information but it cannot be authenticated, and there's nothing we can do but wait for the official announcement, if and when it comes."

Once the Egyptian government lifted the satellite ban, the footage began pouring out, and NBC put it on the air live, and unedited, joined later by ABC and, much later, by CBS, which had hastily returned to the hollow trauma of its daytime soaps *(Search for Tomorrow).* Some of the footage was from Egyptian TV, but all the footage showing the shooting had been filmed by ABC's Moussos. Technically, the other networks did not automatically have the right to air it, but an NBC News spokesman said later that everything was declared "pool stuff" as it came over on "the bird."

The rules were, an ABC spokesman said, in the tech-talk of global video, "Whoever got birded out first would be pooled." At first ABC said the other networks could use its footage only once, and a spokesman said ABC was miffed that NBC had identified the footage as "Egyptian Television," when it had been shot for ABC News. Later ABC News decided to let the other networks continue to use the footage as long as it was attributed to ABC.

By the time Americans returned home to their TV sets last evening, that footage had already been played, replayed, freeze-framed and edited, and joined by the Krauss footage, which had made it to Rome. Soon scenes that were monstrous and horrifying the first time would grow tame through repeated exposure. Those who saw the scenes on the evening news would never know the suspense, or the shock, of experiencing them as the finale to a long day's vigil before the television set, or of not only seeing but feeling the story unfold from a distant region still considered by many Americans to be unpredictable and inscrutable.

"Tragically," said Reynolds, as he left the air, "we know what our lead story is going to be tonight." A long day's television was almost over. How many more days like it will we see in our lifetimes?
October 7, 1981

Report from the Betacombs

NINETEEN EIGHTY-FOUR. It is the third year of our persecution, O my brothers, O Betanauts and Betalogues and fellow members of the Betanese Liberation Front. Still they come, the gray men in the greatcoats, the storm troopers in their clodhoppers, and the brownshirts, and the grayshirts in the brown coats and still they seek us out and pick us off and cart away our *Goldfinger* and our *Roots* and our *Great Muppet Caper*.

Three years, O my brothers, since the decision banning home video recording of TV shows was handed down by a three-judge panel (combined I.Q.: 30) of the U.S. Court of Appeals in San Francisco. Three years since 5 million of us went underground with our Betamaxes, VHSes, our blank tapes, our patch cords; our satellite dishes and our whizzmagidgets. Three years on horizontal hold.

They staged another air raid last week, my brothers; they flew low over the subterranean cubicle in the dread bulk-eraser plane, another of those converted AWACS they never did sell to Saudi Arabia. Their giant magnets swept our Betacombs, hoping to wipe away our *Fantasy Islands*, our Johnny Carsons, our *Masterpiece Theatres,* our Mister Bills, and our Richard Simmons shows.

But we of the fourth sector of the third quadrant of the 17th collective of the underground guerrilla band known as Betanoids, we cling to the words of wisdom of our spiritual leader whom we have seen on the tape called World War II. It was our beloved Sir Winston S. Churchill who said, "We shall fight on the beaches, we shall fight on the landing ground, we shall fight in the field and in the street, we shall fight in the hills.

"We shall never surrender."

The news is not good, O my brothers. Comrade Joseph K returned from the front yesterday and reported that the combined military forces of Walt Disney productions and Universal Studios moved in with their dwarfs and mice and incredible hulks and let fly with the dread bulk erasers on a hidden cache of tapes stored behind a Piggly Wiggly. There went 132 episodes of *The Mary Tyler Moore Show,* up in a cloud of electrons. It was almost more than Joseph K could take, and this is a man who bought Polaroid at 122—the camera, not the stock.

Worse news was yet to come. Also seized by the dread copyright-infringement police was Comrade Gonzo K's entire collection of Betamania—Hank Aaron breaking Babe Ruth's home-run record, the U.S. hockey team winning the 1980 Olympics, Superbowl XI and the third Ali–Frazier fight. We are not in Schaefer City, O my brothers.

They even got our last surviving copy of Ronald Reagan's first inaugural address. Brothers, it was so much better than this year's election-night victory speech.

But as our spiritual leader the beloved Winston S said, "For each and for all, as for the Royal Navy, the watchword should be 'Carry on and dread naught.' "

There was another speech on the radio today by Jack J. Valenti, president of the Motion Picture Association of America. He called for us to come out of hiding, carrying our tapes over our heads. He said the war against video liberation was costing the movie companies billions of dollars a year—a full 0.3 percent of their profits—and he said again, "The petty interests of two hundred and forty million Americans must not be allowed to stand in the way of private enterprise and big business."

Valenti! We tried to kidnap the corporate imperialist lackey once, but—he was too short. We couldn't find him. Comrade Gunther K thinks he saw the top of Valenti's head through the back window of his limousine. We will try again. Next time we will bring a smaller laundry bag.

United States Chief Justice Warren Burger also spoke to us today. It was early 1982 when the Burger court upheld the lower court's ruling. If only Sandra Day O'Connor had not disqualified herself on the ground that she had once seen a TV commercial for a Betamax machine!

The fight goes on. Only yesterday Sister Henrietta K was charged with illegal time-shifting. She had been caught red-handed setting her Betamax timer to record soap operas in the afternoon so that she could watch them later that night when she got home. She pleaded guilty to conspiring to watch the soaps without sitting through the commercials for Stayfree Maxi-pads, Massengill douche and Porcelana fade cream.

They not only confiscated her Betamax, they appropriated her Trinitron.

Poor Henrietta was sentenced to three hours of hard labor a night—watching the network prime-time schedule exactly as the network scheduled it, and with no fast-forwarding through the commercials. O my brothers! They propped her peepers open with toothpicks and dabbed her face with Kleenex as the tears of boredom rolled down her cheeks.

What was it our beloved Winston S said? "And now they even attack my little dog Fala." No, no—it was "Never give in. Never give in. Never, never, never, never." Or was it "Never, never, never, never, never"? Well, it was never give in just the same.

And so we wait, O my brothers, we wait for the terror from Hollywood, our nation's capital, to come again in the night. Even Mike Wallace is on our trail now; creepy-peepy cameras roam the countryside; the *Eyewitness News* jet-propelled traffic copter scours the landscape. Comrade Hector K thinks he even saw Magnum, P.I. casing the terrain in his Ferrari.

Charlie's Angels are hidden under the bed. Benny Hill is in the closet. *The Ten Commandments* are buried in the backyard. I have cleverly disguised a videotape of *Fahrenheit 451* as a book. Yesterday brother Raoul K asked us to conceal his collection of *Hollywood Squares* and *Family Feud*.

They only told us we could pursue happiness, O my brothers; they never did say we could record it and play it back.
October 22, 1981

Gimme an Axe

I WISH I COULD SUE NBC for the grievous consternation, intestinal distress and aggravated low moaning I have suffered as a result of *Gimme a Break*, the paleolithic comedy premiering tonight.

Indeed, on the basis of this half-hour, it is not too much to ask of RCA that it close down the network and find something more useful to do with 30 Rock. Perhaps a condo.

Nell Carter, the balloonish actress of *Ain't Misbehavin'* fame, plays housekeeper to a police chief and his three sex-obsessed teen-age daughters in this coarse insult, a holdover from the Silverman era of wan wanton pandering. In the premiere, "Nell," as she is called in the script, vacuums the family goldfish out of the tank and patches up a dispute between Dad and a daughter caught shoplifting.

The housekeeper as conceived and played is a combination of Hattie McDaniel and Donna Summer; two, or maybe three, racial stereotypes in one. Carter plays it as broadly and with as much sensitivity as Willie Best played a shufflin' handyman on *Life with Father* nearly three decades ago.

But let's get to the sex jokes.

Nell is teaching the tomboyish daughter how to beat up

little boys. "When everything else fails, you've got to kick him where it hurts." "Where's that?" "That's another lesson."

The tomboy is asked to put on a dress. "I hate dresses. They show off your boobies. That turns boys into animals." Later she declares, "I know about sex. It's what you do when you're sixteen."

Another daughter and her boyfriend are reading *The Official Sex Manual*, which tells how women get pregnant: "polliwogs" from the man make their way into the woman's "oven." When the father catches the daughter and the boy kissing and flies into a rage, the daughter snaps back to Dad, "Didn't *you* ever suck face?"

When a cop brings home the daughter accused of shoplifting, he says she "kicked a store manager in the—[pause] where it hurts." The chief complains that one of his cops has come out of the closet. "A gay cop. Is there nothin' sacred? How do I know he's not in there kissin' a suspect?"

The writers of this were Sy Rosen and Mort Lachman; the director was Howard Storm. I wish I could publish their addresses and their home phone numbers. And as for the studio audience, or the machine, that laughed at this, that went "Awww" when the daughters hugged and when father and shoplifting daughter kissed and made up—deportation proceedings should begin at once.

If I thought television could get substantially worse than this, I am not sure I would have the courage or desire ever to turn the set on again.

October 29, 1981

A Tale of Two Toms

It was the best of Toms, it was the worst of Toms. It was the end, it was the beginning. It was breakfast, it was dinner. It was six of one, it was half a dozen of the other.

Things will never be exactly the same as they were 30 seconds ago, and we will all survive the departures of Tom Brokaw from the *Today* show and Tom Snyder from the *Tomorrow* show. But you had to get a little lumpy when both said their farewells on NBC last week within a few hours of each other.

There was Snyder, riding his last herd over the lobster shift, his hair grayer and his chin wearing a bit more blubber than when he began 8½ years ago, but as always, a comet, something to behold with awe and fear. And there was Brokaw, the lethal tot, still sporting a face of purest baby and baritoning his bye-byes to Jane and Willard and Gene and us, with whom he has spent 5½ years of morning glory. Not similar, not of the same stripe, not even employed by the same division at NBC (Brokaw is an NBC News man), Tom and Tom both bat in the same league. They are *broadcasters*. Snyder in particular epitomizes the difference between Real Broadcasting and mere television. It has to do with a way of thinking, and of knowing when not to think; it's a blind faith in the belief that communicating actually accomplishes something, and it might.

And if the world were to be divided between the boring and the never boring, there is no question that Snyder would be among the latter. And probably Brokaw, too.

"Good luck in the new work schedule," President Reagan said Friday to Brokaw during Brokaw's last hour as host of *Today*. From the Ellipse, weatherman and philosopher-poet Willard Scott had led a serenade to the departing Brokaw by the University of Maryland chorus, to the tune of "We Wish You a Merry Christmas": "You're leaving *Today*, and we've got the blues, but we'll see you nightly on NBC News."

In March, Brokaw becomes coanchor, with Roger Mudd, of *NBC Nightly News*. "Godspeed to Brokaw, one great guy," said Willard, who credited Brokaw with helping him join the *Today* show and said, "I expect to get on *Nightly News* in about six months." Willard was in town to help light the national Christmas tree; but of course, in reality, Willard *is* the national Christmas tree.

While he was delivering his au revoir, Brokaw was interrupted on-camera by friend and skiing buddy Robert Redford (a famous actor), who joked, "Tom, Rona couldn't be here, so . . ."—a reference to *Today* show gossip Rona Barrett, one of the show-bizzy things about the program that a newsy type like Brokaw is duty-bound to deplore. Quietly, of course.

"Tab Hunter, ladies and gentlemen, making his first appearance on the *Today* program," said Brokaw as Redford exited stage right. But Jane Pauley had the funniest line—a reference to the unsuccessful attempts of a certain network news president to lure Brokaw away from NBC: "I'd like to say that, as bad as I do feel, I'm glad at least to know that Roone Arledge feels worse." Ho-*ho!*

The mood had not been as festive much earlier that morning —so early it was almost still Thursday—when Tom Snyder signed off the *Tomorrow* show after, by his own estimate, 1,700 appearances. Snyder was never the glass of warm milk one might expect a late-night TV confidant to be, and his program was never, ever dull—infuriating maybe, but it kept you at attention. There has not been quite so magnificent and exasperating a creature of television since, perhaps, Jack Paar, who nearly 20 years ago whispered his own goodbye as host of the *Tonight* show.

For Paar, NBC took out full-page newspaper ads that day which said, "Hail and farewell!" There were no hail-and-farewell ads for Snyder. NBC management had ruined his program, driven much of its audience away and infuriated Snyder, but he was playing it cool on the way out, even when guest Chevy Chase grumbled on the air about how "dumb" NBC was. Actually, Fred Silverman was the dumb one; he added Rona Barrett to Snyder's show (a disaster) and brought in rock stars and a studio audience, which shattered the splendid intimate rapport Snyder had built up with the proverbial folks at home.

The morning after the broadcast, Snyder said from his office in New York that he is not bitter at NBC, but also strongly suggested his contract, which has a year to go, may be renegotiated to permit him to go to another network. He said he would like to try "something a little quieter ... something that doesn't go on the air every single day." He didn't suggest what that might be.

Of past skirmishes: "Fred Silverman forgot the first law of television, which is, If it ain't broke, don't fix it. I was never comfortable with all the ——ing glitz and bumpers and the rock stars and the studio audience, but Fred said Let's try it and I did it, and I finished it and—I killed it! Hahahahahahaha!"

And Ms. Barrett: "Poor Rona. I mean it. Poor Rona."

Poor Tom? No. "I feel great today. I feel like I finished my novel. Hey, I'm not bitter. I've got too many friends here. We did eight and a half years almost—with the exception of *Today* and *Tonight,* that's longer than almost anybody at NBC. I'm declaring victory! I really think now is the time. Television is changing; something is going on that is not making me very comfortable in television. When I hear them say now that they're going to 'fix' the *CBS Morning News,* I get very nervous."

At least, Snyder let his guests—most of them, anyway (even Charles Manson, for which Snyder took critical brickbats and got his highest rating ever)—have their says. "We're the last ones to give 'em time," he said. "Everything from now on is gonna be six minutes and out the door."

There is another law of television that ought to be brought to the attention of those who thought Tom Snyder was just a loud and obnoxious ham: Whatever comes next will be *much, much worse.* And will probably not have Snyder's affection for, and gift for, scintillating hurly-burly. On the air, Snyder said to his viewers, "I thank you for the good times and for the ride, and I'll be right around the corner." Then, to his director, George Paul: "George, a slow fade to black. Thank you all for watching—and good night, everybody."

On the air, Brokaw said to his viewers, "More than any other news program of which I'm aware, there's a personal bond between *here* and *out there,* and I have learned from all of you as well."

Not an occasion for unkempt sentiment, perhaps? No, but

when these fixtures leave, when they disassemble and their roles in the daily rituals of broadcasting are assumed by others, it is a little like parting with a friend or even, maybe, a member of the electronically extended family. On the last episode of *Mary Tyler Moore*, Mary Richards said to her co-workers, "After all, what is a family but people who help you feel . . . a little less . . . alone?"

And that, after all, is why we have television.

December 21, 1981

Uncle President

EVERY NOW AND THEN, a president risks upsetting the balance of power in this country by trying to take a little of it back from television. Really, such impudence! But when the president himself is almost as much a creation of television as Fonzie, Archie Bunker, Scooby-Doo or Winky-Dink, the tussle does take on a certain irony.

Perhaps the irony has occurred to Ronald Reagan—though he's never seemed much of an irony aficionado—or, more likely, to his advisers, because yesterday, in remarks to the National Association of Manufacturers here, Reagan beat a retreat from the attack on the networks he'd made earlier in interviews with the *Daily Oklahoman* and *TV Guide*. Reagan had complained to the *Oklahoman* that TV news was on a "constant downbeat" bender in reporting on the economy. He said in *TV Guide* that there is "a tendency to editorialize in the media" and counseled more "editorial self-censorship" at the networks.

He also said in *TV Guide* that there's too much sex and violence on TV but that he likes *Charlie's Angels* because, ahem, "there's something about a detective story." Yup, that's our president!

You know that a TV comedy or drama series is in trouble when the writers whip up a wedding or a childbirth for one of the continuing characters. You know an administration is in trouble when it starts blaming others for the nation's woes. When the informal statute of limitations on blaming previous administrations looms in the distance, target No. 1 is always the media. Perhaps the most notable things about Reagan's attack are, one, that the networks didn't even trouble themselves with a response and, two, that Reagan all but gosh-a-mighty'd an "I'm sorry" lickety-split.

The same week Reagan attacked television news as unfair and too negative he appeared on network newscasts lifting sandbags to help stem a Midwestern flood (Whew, such symbolism!) and, on ABC's *Good Morning, America,* he beguiled one and all with a presentable impersonation of his old movie-star pal Jimmy Stewart.

Love That President!

Of course, no president, not even Kennedy, has ever been quite so masterly on television as Reagan. Time and again he has soared over the heads of Congress on wings of electrons and disarmed his way into the American living room, TV set and heart, putting over programs that might otherwise have floundered. If network correspondents begrudge him anything, it's his mistress, the camera.

It has become not so much an administration as a TV series, and Reagan not so much a distant national leader as the one and only Uncle President. The camera loves him so much that he can't understand why other people have to intrude on this chummy relationship. He's a tongue-tied disaster at press conferences, but put him in a room—just him and a camera and 80 million folks out there in television land—and he's Johnny Carson, Grandpa Walton and Big Bird all rolled into one.

Now, it is being widely speculated—on the basis of ample evidence, one might add—that the President is not possessed of a large capacity for deepthink. This is relevant to his performance as U.S. president, but irrelevant to his performance as Television President. He's just doing what he, and much better actors, have done for half a century or so in the talkies:

faking it so appealingly that he can scarcely be doubted. It's like Bette Davis in *Jezebel*—the perfect combination of artistry and chemistry. Intelligence has nothing to do with it.

Ronald Reagan may be the first true Prop President, one whose real self is the image on the TV screen and whose shadow self is the man in the White House. Behind the scenes, the counselors take over; out in front of the curtain, Ronald Reagan is wowing the crowd.

Perhaps the performance is beginning also to resemble Mary Martin's in *Peter Pan*. When the President and his advisers start advancing the notion that the media promote a gloomy national mind-set about the economy and this makes the economy worse, the next step may be for Reagan to go on television and ask viewers to clap if they believe in his economic package, the way Peter asked us to clap if we believed in fairies. It's not likely the economy will respond as dramatically to such a show of faith as Tinker Bell did.

Current talk about the honeymoon's being over between the President and Congress isn't very interesting, except to Congress. The honeymoon to worry about is the one between Smilin' Ron and the American viewer. Charisma is enchanting, but eventually people realize that you can't eat it and it doesn't heat the house. As former White House press secretary George Reedy told Bob Schieffer on a particularly salient segment of *The CBS Evening News with Dan Rather* last September, "The public can be sold by clever communications at a period when it has not had actual experience with what it's buying. But once it has some actual experience, then the whole scene shifts. You see, what a president does speaks so much louder than anything he can say that once he starts doing things, that's what people believe."

Reagan knows deep in his heart that he has very little real complaint with television. Like all presidents, he has more access to it than anyone else, and unlike most presidents—especially his decidedly nontelegenic predecessor—he uses it brilliantly, so long as he controls the format. During the 1980 campaign, Ken Towery, a Reagan aide, grumped about Jimmy Carter's access to the almighty airwaves and the fact that even Carter's gripes about press coverage got more respect than Reagan's. "The president can complain and almost make the press look like they're being unpatriotic," Towery said.

Obviously, Reagan's advisers have not forgotten that—hence the Reagan attack. And perhaps they subsequently counseled yesterday's hasty retreat not because they fear the power of the networks (though there are fearsome things about that power indeed) but because they began to feel the shock waves that a display of temper and pique by beloved Uncle President could generate. The man who wanted to ride the white horse to that oft-invoked "shining city on a hill" can't start sounding churlish or grouchy or panicked. That *would* shake the national confidence. It would be like the moment when the senator played by Melvyn Douglas in *The Seduction of Joe Tynan* suddenly lapsed into French at a committee session.

Enter Robert Young.

"Say! Why's my favorite president so nervous?"

"*Wehl,* it's these darn television newscasts and their unemployed workers in South Succotash."

"Whoa there, Ron—here, try some of this Sanka."

Three weeks later. "So, how's my favorite president getting along with the media?"

"Just fine. I think I've come to my senses."

"I knew you would. *Ha ha ha ha ha.*"

March 19, 1982

Farewell to Brideshead

A JOURNEY OF A thousand miles that began with a single episode ends tonight with an 11th. *Brideshead Revisited* concludes with a 90-minute chapter that takes place in the winter of 1939, when Lord Marchmain (Laurence Olivier) comes home to die.

Unfortunately for *Brideshead* and its small but intensely loyal legion of followers, the demise of Lord Marchmain and the series occurs on a day abnormally overstocked with momentous television. In fact, David Brinkley reported yesterday on ABC's *This Week* [with him] that President Reagan had decided to postpone a press conference planned for today because he didn't want to compete for television attention with the Oscars, the NCAA championship and the scheduled landing of the space shuttle *Columbia*.

For the true *Brideshead* loyalist, the choice will not be so difficult. Having come this far with Charles, and Julia, and that besotted sprite Sebastian (gone, but hardly forgotten), one feels obliged and privileged to see things through. It's not a matter of just learning what becomes of Charles Ryder (Jeremy Irons), because we know little will become of him. "I'm homeless; childless, middle-aged and loveless," he announces near the journey's end. But he is also the quintessential outsider, and this gives him a certain doomed pathos.

Those who have remained faithful to the series will find this a fittingly rewarding and cathartically traumatic conclusion. Lord Marchmain's condition worsens until, says Charles in his narration, "presently there were no good spells, only brief fluctuations in the speed of his decline." The central question is whether Marchmain will consent to receive the last rites from a nearby parish priest. At the first attempt, he sends the priest away, but the priest remarks, "I've known worse cases to make beautiful deaths."

One of the longest flashbacks ever recorded on film concludes, and the series ends almost exactly the way Evelyn Waugh ended the novel on which it is based.

The surface glories of *Brideshead* are obvious and have been adequately celebrated. But they are not the principal reason for the impact or popularity of the program. A frump or a heretic here and there has tried to gain a little notoriety for himself by scoffing at *Brideshead* in print; these people think themselves courageous in standing on the sidelines and jeering that the empress has no clothes. But she does, and what clothes, and how sad not that some people don't appreciate *Brideshead*—for that is their right—but that a supercilious few choose to interpret this attitude as a sign of shrewd sophistication.

Among the foolish charges made are that the popularity of *Brideshead* can be attributed purely to anglophilia and that the program is nothing but a fancy-dress soap opera. Both allegations are ridiculous. A passion for British telly may have explained the success here of *Upstairs, Downstairs* and many of the *Masterpiece Theater* pomposities, but *Brideshead* is not about England or the English to any limiting degree. It's about so much more.

And there's also much more to it than a soap-operatic what-happens-next. Purely as a plot, it meanders, or makes sudden leaps over unexplored chasms. These are not the adventures of Charles Ryder; Charles is too passive, for one thing, and at times he is even a bit of a cad (although he is always sympathetic as played by Irons, in a vaguely victimized style that recalls Leslie Howard, especially in *Of Human Bondage*).

On its most general level, *Brideshead* is about remembering something and being unable to recapture it—a lament for lost grace, a graphic confirmation of our suspicion that beauty gets a little less plentiful in the world with the ascent of each succeeding generation. A devotee of the program will find it hard to comprehend how some people are unable to see and appreciate not only the elegance of it but also the depth of it —the charm of it, the power of it, the Catholicism of it, the wisdom of it.

The word "nostalgia" has taken on such a cloying, superficial meaning through overuse that you wouldn't want to apply it to *Brideshead*, except that the program does evoke, sensually and spiritually, the particular mood of the world between wars, and also of a time when—or so it now seems—people still controlled technology, rather than the other way around.

Not the greatest TV program ever made? Slow-moving and dry? These things can be said of *Brideshead*, but they're irrelevant. On television, it's not what things are but what they represent. *Brideshead* for many goes beyond esthetic considerations; it's one of those rare works that insinuate themselves into memory alongside primary experiences. In the future, it will jiggle around in the memory bank like a first date or a lost love or one particular night of good company and laughter. Or one particular morning of rueful realization.

There are so few basic pleasures in life, really. Sex, money, chocolate and *Brideshead Revisited*. It's partly a tribute to the mercurial allure of the program that, finally, its appeal and its magical spell cannot be fully explained by anybody. Very soon it will be something to look back on, and something to hope public TV might repeat annually, or once every five years, or eventually, at least—though the first time will always have been the best. At least, it meets a beautiful death tonight.

Farewell to Brideshead, farewell to the chapel, farewell to Oxford, and Cointreau, and Venice, and Aloysius, and Mr. Samgrass, and the monogrammed turtle, and "such a lot of nonsense," and wine and strawberries under a tree, and innocence and youth and duty and honor, and to all we hoped we one day would become, farewell.

March 29, 1982

About The Author

AS EDITOR OF HIS HIGH SCHOOL NEWSPAPER, Tom Shales appointed himself movie critic and did the same thing at the American University in Washington, D.C. He is film critic for National Public Radio and spent one season as a panelist on a Washington public TV show, which taught him a great deal about what makes a television program truly bad. Now a nationally syndicated columnist, Shales joined *The Washington Post* in 1972 and became television editor and chief television critic in 1979.

Shales lives in Arlington, Virginia, with three television sets.

LAGRANGE COUNTY LIBRARY

791.45
88684

791.45 88684

SHALES, TOM

ON THE AIR!

DATE DUE			

OFFICIAL DISCARD
LAGRANGE COUNTY LIBRARY